High Score
iBT TOEFL READING
For Junior

High Intermediate

Dear Teachers and Parents,

Welcome to Darakwon's *High Score iBT TOEFL Reading for Junior* series.

When people study English, they often focus on learning the same topics that appear in all English textbooks. So while they learn how to have basic conversations with people, that is about all that they can do. The *High Score iBT TOEFL Reading for Junior* series hopes to change the way that students study English. This series focuses on teaching students English by introducing them to a wide number of topics. By learning about new and different subjects, students will not only become more interested in learning English but will also be able to greatly expand their English vocabulary and their knowledge base in general.

The *High Score iBT TOEFL Reading for Junior* series is written as a junior iBT TOEFL textbook. The books in this series cover topics that appear on the actual iBT TOEFL test. The questions in the books are also phrased just like those that students will find on the iBT TOEFL test. This should help familiarize students with the iBT TOEFL test and prepare them for when they take it in the future. By learning as much as they can about the iBT TOEFL test prior to taking it, the students will ensure that they will have some knowledge of many of the topics on the test and will be comfortable with the style of the test and the questions on it. All of these factors should lead to higher scores for the students.

It is my hope that students will use this series first to improve their knowledge of English. They will find the passages have been written at a level that they will be able to understand, and the students should find the passages themselves to be fun to read and full of interesting facts and information. Or course, as a junior iBT TOEFL book, a major emphasis of the series is to familiarize the students with the iBT TOEFL test. Most of all, I hope that this series will instill a love of English in students and inspire them to continue and to advance their studies of the English language.

Michael A. Putlack

Table of CONTENTS

About the TOEFL 4

How to Use This Book 8

Chapter 1 Literature (Chronological Order) 13

Chapter 2 Astronomy (Comparison and Contrast) 39

Chapter 3 Zoology (Classification) 65

Chapter 4 Art (Cause and Effect) 91

Chapter 5 Physiology (Guessing Unknown Words) 117

Chapter 6 Archaeology (Mapping) 139

Chapter 7 Physics (Identifying Cohesive Devices) 165

Chapter 8 Political Science (Outlining) 191

Actual Test 217

About the TOEFL

The TOEFL iBT

TOEFL is the Test of English as a Foreign Language. It measures the test taker's ability in English. Foreign students often need to take the TOEFL to get into an American college or university. For that reason, the TOEFL exam is very important.

The TOEFL iBT is an Internet-based test (iBT). Students take the TOEFL iBT on a computer at one of the test centers.

The TOEFL iBT tests four language skills. These skills are reading, listening, speaking, and writing. There are many different kinds of passages, lectures, conversations, and questions. Many sections combine two or more of these skills. So students must be capable in several English skills to get high scores on the exam.

The Format of the TOEFL iBT

There are four sections on the TOEFL iBT. These sections are Reading, Listening, Speaking, and Writing.

The Reading section has two passages. These passages are around 700 words long with 10 questions per passage. The Reading section of the test takes 35 minutes.

The Listening section has two types of passages. They are lectures and conversations. Each Listening section has 3 lectures. The lectures are 3-5 minutes each with 6 questions per lecture. Each Listening section has 2 conversations. The conversations are 3 minutes each with 5 questions per conversation. The Listening section of the test takes 36 minutes.

The Speaking section has two types of questions. They are independent and integrated questions. There is 1 independent question. The independent question asks about your own ideas, opinions, and experiences. There are 3 integrated questions. The integrated questions consist of conversations, reading passages, lectures, or combinations of them, just as you would see in or out of a classroom. They ask questions based on the reading and listening passages. The Speaking section of the test takes 16 minutes.

The Writing section has two types of questions: 1 integrated task and 1 academic discussion task. The integrated task combines a short reading passage and a short lecture. The test taker must then write an essay about these two. The academic discussion task asks a question about a personal experience or opinion. The test taker must then write an essay about this question. The Writing section of the test takes 29 minutes.

The Test Format

Test Section	Number of Questions	Timing	Score
Reading	• 2 passages, 10 questions each	35 minutes	30
Listening	• 3 lectures, 6 questions each • 2 conversations, 5 questions each	36 minutes	30
Speaking	• 1 independent task • 3 integrated tasks	16 minutes	30
Writing	• 1 integrated task • 1 academic discussion task	29 minutes	30

The Reading Section

There are 10 different kinds of questions in the Reading section. Each question appears a different number of times.

The different kinds of questions are:

1 Factual Information Questions

These ask about the facts in the passage.
There are 1-3 of these questions in each passage.

2 Negative Factual Questions

These ask about information that is NOT in the passage or which is NOT true.
There are 0-2 of these questions in each passage.

3 Rhetorical Purpose Questions

These ask about the reason why the author includes some information in the passage.
There are 0-2 of these questions in each passage.

4 Inference Questions

These ask about information the test taker must infer from the passage.
There are 0-2 of these questions in each passage.

5 Vocabulary Questions

These ask about the definitions of words or phrases in the passage.
There are 1-3 of these questions in each passage.

6 Reference Questions

These ask which word or words in the passage refers to.
There are 0-1 of these questions in each passage.

About the TOEFL

7 Sentence Simplification Questions
These take one long sentence from the passage and ask the test taker to find a simplified version of that sentence. There are 0-1 of these questions in each passage.

8 Insert Text Questions
These show the test taker a new sentence and ask the test taker to determine where the sentence would fit best in the passage. There are 0-1 of these questions in each passage.

9 Prose Summary Questions
These provide a summary of the passage and then ask the test taker to choose 3 of 6 sentences that best relate to the summary. There are 0-1 of these questions in each passage.

10 Fill in a Table Questions
These ask the test taker to categorize various facts and information that appear in the passage. There are 0-1 of these questions in each passage.

How to Use This Book

Question Types
This section describes the question or questions covered in the chapter. It provides an explanation of each question and how to try to answer it.

Example Questions
This section shows the different ways that the questions appear on the TOEFL test. Students can learn how to recognize the different types of questions in this section.

Useful Tips for Your Success
This section provides various tips on how to answer questions properly. It also provides hints on right and wrong approaches to answering each question.

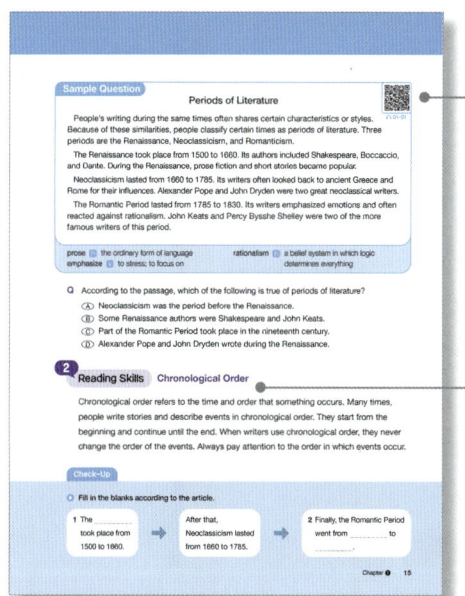

Sample Question

This is a medium-length 120-word passage on one of the topics in the unit. It has one TOEFL question and one reading skills question.

Reading Skills

This is an explanation of the reading skill that the chapter covers.

Exercises

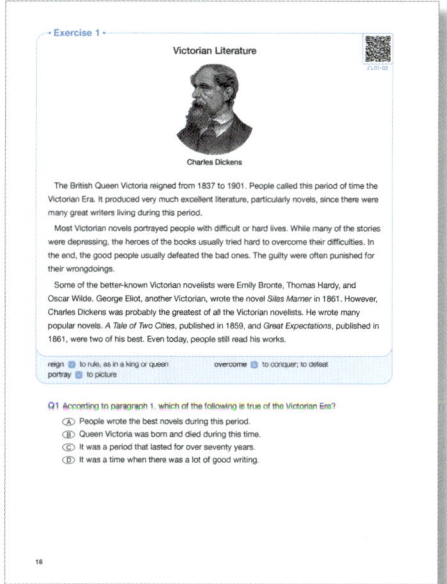

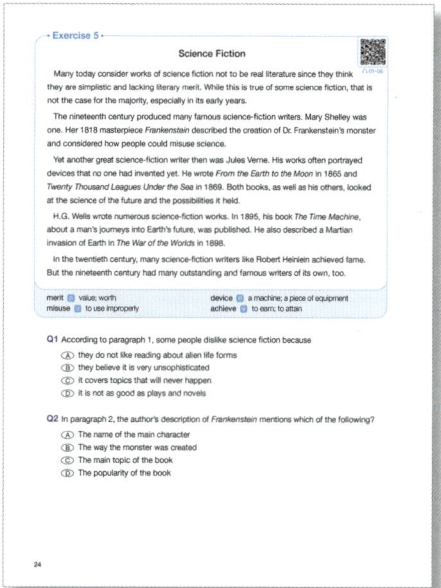

Long Passages

There are four long passages with 120-160 words each. Each passage is on a topic that concerns the subject of the unit and has three TOEFL questions and one reading skills question.

Longer Passages

There are four longer passages with 160-200 words each. Each passage is on a topic that concerns the subject of the unit and has four TOEFL questions and one reading skills question.

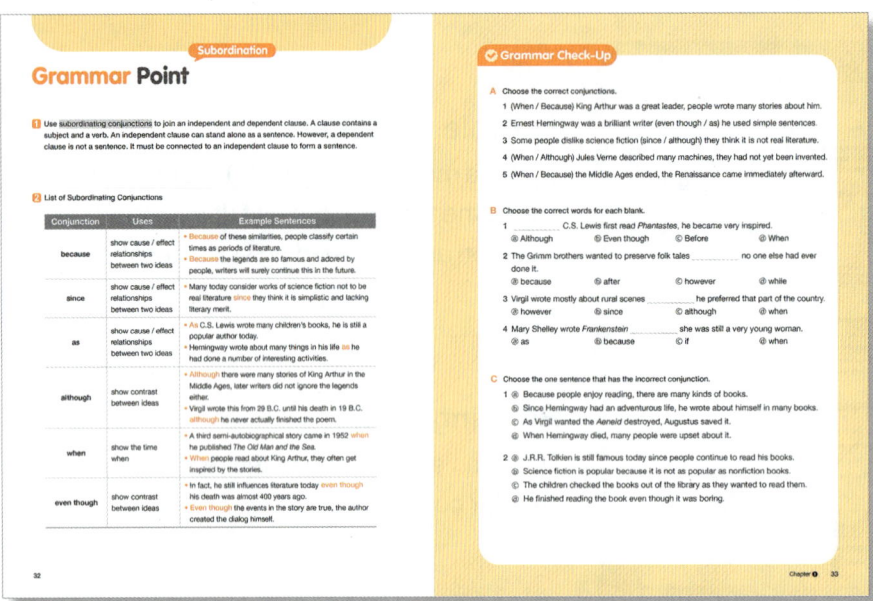

Grammar Point

This section explains a certain part of speech. It has one page of explanations and one page of various exercises for students to answer.

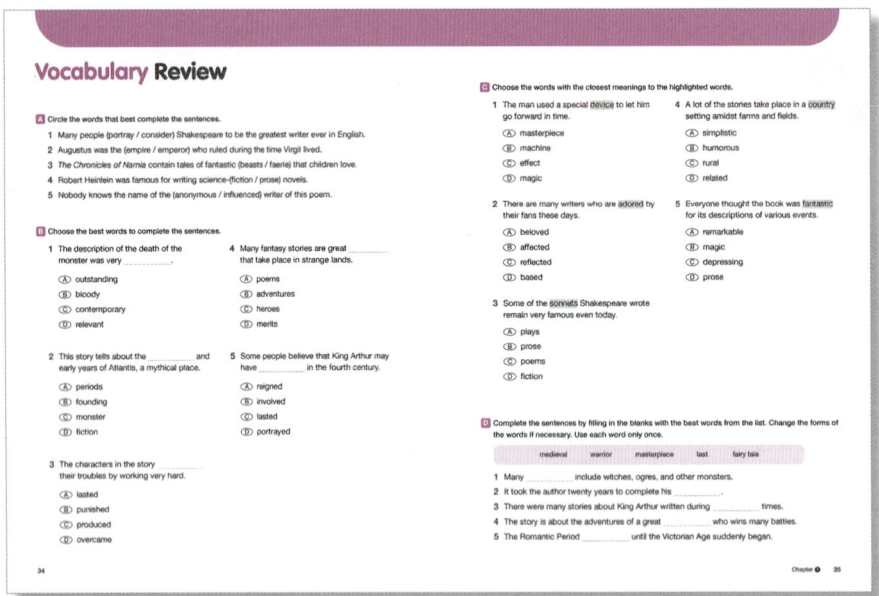

Vocabulary Review

This section provides a comprehensive review of the vocabulary found in the various passages in the unit. Each unit has twenty vocabulary review questions, and all of the answer choices are words that appear in the passages in the unit.

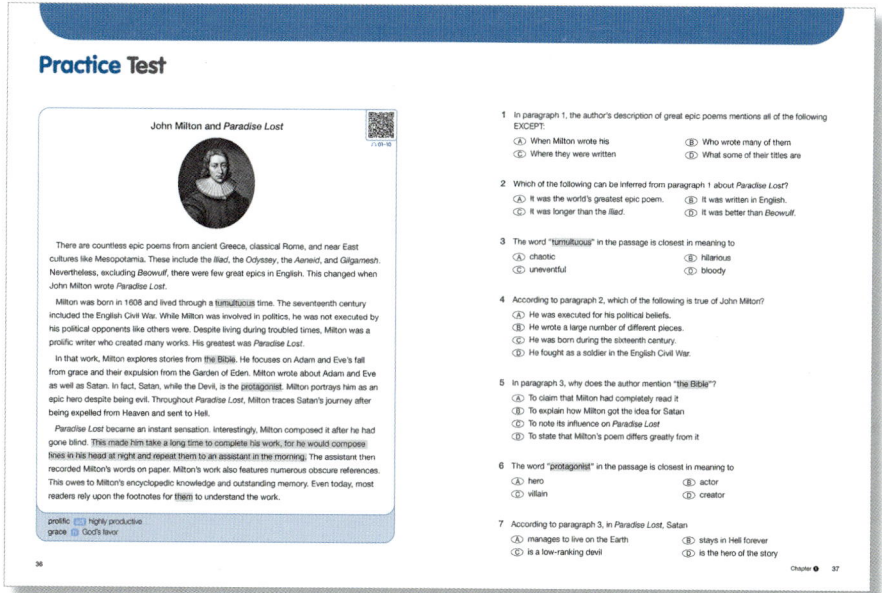

Practice Test

There is one passage with 200-250 words. The passage is on a topic that concerns the subject of the unit and has ten TOEFL questions.

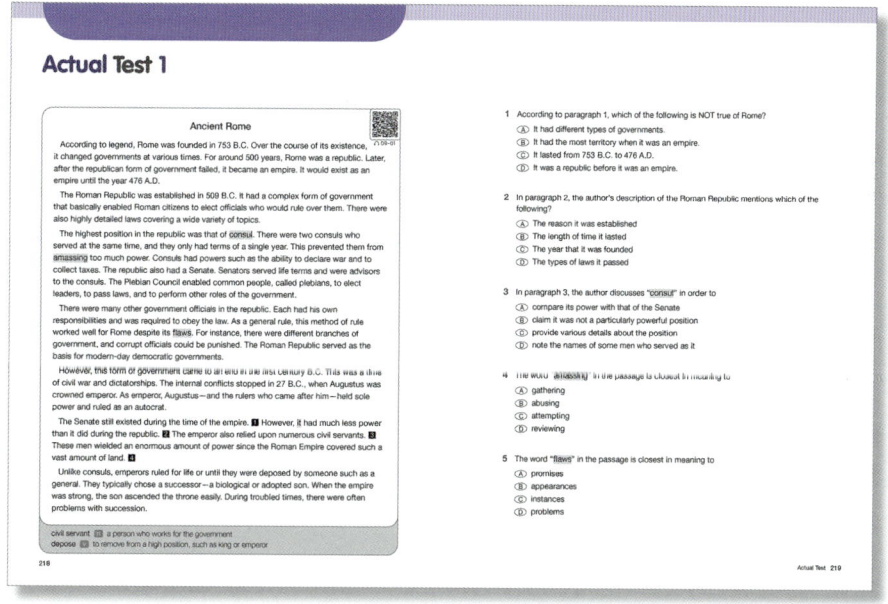

Actual Test

This section includes 3 passages with 300-400 words with 10 questions each. Every passage has different kinds of questions. There are questions from all 10 types found in the Reading section. Additionally, all of the passages are from topics that appear in the book. These passages and questions are shorter versions of a typical TOEFL iBT Reading section.

CHAPTER

01

Literature
(Chronological Order)

1. Victorian Literature
2. William Shakespeare
3. Grimm's Fairy Tales
4. Medieval English Literature
5. Science Fiction
6. The Legends of King Arthur
7. Virgil
8. Fantasy Writers

CHAPTER 1 **Literature** (Chronological Order)

Understanding TOEFL Question Types & Reading Skills

1 Question Types — Factual Information Questions

Factual Information questions ask about the facts, details, definitions, or other information in the passage. They ask you to identify names, dates, places, or reasons why something happened. Read the facts in the passage carefully, and then you can answer the questions easily.

- **Example Factual Information Questions**
    - According to paragraph 1, what is true of X?
    - The author's description of X mentions which of the following?
    - According to the paragraph, X did Y because ~

- **Useful Tips for Your Success**
    - Pay attention to
        - → any places the passage mentions.
        - → the names the passage gives.
        - → any dates in the passage.
    - Always
        - → try to find the details in the passage.
        - → pay attention to the facts in the passage.

Sample Question

Periods of Literature

People's writing during the same times often shares certain characteristics or styles. Because of these similarities, people classify certain times as periods of literature. Three periods are the Renaissance, Neoclassicism, and Romanticism.

The Renaissance took place from 1500 to 1660. Its authors included Shakespeare, Boccaccio, and Dante. During the Renaissance, prose fiction and short stories became popular.

Neoclassicism lasted from 1660 to 1785. Its writers often looked back to ancient Greece and Rome for their influences. Alexander Pope and John Dryden were two great neoclassical writers.

The Romantic Period lasted from 1785 to 1830. Its writers emphasized emotions and often reacted against rationalism. John Keats and Percy Bysshe Shelley were two of the more famous writers of this period.

prose (n) the ordinary form of language
emphasize (v) to stress; to focus on
rationalism (n) a belief system in which logic determines everything

Q According to the passage, which of the following is true of periods of literature?
- Ⓐ Neoclassicism was the period before the Renaissance.
- Ⓑ Some Renaissance authors were Shakespeare and John Keats.
- Ⓒ Part of the Romantic Period took place in the nineteenth century.
- Ⓓ Alexander Pope and John Dryden wrote during the Renaissance.

2 Reading Skills — Chronological Order

Chronological order refers to the time and order that something occurs. Many times, people write stories and describe events in chronological order. They start from the beginning and continue until the end. When writers use chronological order, they never change the order of the events. Always pay attention to the order in which events occur.

Check-Up

▶ Fill in the blanks according to the article.

1 The _____ took place from 1500 to 1660. After that, Neoclassicism lasted from 1660 to 1785. 2 Finally, the Romantic Period went from _____ to _____.

Exercise 1

Victorian Literature

Charles Dickens

The British Queen Victoria reigned from 1837 to 1901. People called this period of time the Victorian Era. It produced very much excellent literature, particularly novels, since there were many great writers living during this period.

Most Victorian novels portrayed people with difficult or hard lives. While many of the stories were depressing, the heroes of the books usually tried hard to overcome their difficulties. In the end, the good people usually defeated the bad ones. The guilty were often punished for their wrongdoings.

Some of the better-known Victorian novelists were Emily Bronte, Thomas Hardy, and Oscar Wilde. George Eliot, another Victorian, wrote the novel *Silas Marner* in 1861. However, Charles Dickens was probably the greatest of all the Victorian novelists. He wrote many popular novels. *A Tale of Two Cities*, published in 1859, and *Great Expectations*, published in 1861, were two of his best. Even today, people still read his works.

---

reign v to rule, as in a king or queen   **overcome** v to conquer; to defeat
portray v to picture

Q1 According to paragraph 1, which of the following is true of the Victorian Era?

Ⓐ People wrote the best novels during this period.
Ⓑ Queen Victoria was born and died during this time.
Ⓒ It was a period that lasted for over seventy years.
Ⓓ It was a time when there was a lot of good writing.

Q2 The author's description of Victorian novels mentions which of the following?

- Ⓐ How guilty people suffered in them
- Ⓑ The type of story they usually were
- Ⓒ Why they featured few heroes
- Ⓓ The average number of copies they sold

Q3 According to paragraph 3, which of the following is true of Charles Dickens?

- Ⓐ He wrote the Victorian novel *Silas Marner*.
- Ⓑ He was a contemporary of George Eliot.
- Ⓒ His favorite novel was *Great Expectations*.
- Ⓓ He wrote *A Tale of Two Cities* in 1861.

Reading Skills | **Chronological Order**

Check-Up Insert a number from 1 to 4 in the correct order according to the article.

_____ Queen Victoria's reign in Britain ended.
_____ Charles Dickens published *A Tale of Two Cities*.
_____ Victoria became the queen of England.
_____ George Eliot wrote the book *Silas Marner*.

• **Exercise 2** •

William Shakespeare

Born in 1564 and dying in 1616, William Shakespeare had a tremendous effect on the world of literature. In fact, he still influences literature today even though his death came almost 400 years ago.

Including plays and poems, many of Shakespeare's works remain not only famous but also relevant. Among his plays, many consider 1595's *Romeo and Juliet* to be the greatest love story of all time. Around 1600, Shakespeare wrote *Hamlet*. Critics often cite that as his best play. Altogether, Shakespeare wrote thirty-seven plays in his life.

Beginning in 1593, he also composed a number of poems, including numerous sonnets. These are fourteen-line poems. People still quote many of Shakespeare's lines from his poems.

Interestingly, Shakespeare was also a great contributor to the English language. During his life, English was still a developing language. Some experts believe Shakespeare introduced more than 1,700 words into English. Whatever the case, his influence on English language and literature was remarkable.

---

relevant adj related; significant
cite v to mention; to name
remarkable adj great; huge

Q1 According to paragraph 1, Shakespeare is an important writer because

Ⓐ he wrote more than 400 years ago
Ⓑ he wrote many genres of literature
Ⓒ he affects many of today's writers
Ⓓ he was born in the sixteenth century

Q2 In paragraph 2, the author's description of *Romeo and Juliet* mentions which of the following?

- Ⓐ The reason it is Shakespeare's best play
- Ⓑ The first year it was performed
- Ⓒ The city where it takes place
- Ⓓ What many people think of it

Q3 According to paragraph 4, which of the following is true of Shakespeare?

- Ⓐ He added many new words to English.
- Ⓑ He largely created the English language.
- Ⓒ He no longer has an influence on English.
- Ⓓ Others influenced English more than he did.

Reading Skills | Chronological Order

Check-Up Fill in the blanks according to the article.

| William Shakespeare was born in 1564. | → | 1 Beginning in _____, he composed many poems. | → | 2 He composed _____ _____ in 1595. | → | He wrote his best work, *Hamlet*, around 1600. |

• **Exercise 3** •

Grimm's Fairy Tales

🎧 01-04

Today, parents often read their children fairy tales before bed. So children are familiar with stories like *Cinderella*, *Rapunzel*, and *Snow White*. Actually, these stories and other similar ones are quite old. However, no one had ever recorded them until the nineteenth century.

Jacob and Wilhelm Grimm, two German brothers, became interested in children's stories in 1803. People had passed these stories on for generations, yet no one had written them down anywhere. The Grimm brothers changed that.

In 1812, they published their first volume of fairy tales, which had eighty-six stories. They published a second volume in 1814 and a third in 1822. Altogether, there were around 170 stories in their books.

The Grimm's fairy tales are often quite violent. The stories contain many deaths and extremely bloody scenes. They were much unlike the nonviolent fairy tales people tell nowadays. Despite the differences, the Grimm brothers provided an invaluable service by recording so many stories for people to enjoy.

---

record v to write down
generation n all the people born at a certain time

nonviolent adj peaceful

Q1 According to paragraph 2, the Grimm brothers wrote down many fairy tales because

Ⓐ they recorded them for their children
Ⓑ they really enjoyed children's stories
Ⓒ no one had ever done it before
Ⓓ they liked the history of fairy tales

Q2 In paragraph 3, the author's description of the Grimm brothers' books mentions which of the following?

- Ⓐ The total number of volumes
- Ⓑ The company that published the books
- Ⓒ The names of all the stories in the books
- Ⓓ The number of stories in each volume

Q3 According to paragraph 4, which of the following is true of the Grimm brothers' stories?

- Ⓐ They were similar to stories people tell today.
- Ⓑ Most of the stories were very peaceful.
- Ⓒ A lot of people perished in their stories.
- Ⓓ Children today love to read their stories.

Reading Skills — Chronological Order

Check-Up Insert a number from 1 to 4 in the correct order according to the article.

_____ The Grimm brothers became interested in children's stories.
_____ They completed their second volume.
_____ They published a book with eighty-six stories.
_____ The Grimm brothers finished writing their entire series.

Exercise 4

Medieval English Literature

The medieval period lasted from 476 to roughly 1500. During that time, there were many impressive works of literature written in English. Most of them were poems.

The first great work composed in the English language was the epic poem *Beowulf*. Most scholars believe it was written in the eighth century. The poem tells the story of a great Scandinavian warrior named Beowulf. He defeats monsters, including a dragon, and becomes king.

At the end of the tenth century, the poem *The Battle of Maldon* was composed. Sometime around the year 1370, William Langland wrote *Piers Plowman*. At the end of the fourteenth century, *Pearl*, another poem, was composed by an anonymous poet. One of the greatest poems of the Middle Ages was written around 1392. It was *The Canterbury Tales*, which was composed by Geoffrey Chaucer. It is a collection of stories about a group of people on a pilgrimage to Canterbury, England.

---

roughly adv around; about; approximately
dragon n a mythical monster that looks like a giant lizard with wings
anonymous adj of unknown name

Q1 According to paragraph 1, which of the following is true of the medieval period?

Ⓐ It lasted for around two thousand years.
Ⓑ Many great poems were written then.
Ⓒ Not much literature was composed during it.
Ⓓ It started around the year 1500.

Q2 According to paragraph 2, what did Beowulf do?

- Ⓐ He fought and won against a monster.
- Ⓑ He led an army to victory.
- Ⓒ He became the king of Scandinavia.
- Ⓓ He built a large castle to live in.

Q3 In paragraph 3, the author's description of *Pearl* mentions which of the following?

- Ⓐ The type of poem it is
- Ⓑ The subject it covers
- Ⓒ The time it was written
- Ⓓ The name of its writer

Reading Skills | Chronological Order

Check-Up Fill in the blanks according to the article.

| 1 _____ was written in the eighth century. | → | *The Battle of Maldon* was composed at the end of the tenth century. | → | William Langland wrote *Piers Plowman* in 1370. | → | 2 Geoffrey Chaucer wrote _____ _____ in 1392. |

• **Exercise 5** •

Science Fiction

Many today consider works of science fiction not to be real literature since they think they are simplistic and lacking literary merit. While this is true of some science fiction, that is not the case for the majority, especially in its early years.

The nineteenth century produced many famous science-fiction writers. Mary Shelley was one. Her 1818 masterpiece *Frankenstein* described the creation of Dr. Frankenstein's monster and considered how people could misuse science.

Yet another great science-fiction writer then was Jules Verne. His works often portrayed devices that no one had invented yet. He wrote *From the Earth to the Moon* in 1865 and *Twenty Thousand Leagues Under the Sea* in 1869. Both books, as well as his others, looked at the science of the future and the possibilities it held.

H.G. Wells wrote numerous science-fiction works. In 1895, his book *The Time Machine*, about a man's journeys into Earth's future, was published. He also described a Martian invasion of Earth in *The War of the Worlds* in 1898.

In the twentieth century, many science-fiction writers like Robert Heinlein achieved fame. But the nineteenth century had many outstanding and famous writers of its own, too.

---

merit n value; worth
misuse v to use improperly
device n a machine; a piece of equipment
achieve v to earn; to attain

Q1 According to paragraph 1, some people dislike science fiction because

Ⓐ they do not like reading about alien life forms
Ⓑ they believe it is very unsophisticated
Ⓒ it covers topics that will never happen
Ⓓ it is not as good as plays and novels

Q2 In paragraph 2, the author's description of *Frankenstein* mentions which of the following?

Ⓐ The name of the main character
Ⓑ The way the monster was created
Ⓒ The main topic of the book
Ⓓ The popularity of the book

Q3 According to paragraph 3, which of the following is true of Jules Verne?

Ⓐ Many of his works had to do with the future.
Ⓑ He wrote about inventions people had already made.
Ⓒ He published *Twenty Thousand Leagues Under the Sea* in 1865.
Ⓓ He was the coauthor of *From the Earth to the Moon*.

Q4 In paragraph 4, the author's description of H.G. Wells mentions which of the following?

Ⓐ The way he wrote his stories
Ⓑ The settings of his works
Ⓒ The topics of two of his books
Ⓓ The number of books he wrote

Reading Skills   Chronological Order

Check-Up Insert a number from 1 to 4 in the correct order according to the article.

_____ Jules Verne's book *From the Earth to the Moon* came out.
_____ Robert Heinlein became a famous science-fiction writer.
_____ Mary Shelley published her masterpiece *Frankenstein*.
_____ H.G. Wells wrote the book *The War of the Worlds*.

• Exercise 6 •

The Legends of King Arthur

For hundreds of years, people have read stories about King Arthur and the Knights of the Round Table. No one is sure if King Arthur was an actual person. Some believe he lived in Britain in the fourth or fifth century. But there have been countless stories written about his adventures.

In the Middle Ages, there were many great tales of King Arthur. Geoffrey of Monmouth, writing in the early twelfth century, wrote about Arthur in his *History of the Kings of Britain*. In the late twelfth century, Chrétien de Troyes, a Frenchman, created several poems about Arthur's knights' feats. In 1485, Thomas Malory wrote *The Death of Arthur*, one of the greatest of all medieval works.

Although there were many stories of King Arthur in the Middle Ages, later writers did not ignore the legends either. For example, in 1885, Alfred, Lord Tennyson completed publishing his work *The Idylls of the King*. And Mark Twain wrote a humorous variation of the Arthur legend with *A Connecticut Yankee in King Arthur's Court* in 1889.

Even today, many writers focus on King Arthur. Because the legends are so famous and adored by people, writers will surely continue this in the future.

legend n a myth; a story that is probably not true
feat n a deed; an act
medieval adj relating to the Middle Ages
humorous adj funny

Q1 According to paragraph 1, which of the following is true of King Arthur?

Ⓐ He lived sometime during the fourth century.
Ⓑ He was definitely not a real person.
Ⓒ He lived to be one hundred years old.
Ⓓ There are many tales about him and his knights.

Q2 In paragraph 2, the author's description of Chrétien de Troyes mentions which of the following?

- Ⓐ The language that he wrote his work in
- Ⓑ The work he did together with Thomas Malory
- Ⓒ The type of work about King Arthur that he wrote
- Ⓓ The lengths of the stories that he wrote

Q3 According to paragraph 3, which of the following is true of later authors?

- Ⓐ They entirely ignored the King Arthur legends.
- Ⓑ Most of their stories about King Arthur were funny.
- Ⓒ They wrote some stories about King Arthur.
- Ⓓ Mark Twain wrote the most famous Arthur story.

Q4 According to paragraph 4, writers will continue making stories about King Arthur because

- Ⓐ people enjoy reading about the legends
- Ⓑ there is much material for them to use
- Ⓒ they can sell very many books this way
- Ⓓ they like writing stories about him

Reading Skills | Chronological Order

Check-Up Fill in the blanks according to the article.

| King Arthur may have lived in the fourth or fifth century. | → | **1** _____ wrote *History of the Kings of Britain*. | → | Thomas Malory published *The Death of Arthur* in 1485. | → | **2** _____ wrote *A Connecticut Yankee in King Arthur's Court* in 1889. |

Exercise 7

Virgil

Rome produced one of the world's largest and longest-lived empires. It created a brilliant civilization and many outstanding writers, which included Cicero, Suetonius, and Livy. But the greatest of all the Roman writers was Publius Vergilius Maro, called Virgil.

Born in 70 B.C., Virgil wrote a number of different works. But people mostly know him for three epic works. The first were the *Bucolics*, which Virgil wrote from 44 to 38 B.C. These were mostly poems in rural settings, but they also focused on politics. After completing the *Bucolics*, Virgil subsequently began working on the *Georgics*. The subjects of these poems were rural life and farming, and he published them in 29 B.C.

But Virgil's best and most famous work was the *Aeneid*. Virgil wrote this from 29 B.C. until his death in 19 B.C. although he never actually finished the poem. The *Aeneid* told the story of the founding of Rome. It began with the fall of Troy and traced the travels of the hero Aeneas as he finally made it to Italy. While Virgil wanted the poem destroyed when he died, the emperor saved it. So the world managed to gain an exceptional piece of literature.

---

epic adj great; tremendous
rural adj related to the countryside
subsequently adv next; later
trace v to outline; to follow

Q1 In paragraph 1, the author's description of the Roman Empire mentions which of the following?

Ⓐ The amount of land it ruled over
Ⓑ The names of some of its great writers
Ⓒ The titles of several famous written works
Ⓓ The years during which it existed

Q2 According to paragraph 2, which of the following is true of Virgil?
- Ⓐ He only wrote three works in his life.
- Ⓑ The *Georgics* looked at life in the city.
- Ⓒ He took five years to write the *Bucolics*.
- Ⓓ The *Bucolics* were mostly about politics.

Q3 In paragraph 3, the author's description of the *Aeneid* mentions which of the following?
- Ⓐ The number of lines it contained
- Ⓑ The place where the story begins
- Ⓒ The manner in which Virgil finished it
- Ⓓ The history of the Roman Empire it covers

Q4 According to paragraph 3, people were able to read the *Aeneid* because
- Ⓐ it was written in Latin, the language of Rome
- Ⓑ Virgil had it published after his death
- Ⓒ the emperor would not let it be destroyed
- Ⓓ the people demanded that Virgil publish it

Reading Skills | Chronological Order

Check-Up Insert a number from 1 to 4 in the correct order according to the article.

_____ Virgil wrote the *Bucolics* during a six-year period.
_____ Virgil died before finishing the *Aeneid*.
_____ The Roman emperor refused to have the *Aeneid* destroyed.
_____ Virgil published the *Georgics* in 29 B.C.

• Exercise 8 •

Fantasy Writers

Fantasy literature often involves magic, strange lands, and fantastic beasts. Many ancient works of literature were fantasy works. However, modern fantasy stories did not begin until around the nineteenth century. Since then, three writers have greatly affected the fantasy genre. They are George MacDonald, C.S. Lewis, and J.R.R. Tolkien.

George MacDonald lived from 1824 to 1905. A Scottish minister, he wrote novels and children's books. He also helped restart the fantasy genre. Among his fantasy works was *Phantastes*, an 1858 novel about a man's adventures in the world of faerie. Another fantasy novel he wrote was *Lilith*, written in 1895.

Phantastes greatly influenced C.S. Lewis, one of the twentieth century's most famous writers. Lewis wrote many Christian works, but he is best known for *The Chronicles of Narnia*, a seven-book series. Written between 1949 and 1954, they describe the adventures of some children in the land of Narnia. The first book, *The Lion, the Witch, and the Wardrobe*, has both child and adult fans.

Finally, J.R.R. Tolkien, a contemporary of Lewis's, published *The Lord of the Rings* series in 1954 and 1955. A fantasy work that is similar to ancient epic poems, Tolkien's works have influenced countless modern writers.

---

fantastic adj incredible; amazing
genre n a type; a kind
restart v to begin again; to start again
faerie n the land where fairies live; fairyland

Q1 In paragraph 1, the author's description of fantasy works mentions which of the following?

Ⓐ The most popular ancient fantasy works
Ⓑ The name of the first person to write some
Ⓒ The reason few people write them
Ⓓ The types of animals that they include

Q2 According to paragraph 2, which of the following is true of George MacDonald?

Ⓐ He was the first man to write fantasy novels.
Ⓑ He published the book *Phantastes* in 1895.
Ⓒ He wrote fantasy books and also novels.
Ⓓ He wrote children's books and then became a minister.

Q3 According to paragraph 3, C.S. Lewis's popularity mainly occurred because

- Ⓐ he wrote *The Chronicles of Narnia*
- Ⓑ he wrote many books on Christianity
- Ⓒ he read *Phantastes* as a young man
- Ⓓ he wrote for both children and adults

Q4 In paragraph 4, the author's description of J.R.R. Tolkien mentions which of the following?

- Ⓐ The influence George MacDonald had on him
- Ⓑ The title of each book in *The Lord of the Rings*
- Ⓒ The fact he lived at the same time as C.S. Lewis
- Ⓓ The subjects of the epic poems he wrote

Reading Skills | Chronological Order

Check-Up Fill in the blanks according to the article.

| George MacDonald published *Phantastes* in 1858. | ➡ | **1** MacDonald wrote _____ in 1895. | ➡ | C.S. Lewis came out with *The Chronicles of Narnia* from 1949 to 1954. | ➡ | **2** _____ published *The Lord of the Rings* in 1954 and 1955. |

Subordination

Grammar Point

1 Use **subordinating conjunctions** to join an independent clause and a dependent clause. A clause contains a subject and a verb. An independent clause can stand alone as a sentence. However, a dependent clause is not a sentence. It must be connected to an independent clause to form a sentence.

2 List of Subordinating Conjunctions

Conjunction	Uses	Example Sentences
because	show cause/effect relationships between two ideas	• Because of these similarities, people classify certain times as periods of literature. • Because the legends are so famous and adored by people, writers will surely continue this in the future.
since	show cause/effect relationships between two ideas	• Many today consider works of science fiction not to be real literature since they think they are simplistic and lacking literary merit.
as	show cause/effect relationships between two ideas	• As C.S. Lewis wrote many children's books, he is still a popular author today. • Hemingway wrote about many things in his life as he had done a number of interesting activities.
although	show contrast between ideas	• Although there were many stories of King Arthur in the Middle Ages, later writers did not ignore the legends either. • Virgil wrote this from 29 B.C. until his death in 19 B.C. although he never actually finished the poem.
when	show the time when	• A third semi-autobiographical story came in 1952 when he published *The Old Man and the Sea*. • When people read about King Arthur, they often get inspired by the stories.
even though	show contrast between ideas	• In fact, he still influences literature today even though his death came almost 400 years ago. • Even though the events in the story are true, the author created the dialog himself.

Grammar Check-Up

A Choose the correct conjunctions.

1 (When / **Because**) King Arthur was a great leader, people wrote many stories about him.

2 Ernest Hemingway was a brilliant writer (**even though** / as) he used simple sentences.

3 Some people dislike science fiction (**since** / although) they think it is not real literature.

4 (When / **Although**) Jules Verne described many machines, they had not yet been invented.

5 (**When** / Because) the Middle Ages ended, the Renaissance came immediately afterward.

B Choose the correct words for each blank.

1 _____ C.S. Lewis first read *Phantastes*, he became very inspired.
  ⓐ Although ⓑ Even though ⓒ Before ⓓ When

2 The Grimm brothers wanted to preserve folk tales _____ no one else had ever done it.
  ⓐ because ⓑ after ⓒ however ⓓ while

3 Virgil wrote mostly about rural scenes _____ he preferred that part of the country.
  ⓐ however ⓑ since ⓒ although ⓓ when

4 Mary Shelley wrote *Frankenstein* _____ she was still a very young woman.
  ⓐ as ⓑ because ⓒ if ⓓ when

C Choose the one sentence that has the incorrect conjunction.

1 ⓐ Because people enjoy reading, there are many kinds of books.
  ⓑ Since Hemingway had an adventurous life, he wrote about himself in many books.
  ⓒ As Virgil wanted the *Aeneid* destroyed, Augustus saved it.
  ⓓ When Hemingway died, many people were upset about it.

2 ⓐ J.R.R. Tolkien is still famous today since people continue to read his books.
  ⓑ Science fiction is popular because it is not as popular as nonfiction books.
  ⓒ The children checked the books out of the library as they wanted to read them.
  ⓓ He finished reading the book even though it was boring.

Vocabulary Review

A Circle the words that best complete the sentences.

1 Many people (portray / consider) Shakespeare to be the greatest writer ever in English.
2 Augustus was the (empire / emperor) who ruled during the time Virgil lived.
3 *The Chronicles of Narnia* contain tales of fantastic (beasts / faerie) that children love.
4 Robert Heinlein was famous for writing science-(fiction / prose) novels.
5 Nobody knows the name of the (anonymous / influenced) writer of this poem.

B Choose the best words to complete the sentences.

1 The description of the death of the monster was very _____.
   A outstanding
   B bloody
   C contemporary
   D relevant

2 This story tells about the _____ and early years of Atlantis, a mythical place.
   A periods
   B founding
   C monster
   D fiction

3 The characters in the story _____ their troubles by working very hard.
   A lasted
   B punished
   C produced
   D overcame

4 Many fantasy stories are great _____ that take place in strange lands.
   A poems
   B adventures
   C heroes
   D merits

5 Some people believe that King Arthur may have _____ in the fourth century.
   A reigned
   B involved
   C lasted
   D portrayed

C Choose the words with the closest meanings to the highlighted words.

1. The man used a special device to let him go forward in time.
   - Ⓐ masterpiece
   - Ⓑ machine
   - Ⓒ effect
   - Ⓓ magic

2. There are many writers who are adored by their fans these days.
   - Ⓐ beloved
   - Ⓑ affected
   - Ⓒ reflected
   - Ⓓ based

3. Some of the sonnets Shakespeare wrote remain very famous even today.
   - Ⓐ plays
   - Ⓑ prose
   - Ⓒ poems
   - Ⓓ fiction

4. A lot of the stories take place in a country setting amidst farms and fields.
   - Ⓐ simplistic
   - Ⓑ humorous
   - Ⓒ rural
   - Ⓓ related

5. Everyone thought the book was fantastic for its descriptions of various events.
   - Ⓐ remarkable
   - Ⓑ epic
   - Ⓒ depressing
   - Ⓓ prose

D Complete the sentences by filling in the blanks with the best words from the list. Change the forms of the words if necessary. Use each word only once.

> medieval   warrior   masterpiece   last   fairy tale

1. Many _____ include witches, ogres, and other monsters.
2. It took the author twenty years to complete his _____.
3. There were many stories about King Arthur written during _____ times.
4. The story is about the adventures of a great _____ who wins many battles.
5. The Romantic Period _____ until the Victorian Age suddenly began.

Practice Test

John Milton and *Paradise Lost*

    There are countless epic poems from ancient Greece, classical Rome, and near East cultures like Mesopotamia. These include the *Iliad*, the *Odyssey*, the *Aeneid*, and *Gilgamesh*. Nevertheless, excluding *Beowulf*, there were few great epics in English. This changed when John Milton wrote *Paradise Lost*.

    Milton was born in 1608 and lived through a tumultuous time. The seventeenth century included the English Civil War. While Milton was involved in politics, he was not executed by his political opponents like others were. Despite living during troubled times, Milton was a prolific writer who created many works. His greatest was *Paradise Lost*.

    In that work, Milton explores stories from the Bible. He focuses on Adam and Eve's fall from grace and their expulsion from the Garden of Eden. Milton wrote about Adam and Eve as well as Satan. In fact, Satan, while the Devil, is the protagonist. Milton portrays him as an epic hero despite being evil. Throughout *Paradise Lost*, Milton traces Satan's journey after being expelled from Heaven and sent to Hell.

    Paradise Lost became an instant sensation. Interestingly, Milton composed it after he had gone blind. This made him take a long time to complete his work, for he would compose lines in his head at night and repeat them to an assistant in the morning. The assistant then recorded Milton's words on paper. Milton's work also features numerous obscure references. This owes to Milton's encyclopedic knowledge and outstanding memory. Even today, most readers rely upon the footnotes for them to understand the work.

---

prolific *adj* highly productive
grace *n* God's favor

1. In paragraph 1, the author's description of great epic poems mentions all of the following EXCEPT:
   - (A) Which poem John Milton wrote
   - (B) Who wrote many of them
   - (C) Where they were written
   - (D) What some of their titles are

2. Which of the following can be inferred from paragraph 1 about *Paradise Lost*?
   - (A) It was the world's greatest epic poem.
   - (B) It was written in English.
   - (C) It was longer than the *Iliad*.
   - (D) It was better than *Beowulf*.

3. The word "tumultuous" in the passage is closest in meaning to
   - (A) chaotic
   - (B) hilarious
   - (C) uneventful
   - (D) bloody

4. According to paragraph 2, which of the following is true of John Milton?
   - (A) He was executed for his political beliefs.
   - (B) He wrote a large number of different pieces.
   - (C) He was born during the sixteenth century.
   - (D) He fought as a soldier in the English Civil War.

5. In paragraph 3, why does the author mention "the Bible"?
   - (A) To claim that Milton had completely read it
   - (B) To explain how Milton got the idea for Satan
   - (C) To note its influence on *Paradise Lost*
   - (D) To state that Milton's poem differs greatly from it

6. The word "protagonist" in the passage is closest in meaning to
   - (A) hero
   - (B) actor
   - (C) villain
   - (D) creator

7. According to paragraph 3, in *Paradise Lost*, Satan
   - (A) manages to live on the Earth
   - (B) stays in Hell forever
   - (C) is a low-ranking devil
   - (D) is the hero of the story

8 Which of the following best expresses the essential information in the highlighted sentence? *Incorrect* answer choices change the meaning in important ways or leave out essential information.

- (A) Milton really did not write *Paradise Lost* as he would only say a few words, and then an assistant would later write the poem.
- (B) Because *Paradise Lost* took a long time to write, Milton did not write the words himself but made an assistant do it.
- (C) Milton wrote *Paradise Lost* slowly since he made the lines in his head and then repeated them to someone else the next day.
- (D) An assistant wrote *Paradise Lost* after Milton told him the words, so this made him complete the poem faster than he had expected.

9 The word "them" in the passage refers to

- (A) numerous obscure references
- (B) Milton's encyclopedic knowledge and outstanding memory
- (C) most readers
- (D) the footnotes

10 *Directions:* An introductory sentence for a brief summary of the passage is provided below. Complete the summary by selecting the THREE answer choices that express the most important ideas in the passage.

***Paradise Lost*, which is about the fall of man and Adam and Eve's expulsion from the Garden of Eden, was a great epic poem by John Milton.**

-
-
-

Answer Choices

1	John Milton was very much involved in the politics of his day.	4	Some people think Satan is an admirable character in the poem.
2	Milton included many obscure references into his work.	5	Milton describes the actions of Satan after he leaves Heaven.
3	Much of the poem was inspired by stories in the Bible.	6	The poem itself was completed in the late 1660s.

CHAPTER 02

Astronomy
(Comparison and Contrast)

1. Mars and Venus
2. Europa and Io
3. Unmanned and Manned Spaceflights
4. The Planets in the Solar System
5. Asteroids and Comets
6. Telescopes
7. Space Colonies
8. Theories on the Solar System

CHAPTER 2 **Astronomy** (Comparison and Contrast)

Understanding TOEFL Question Types & Reading Skills

1 Question Types — **Negative Factual Questions**

Negative Factual questions ask you to confirm correct information in the passage and then to find the information that is NOT true. One of the answer choices will have incorrect information. This is the correct answer. Pay attention to the facts in the passage. Make sure you can find the answer choice that is incorrect.

- **Example Negative Factual Questions**
  - According to the passage, which of the following is NOT true of X?
  - The author's description of X mentions all of the following EXCEPT:
  - In paragraph 2, all of the following questions are answered EXCEPT:

- **Useful Tips for Your Success**
  - Pay attention to
    - → the facts in the entire passage.
    - → answer choices with information not in the passage.
  - Don't
    - → choose an answer choice with information not from the passage.
    - → choose any answers mentioned in the passage.

Sample Question

Types of Stars

When people gaze at the night sky, they see thousands of stars. These stars may all appear identical, yet they possess diverse characteristics. There are actually several different classes of stars; two are blue stars and red stars.

Blue stars are the hottest in the universe and are extremely bright. People viewing them from Earth perceive them as slightly blue in color. They are actually quite rare since, despite their enormous size, they burn out incredibly quickly because of their high heat.

Meanwhile, red stars, which look orange-red from Earth, are the smallest stars. These are also, without doubt, the most common stars in the galaxy. They are also the coolest because they have already burned most of their energy.

gaze v to look at   **perceive** v to distinguish; to identify   **without doubt** phr surely; definitely

Q According to the passage, which of the following is NOT true of blue stars?
- Ⓐ They are stars of extremely large size.
- Ⓑ They are the most common stars in the galaxy.
- Ⓒ There are no stars in the universe hotter than them.
- Ⓓ They appear blue when people look at them.

2 Reading Skills — Comparison and Contrast

Comparing two or more things shows their similarities. Contrasting two or more things shows their differences. By using comparison and contrast, writers can show relationships between two or more things. Writers often use words such as *more*, *less*, *as ... as*, and *the same as* to make comparisons and contrasts.

Check-Up

▶ Which comparison between blue stars and red stars is accurate?
- Ⓐ Red stars have practically the same temperature as blue stars.
- Ⓑ Blue stars appear in the universe more frequently than red stars.
- Ⓒ Blue and red stars look like they have the same colors when people observe them.
- Ⓓ Red stars are much smaller in size than blue stars are.

• Exercise 1 •

Mars and Venus

02-02

Mars

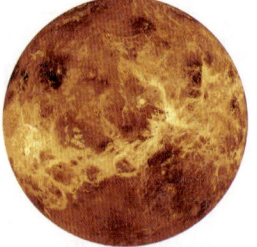
Venus

Mars and Venus are the two planets closest to Earth. They share some similarities yet are actually somewhat different from one another.

Both are classified as terrestrial planets, so this means they are relatively small. Mars is actually quite small, but Venus and Earth are practically identical in size. People even call Venus Earth's "sister planet" because the two planets' sizes are so similar. Earth, however, is almost double the size of Mars. Mars and Venus are also close enough to the sun that they could potentially have life. While scientists have not detected life on either planet, both possibly could have or once have supported life.

However, they also have many differences. For example, Mars has virtually no atmosphere, but Venus's atmosphere is thick in carbon dioxide because of the greenhouse effect there. And Venus's surface is much hotter than Mars's. Finally, Mars has ice, yet any water on Venus evaporated a long time ago thanks to the heat.

potentially adv possibly
detect v to find; to identify
evaporate v to disappear; to vanish

Q1 According to paragraphs 1 and 2, which of the following is NOT true of Earth?

Ⓐ It has been called the sister planet of Venus.
Ⓑ It is located near both Mars and Venus.
Ⓒ It is about two times smaller than Mars.
Ⓓ It is just about the same size that Venus is.

Q2 In paragraphs 2 and 3, the author's description of Venus mentions all of the following EXCEPT:

- Ⓐ The types of life forms that once existed on it
- Ⓑ How the greenhouse effect has changed its atmosphere
- Ⓒ The reason there is no water on the planet
- Ⓓ The large amount of carbon dioxide there

Q3 In paragraph 3, all of the following questions are answered EXCEPT:

- Ⓐ What is the atmosphere of Venus like?
- Ⓑ Where did water once flow on the surface of Mars?
- Ⓒ Which planet has the hotter surface temperature?
- Ⓓ What form of water currently exists on Mars?

Reading Skills Comparison and Contrast

Check-Up Write "D" for difference or "S" for similarity in the blanks for each sentence.

1. _____ Venus has a thick atmosphere, but Mars has almost none.
2. _____ Both Venus and Mars are terrestrial planets.
3. _____ Mars could potentially have life on it, and so could Venus.
4. _____ Venus is similar in size to Earth, but Mars is smaller than both planets.

• **Exercise 2** •

Europa and Io

In the 1600s, astronomer Galileo Galilei used a telescope to observe the planet Jupiter. He noticed four objects orbiting the planet. These were four of the planet's moons, which were called the Galilean moons after him. Two of them are Europa and Io.

Europa is the solar system's brightest moon, but that is not the reason astronomers are interested in it. Europa is incredibly cold, having a high surface temperature of around -160 degrees Celsius. As a result, its surface is frozen ice. Nevertheless, astronomers believe that beneath this layer of ice is a liquid ocean. Some speculate that life may exist there.

As for Io, astronomers are interested in its volcanoes. The moon has more than 400 active volcanoes, making it the most volcanically active place in the solar system. The constant eruptions mean that despite Io's coldness, its surface is mostly liquid. The lava and the molten rock flowing from volcanoes constantly change the appearance of the moon's surface.

---

orbit [v] continually to move around an object in a circular motion

speculate [v] to guess; to estimate

molten [adj] melted

Q1 In paragraph 1, all of the following questions are answered EXCEPT:

Ⓐ What is the connection between Galileo Galilei and Jupiter?
Ⓑ Who were a group of four of Jupiter's moons found by?
Ⓒ What are the names of two of Jupiter's moons?
Ⓓ How many moons does Jupiter have orbiting it?

Q2 In paragraph 2, the author's description of Europa mentions all of the following EXCEPT:

Ⓐ What comprises its surface
Ⓑ What type of life exists there
Ⓒ How bright it is compared to other moons
Ⓓ How cold its surface can get

Q3 According to paragraph 3, which of the following is NOT true of Io?

Ⓐ It is very volcanically active.
Ⓑ Its surface continually changes.
Ⓒ There are hundreds of volcanoes on it.
Ⓓ The lava on it heats the moon's surface.

Reading Skills Comparison and Contrast

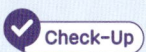 **Which comparison between Europa and Io is accurate?**

Ⓐ Europa and Io were both discovered by the same individual.
Ⓑ Europa is one of the biggest moons in the solar system, and so is Io.
Ⓒ Europa may have life under its surface while Io might have life, too.
Ⓓ Both Io and Europa have active volcanoes on their surfaces.

• **Exercise 3** •

Unmanned and Manned Spaceflights

  Several countries around the world have space programs, so they frequently make excursions into outer space. They accomplish this in two ways: with unmanned flights and manned ones.

  Unmanned flights are easily the most common. Unmanned spaceflight started when the Soviet Union launched the satellite *Sputnik* in 1957. Since then, several countries' space agencies have launched thousands of unmanned flights. Most are satellites which orbit Earth; however, some unmanned missions have sent probes to the moon and even to other planets in the solar system.

  Manned spaceflights have never been very common, especially since they are extremely more expensive and perilous than unmanned flights. The first manned flight was made by Soviet Yuri Gagarin in 1961. After that, several Americans landed on the moon. Nowadays, the United States and Russia make occasional manned missions to the International Space Station. However, there are not as many manned missions today as there once were in the past.

excursion [n] a trip
probe [n] a satellite

perilous [adj] dangerous

Q1 According to paragraph 1, which of the following is NOT true of space programs?
  Ⓐ They sometimes utilize manned flights.
  Ⓑ They exist in some countries.
  Ⓒ They have spent small amounts of money.
  Ⓓ They may involve unmanned flights.

Q2 In paragraph 2, the author's description of unmanned spaceflights mentions all of the following EXCEPT:

- Ⓐ Where some of them have gone
- Ⓑ When the first one happened
- Ⓒ How many of them there have been
- Ⓓ Why they happen less often than manned flights

Q3 In paragraph 3, all of the following questions are answered EXCEPT:

- Ⓐ Where in space do people from Russia go nowadays?
- Ⓑ How are manned flights different from unmanned ones?
- Ⓒ Who was the first person to go into outer space?
- Ⓓ How long does it take manned flights to get into space?

Reading Skills | Comparison and Contrast

Check-Up Write "D" for difference or "S" for similarity in the blanks for each sentence.

1. _____ Both manned missions and unmanned missions have been to the moon.
2. _____ Manned spaceflights are not as common as unmanned spaceflights.
3. _____ Unmanned spaceflights are less dangerous than manned spaceflights.
4. _____ Unmanned spaceflights have visited other planets, but manned ones have not.

Exercise 4

The Planets in the Solar System

There are eight planets in the solar system: Mercury, Venus, Earth, Mars, Jupiter, Saturn, Uranus, and Neptune. While these planets all share some characteristics, there are numerous differences between them. In fact, astronomers have divided the planets into two separate groups: They are the terrestrial planets and the gas giants.

Mercury, Venus, Earth, and Mars are the terrestrial planets. They are composed of rocks and metal. Additionally, they rotate slowly, are fairly small, and have zero, one, or two moons each. These planets are also the closest to the sun.

The gas giants are Jupiter, Saturn, Uranus, and Neptune. They are much larger than the terrestrial planets. Hydrogen and helium mostly comprise these planets. These planets rotate very quickly and have large numbers of moons. Jupiter actually has at least ninety-five. The gas giants are also located rather far from the sun, so they take much longer to orbit the sun than the terrestrial planets do.

---

terrestrial [adj] of or relating to Earth
rotate [v] to turn; to revolve
comprise [v] to make up

Q1 According to paragraph 1, which of the following is NOT true of the eight planets?

Ⓐ They all orbit the sun at similar speeds.
Ⓑ Some of them are considered gas giants.
Ⓒ They all belong to the same solar system.
Ⓓ All of them share some characteristics.

Q2 In paragraph 2, the author's description of terrestrial planets mentions all of the following EXCEPT:

- Ⓐ Their location relative to the sun
- Ⓑ The major component of them
- Ⓒ The type of atmosphere they have
- Ⓓ The total number of them

Q3 According to paragraph 3, which of the following is NOT true of gas giants?

- Ⓐ They spin around much faster than terrestrial planets.
- Ⓑ Their years are long since they are far from the sun.
- Ⓒ These planets all have many moons that orbit them.
- Ⓓ Their atmospheres mostly have three different gases.

Reading Skills Comparison and Contrast

 Which comparison between terrestrial planets and gas giants is accurate?

- Ⓐ All of the gas giants and the terrestrial planets orbit the sun.
- Ⓑ Both terrestrial planets and gas giants are made of rock and metal.
- Ⓒ Terrestrial planets rotate very quickly, but gas giants spin quite slowly.
- Ⓓ Gas giants and terrestrial planets all have at least one moon orbiting them.

• **Exercise 5** •

Asteroids and Comets

There are countless objects orbiting the sun along with the planets and moons. In fact, outer space is not nearly as empty as people believe. Two extremely common objects in the solar system are asteroids and comets. They possess some similarities yet are mostly different.

Asteroids formed around 4.6 billion years ago when the solar system was created. So far, astronomers have identified more than 90,000 asteroids in the asteroid belt, which is located between Mars and Jupiter. Asteroids are simply large chunks of rock; however, they all differ in size. Some are merely several feet long while others stretch for miles. Ceres, the largest known asteroid, has a 590-mile-wide diameter.

Like asteroids, comets also formed during the creation of the solar system. However, their composition is different from asteroids. Comets are large balls of rock and ice. When they near the sun, their melting ice creates million-mile-long tails. Astronomers believe there might be trillions of comets in the solar system. However, most comets are located beyond Pluto. Unlike asteroids, comets all follow various orbits. Some may pass through the solar system, but others always remain outside of it, so some comets' orbits may last thousands of years.

---

chunk n a piece
diameter n width; length
composition n makeup
trillion n one thousand billion; 1,000,000,000,000

Q1 In paragraph 1, all of the following questions are answered EXCEPT:
  Ⓐ What are two common objects in the solar system?
  Ⓑ What are some objects that orbit the sun?
  Ⓒ How are comets and asteroids similar?
  Ⓓ What do some people believe about outer space?

Q2 In paragraph 2, the author's description of asteroids mentions all of the following EXCEPT:

- Ⓐ Where many can be found
- Ⓑ What minerals they contain
- Ⓒ When they were created
- Ⓓ What the biggest one is called

Q3 According to paragraphs 2 and 3, which of the following is NOT true of the creation of the solar system?

- Ⓐ It was the time when many asteroids were formed.
- Ⓑ All of the planets obtained their final forms then.
- Ⓒ It happened sometime around 4.6 billion years ago.
- Ⓓ Most of the solar system's comets formed then.

Q4 According to paragraph 3, which of the following is NOT true of comets?

- Ⓐ They have a composition similar to that of asteroids.
- Ⓑ They can have tails that are millions of miles long.
- Ⓒ They follow individual orbits that go in different directions.
- Ⓓ They formed at around the same time that asteroids did.

Reading Skills | Comparison and Contrast

Check-Up Write "D" for difference or "S" for similarity in the blanks for each sentence.

1. _____ Asteroids are big rocks while comets are balls of rock and ice.
2. _____ Comets formed about 4.6 billion years ago, and so did asteroids.
3. _____ There are about 90,000 asteroids, yet there are trillions of comets.
4. _____ Comets and asteroids are two of the most common objects in the solar system.

• Exercise 6 •

Telescopes

02-07

Ever since the time of Galileo, people have used telescopes to examine the universe. Telescopes allow people to get close-up views of stars, planets, and other objects in the universe. There are several types of telescopes, but the two most common are reflecting and refracting telescopes.

A reflecting telescope uses mirrors to enhance the size of the objects it is observing. The first mirror is spherical and collects the light. It then focuses that light on a secondary mirror. This second mirror focuses the light on the eyepiece, so the observer can then look through it. Reflecting telescopes are good for observing faraway objects and are also somewhat inexpensive. Unfortunately, they do not always work well on the Earth, and they can sometimes provide faulty images.

A refracting telescope utilizes lenses to observe various objects. There are often two lenses at the front, which capture the image and then bend the light to the eyepiece. Refracting telescopes are easy to use and excellent for looking at the moon, planets, and binary stars. However, they can be expensive and are not effective at looking at faraway objects.

refracting adj deflecting something and keeping it from going straight
enhance v to enlarge; to improve
spherical adj circular; shaped like a sphere
faulty adj mistaken; erroneous

Q1 According to paragraph 1, which of the following is NOT true of telescopes?

Ⓐ Galileo was the man who first invented the telescope.
Ⓑ There are two main types of telescopes people use.
Ⓒ People used telescopes during the time Galileo lived.
Ⓓ Telescopes get used to look at many things in the universe.

Q2 In paragraph 2, the author's description of reflecting telescopes mentions all of the following EXCEPT:

- Ⓐ What people think about their prices
- Ⓑ What the purposes of their mirrors are
- Ⓒ What they are good at observing
- Ⓓ What make them produce poor images

Q3 In paragraphs 2 and 3, all of the following questions are answered EXCEPT:

- Ⓐ What are refracting telescopes not good at doing?
- Ⓑ What is the average price of a reflecting telescope?
- Ⓒ How many lenses does a refracting telescope have?
- Ⓓ What does the second mirror in a reflecting telescope do?

Q4 According to paragraph 3, which of the following is NOT true of refracting telescopes?

- Ⓐ They have at least two lenses to help observe the image.
- Ⓑ They may provide faulty images of the planets.
- Ⓒ They are quite simple for people to utilize.
- Ⓓ They are hard to use to see far-off objects.

Reading Skills Comparison and Contrast

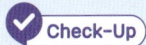 **Check-Up** Which comparison between reflecting and refracting telescopes is accurate?

- Ⓐ Reflecting telescopes observe faraway objects as well as refracting telescopes.
- Ⓑ People created reflecting and refracting telescopes during Galileo's time.
- Ⓒ Refracting telescopes use one lens while reflecting telescopes need two mirrors.
- Ⓓ Reflecting telescopes are cheaper than refracting telescopes are.

Exercise 7

Space Colonies

Eventually, manned space missions will become more common, and humans will begin to settle elsewhere in the solar system and maybe even in the galaxy. For now, the moon and Mars are likely places where humans can establish colonies. Some people are very much in favor of colonizing other planets, but others are strongly against it.

People in favor of space colonies feel that mankind must leave the Earth in order to guarantee the survival of the species. They are afraid that nuclear war or a deadly disease might kill everyone on the planet. Since the Earth's population is increasing, they want to send extra people to colonies on other planets. They also believe that these outposts can be useful to people on the Earth. For example, people could use other planets' natural resources since the Earth's are decreasing. They will let humans finally reach the stars, too.

There are surprisingly large numbers of people who believe space colonies are bad ideas. They think mankind does not have the technology to create them. Everyone knows humans will have to terraform planets to make them more like the Earth. This will cost an incredible amount of money. They also think it is too dangerous, so many people could die.

---

elsewhere adv another place
colonize v to establish or found a colony
outpost n a colony; a fort
terraform v to make something earthlike so that it can support humans

---

Q1 According to paragraph 1, which of the following is NOT true of current space programs?

Ⓐ Humans will someday live in places other than the Earth.
Ⓑ Not everyone supports colonizing other planets.
Ⓒ Manned space missions are very common now.
Ⓓ There are not yet colonies on the moon or Mars.

Q2 In paragraph 2, the author's description of the reason space colonies are necessary mentions all of the following EXCEPT:

- Ⓐ The importance of exploring new worlds
- Ⓑ What could kill everyone on the Earth
- Ⓒ How the Earth's population is a problem
- Ⓓ A possible effect of warfare on the Earth

Q3 According to paragraph 2, which of the following is NOT true of the benefits of space colonies?

- Ⓐ People will be able to encounter other life forms.
- Ⓑ The human species will be able to survive.
- Ⓒ Excess population can live in other colonies.
- Ⓓ People can utilize other planets' natural resources.

Q4 In paragraph 3, all of the following questions are answered EXCEPT:

- Ⓐ What is one problem with terraforming other planets?
- Ⓑ Why might many people in a space colony die?
- Ⓒ How do some people feel about space colonies?
- Ⓓ Which star system is ideal for a space colony?

Reading Skills Comparison and Contrast

Check-Up Write "D" for difference or "S" for similarity in the blanks for each sentence.

1. _____ Supporters of colonies want to send people there, but opponents think the colonists will die.
2. _____ Some people want to colonize planets, but others do not want to.
3. _____ Both supporters and opponents know humans must terraform new worlds.
4. _____ Opponents think colonies are too expensive, yet supporters believe the cost is worth it.

• **Exercise 8** •

Theories on the Solar System

02-09

Ancient societies frequently focused on studying the solar system. They detected several planets and learned very much about the sun and stars. However, their thoughts on Earth's relation to the solar system were quite different from what people believe nowadays.

The ancient Greeks regularly studied astronomy, and they made many accurate hypotheses about the universe. However, they were positive Earth was the center of the universe. People call this a geocentric model of the universe. The Greeks realized that Earth was round and not flat. Nevertheless, they thought that the moon, planets, stars, and even the sun orbited Earth. In their opinion, Earth did not move but remained stationary while everything else moved around Earth.

During the seventeenth century, this style of thinking began changing. Astronomers such as Galileo Galilei and Johannes Kepler proposed new theories, like their belief in a heliocentric solar system. In other words, they thought the planets all orbited the sun, which determined how fast each one moved. They recognized that the planets' orbits were not perfect circles. They could comprehend this thanks to telescopes. People now recognize that Galileo's and Kepler's ideas, while not perfect, were much closer to reality than the ancient Greeks' ideas.

---

hypothesis n a theory; a suggestion
geocentric adj centered around the Earth
stationary adj unmoving
heliocentric adj centered around the sun

Q1 According to paragraph 1, which of the following is NOT true of ancient societies?

Ⓐ They managed to find all of the planets in the solar system.
Ⓑ Their beliefs on the solar system were different from modern ones.
Ⓒ They knew a lot about both the sun and the other stars.
Ⓓ They made it a point to study the solar system.

Q2 In paragraph 2, the author's description of the ancient Greeks' model of the universe mentions all of the following EXCEPT:

- Ⓐ The name people call it
- Ⓑ The way the planets move
- Ⓒ The place that is the center of the universe
- Ⓓ The effect of Earth's motion on other planets

Q3 In paragraph 3, all of the following questions are answered EXCEPT:

- Ⓐ How long did Galileo think it took the planets to orbit the sun?
- Ⓑ What kind of solar system did Johannes Kepler believe in?
- Ⓒ How did Galileo's ideas on the solar system compare to those of the Greeks?
- Ⓓ When did people start believing in the heliocentric theory?

Q4 According to paragraph 3, which of the following is NOT true of a heliocentric solar system?

- Ⓐ The planets all move at different speeds.
- Ⓑ The planets' orbits are not circular.
- Ⓒ The planets all travel around the sun.
- Ⓓ The moons only revolve around the sun.

Reading Skills — Comparison and Contrast

Check-Up Write "D" for difference or "S" for similarity in the blanks for each sentence.

1. _____ Geocentric and heliocentric systems both try to explain how the solar system works.
2. _____ Neither geocentric nor heliocentric solar systems believe that Earth is flat.
3. _____ The sun is the center of a heliocentric system, but Earth is the center in a geocentric one.
4. _____ The Greeks believed in a geocentric system while modern astronomers believe in a heliocentric one.

Grammar Point

Coordination

1 Use **coordinating conjunctions** to join words, phrases, or sentences to one another. Coordinating conjunctions always join similar constructions. In other words, they connect word + word, phrase + phrase, or sentence + sentence.

2 List of Coordinating Conjunctions

Conjunction	Uses	Example Sentences
and	joins two or more similar ideas	• The ancient Greeks regularly studied astronomy, and they made many accurate hypotheses about the universe. • These planets rotate very quickly and have large numbers of moons.
but	joins two opposing ideas	• Mars is actually quite small, but Venus and Earth are practically identical in size. • There are several types of telescopes, but the two most common are reflecting and refracting telescopes.
so	shows cause and effect	• They also think it is too dangerous, so many people could die. • Several countries around the world have space programs, so they frequently make excursions into outer space.
for	explains a reason for something	• Astronauts are careful in space, for it can be very dangerous there. • Most space missions are unmanned, for they are cheaper than manned missions.
yet	joins two opposing ideas	• They possess some similarities yet are mostly different. • These stars may all appear identical, yet they possess diverse characteristics.
or	joins two or more differing choices	• Astronomers want to send a probe to an asteroid or send one to a comet.

Grammar Check-Up

A Choose the correct conjunctions.

1 Comets (and / but) asteroids both orbit the sun.

2 Astronomers look at the stars with telescopes, (so / but) they can see the stars more clearly.

3 The terrestrial planets are small, (yet / or) the gas giants are big planets.

4 Colonists will have to terraform planets, (for / but) it will not be easy.

5 Most people use either reflecting (and / or) refracting telescopes.

B Choose the correct words for each blank.

1 The USSR launched the first satellite, _____ the United States went to the moon first.
   ⓐ so   ⓑ but   ⓒ or   ⓓ for

2 Red stars are very small _____ are also the coolest of all stars.
   ⓐ but   ⓑ for   ⓒ and   ⓓ or

3 The Greeks knew that Earth was round _____ was not flat.
   ⓐ and   ⓑ or   ⓒ for   ⓓ but

4 Colonies on other planets will be expensive, _____ they will help humans reach the stars.
   ⓐ so   ⓑ yet   ⓒ and   ⓓ or

C Choose the sentences that have the incorrect conjunctions.

1 ⓐ The Greeks believed Earth was the center of the universe, but Kepler disagreed.
   ⓑ Some people are afraid of nuclear war, so they want to colonize other planets.
   ⓒ Reflecting telescopes can see faraway objects well, for they are inexpensive.
   ⓓ There are thousands of asteroids, so astronomers have not found them all yet.

2 ⓐ Asteroids are chunks of rocks, or comets are made of rock and ice.
   ⓑ Blue stars and red stars are two different classes of stars in the universe.
   ⓒ Venus is Earth's sister planet, but Earth is still slightly bigger than it.
   ⓓ Many people support SETI's mission, yet others feel that SETI is wasting its time.

Vocabulary Review

A Circle the words that best complete the sentences.

1 (Reflecting / Refracting) telescopes have mirrors to help look at faraway objects.
2 Some planets and moons are known to have active (volcanoes / volcanic) on them.
3 Humans will have to (terraform / colonize) other planets before they can live on them.
4 Satellites are one example of (manned / unmanned) missions that go into space.
5 Earth (rotates / orbits) one full time every twenty-four hours.

B Choose the best words to complete the sentences.

1 The amateur astronomer _____ the comet that was heading toward Earth.
 Ⓐ focused
 Ⓑ rotated
 Ⓒ detected
 Ⓓ bent

2 Some astronomers believe one of Saturn's moons may be able to _____ life.
 Ⓐ guarantee
 Ⓑ focus
 Ⓒ view
 Ⓓ support

3 Many people are interested in _____ on a different planet or moon.
 Ⓐ colonizing
 Ⓑ settling
 Ⓒ observing
 Ⓓ enhancing

4 Many people _____ that life might exist on other planets.
 Ⓐ study
 Ⓑ speculate
 Ⓒ remain
 Ⓓ favor

5 Telescopes let people get a _____ look at various objects in the sky.
 Ⓐ divided
 Ⓑ rare
 Ⓒ diverse
 Ⓓ close-up

C Choose the words with the closest meanings to the highlighted words.

1. Right now, traveling to another star system is virtually impossible.
   - Ⓐ potentially
   - Ⓑ relatively
   - Ⓒ practically
   - Ⓓ extremely

2. All of the planets were created several billion years in the past.
   - Ⓐ formed
   - Ⓑ terraformed
   - Ⓒ classified
   - Ⓓ launched

3. The galaxy is a big place, and Earth is a very small part of it.
   - Ⓐ comet
   - Ⓑ universe
   - Ⓒ solar system
   - Ⓓ star system

4. Saturn and Jupiter possess many characteristics Earth does not.
   - Ⓐ have
   - Ⓑ identify
   - Ⓒ perceive
   - Ⓓ support

5. The space agency sent a probe to explore the other planets in the solar system.
   - Ⓐ flight
   - Ⓑ rocket
   - Ⓒ space shuttle
   - Ⓓ satellite

D Complete the sentences by filling in the blanks with the best words from the list. Change the forms of the words if necessary. Use each word only once.

| heliocentric | terrestrial | comprise | orbit | evaporate |

1. Galileo believed in a(n) _____ model of the universe.
2. It takes Earth slightly over 365 days for it to _____ the sun.
3. Mars and Mercury are both considered _____ planets by astronomers.
4. Gas giants are mostly _____ of hydrogen, helium, and other gases.
5. If water is exposed to heat, it will soon _____ and disappear.

Practice Test

Problems with Interstellar Travel

The United States, the former Soviet Union, and other countries have sent probes to some planets, particularly Venus and Mars. Additionally, astronauts from the United States visited the moon a few times. However, visiting other star systems is presently impossible.

The primary reason is the vast distances involved. The distance from the sun to Earth is approximately 93,000,000 miles—one astronomical unit (AU). The *Apollo 11* mission to the moon took four days to arrive. A spaceship traveling to the sun at the same speed would take more than two years. Neptune, the farthest planet from Earth, is about twenty-nine AU distant. A trip at speeds comparable to *Apollo*'s would take decades.

As for stars, the closest one is Proxima Centauri, which is 4.2 light years away. A trip there at *Apollo*-like speeds would require thousands of years. Simply put, until spaceships can fly close to the speed of light, traveling to another star system will take too long.

Additionally, a spaceship traveling at light speed would arrive at Proxima Centauri in 4.2 years. The astronauts would need to carry enough food or have a place to grow it. They must also have abundant oxygen and water. Most people could not handle being confined in a small space for many years. While some have suggested putting astronauts into a hibernating sleep mode, this technology does not currently exist.

The distances involved present too many hurdles for interstellar travel. Until man's technological level improves tremendously, humans will remain in their solar system.

---

abundant *adj* in a large amount; plenty of
confine *v* to capture; to imprison

1. Which of the following can be inferred from paragraph 1 about the United States?
   - Ⓐ It is the only country to have sent men into outer space.
   - Ⓑ It has done the most out of all the world's space programs.
   - Ⓒ It will send another man to the moon in the near future.
   - Ⓓ It was the first country to send satellites to orbit the Earth.

2. According to paragraph 1, which of the following is true of humans' accomplishments in space?
   - Ⓐ They have sent probes to every planet in the solar system.
   - Ⓑ They have managed to visit another star system.
   - Ⓒ They have put people on the moon on several occasions.
   - Ⓓ They are currently putting together a plan to visit the stars.

3. The word "comparable" in the passage is closest in meaning to
   - Ⓐ similar
   - Ⓑ faster
   - Ⓒ nearer
   - Ⓓ slower

4. In paragraph 2, why does the author mention the distance from the Earth to the sun?
   - Ⓐ To show how long one astronomical unit is
   - Ⓑ To explain why men can never visit the sun
   - Ⓒ To note why it would take four days to get there
   - Ⓓ To compare it with the size of the Earth

5. According to paragraph 2, which of the following is NOT true of astronomical units?
   - Ⓐ There are almost thirty of them from Earth to Neptune.
   - Ⓑ One of them is equal to 93,000,000 miles.
   - Ⓒ They refer to the distance from the Earth to the sun.
   - Ⓓ It would take four days to cover the length of one AU.

6 Which of the following best expresses the essential information in the highlighted sentence? *Incorrect* answer choices change the meaning in important ways or leave out essential information.
   - (A) Spaceships take too long to get to other planets, so they must fly at light speed.
   - (B) Only a ship traveling faster than light speed will get to other stars fast enough.
   - (C) Flying near the speed of light will make a ship get to a star at much faster speeds.
   - (D) A trip to another star will take too long unless spaceships can fly near light speed.

7 The word "it" in the passage refers to
   - (A) a spaceship
   - (B) Proxima Centauri
   - (C) enough food
   - (D) a place

8 According to paragraph 4, which of the following is true of a ship traveling to another star?
   - (A) It must be able to make its own oxygen.
   - (B) It will have to put its crew in extended sleep.
   - (C) It will need to be able to make its own food.
   - (D) It will cost an incredible amount of money.

9 The word "hurdles" in the passage is closest in meaning to
   - (A) obstacles
   - (B) conditions
   - (C) opportunities
   - (D) expenses

10 *Directions:* An introductory sentence for a brief summary of the passage is provided below. Complete the summary by selecting the THREE answer choices that express the most important ideas in the passage.

While men may wish to visit other star systems, the technology to do so does not currently exist.

-
-
-

Answer Choices

1. A trip to a nearby star at light speed would take more than four years.
2. Taking supplies on a ship to another star would be a problem.
3. The United States has managed to send people to the moon in the past.
4. There is no spaceship yet that can travel near the speed of light.
5. A trip to another star in an *Apollo 11*-like craft would take thousands of years.
6. The planet Neptune is about twenty-nine AU distant from Earth.

CHAPTER 03

Zoology
(Classification)

1. Fields of Zoology
2. Shellfish
3. Primates
4. Vertebrates and Invertebrates
5. Native and Invasive Species
6. Predators and Prey
7. Cetaceans
8. Animal Evolution

CHAPTER 3   Zoology (Classification)

Understanding TOEFL Question Types & Reading Skills

1 Question Types   Rhetorical Purpose Questions

Rhetorical Purpose questions ask the reason why the author mentions certain information in the passage. These questions ask you to understand the function of a word or phrase. Try to understand the logic in why the author mentions various facts or incidents.

- **Example Rhetorical Purpose Questions**
    - The author discusses "X" in paragraph 2 in order to ~
    - Why does the author mention "X"?
    - The author uses "X" as an example of ~

- **Useful Tips for Your Success**

    - Learn to
        → recognize important words and phrases.
        → understand the meanings of these words and phrases.

    - Think about
        → the connections between sentences.
        → the connections between paragraphs.

Sample Question

Reptiles and Amphibians

People visiting lakes can typically see frogs, toads, turtles, lizards, and even snakes. These animals are not identical though as biologists have classified them separately. Some are reptiles while others are amphibians.

Reptiles and amphibians are both cold blooded, and they can all survive either on land or in water. Nevertheless, snakes, lizards, and turtles—the reptiles—are classified as separate species than frogs and toads—the amphibians.

Reptiles and amphibians are born from eggs. But reptile eggs hatch on land; amphibian eggs hatch underwater. Young amphibians even temporarily possess gills to allow them to breathe underwater. Amphibians also have smooth, moist skin that is unlike reptiles' dry, scaly skin. Additionally, amphibians can drink water and breathe through their skin.

hatch v to come out from an egg   temporarily adv for a short time

Q The author discusses "gills" in paragraph 3 in order to

Ⓐ mention amphibians' most important characteristic
Ⓑ explain how baby amphibians can survive in the water
Ⓒ describe the biggest difference between reptiles and amphibians
Ⓓ account for the reason why amphibians hatch underwater

2 Reading Skills Classification

Classification is organizing similar things or ideas into groups. People use classification to understand how two or more things or ideas relate to each other. When a writer uses classification, you should be able to notice the similarities in different things.

Check-Up

▶ The following are classified according to the article. Choose one characteristic to fill in the blank below.

Reptiles	Amphibians
Are cold blooded Hatch from eggs on land Have dry, scaly skin	Are cold blooded Hatch from eggs underwater _____

Ⓐ Have tough, scaly skin   Ⓑ Have smooth, dry skin
Ⓒ Have scaly, moist skin   Ⓓ Have smooth, moist skin

• Exercise 1 •

Fields of Zoology

People refer to the study of animals as zoology. As they work though, zoologists take many different approaches to studying animals. The result is that there are several different fields of zoology. Two are comparative anatomy and ethology.

In comparative anatomy, zoologists research the bodies of various animals. They can do this in many ways. They catalog the individual characteristics of each animal. Zoologists examine animals to see how they differ from other animals in the same or related genera. They also note the similarities between animals.

Ethology is a relatively new branch of zoology. It examines animal behavior. Ethologists are interested in how animals communicate with one another and with humans. They research animal culture and how animals get along with one another. They even look at the emotions of animals and how they react in different situations.

There are many other fields of zoology. These two, however, are ones that are relatively popular nowadays.

---

approach [n] a way of doing something
catalog [v] to record; to list
note [v] to pay attention to

Q1 In paragraph 1, why does the author mention "zoologists"?

Ⓐ To explain why they study animals
Ⓑ To mention that their field is zoology
Ⓒ To say they study animals in many ways
Ⓓ To describe them as kinds of scientists

Q2 The author discusses "comparative anatomy" in paragraph 2 in order to

- Ⓐ explain one of the fields of zoology
- Ⓑ claim it is the most popular field of zoology
- Ⓒ note that it is a difficult part of zoology
- Ⓓ explain that it only concerns cataloging animals

Q3 In paragraph 3, the author uses "animal behavior" as an example of

- Ⓐ one important aspect of ethology
- Ⓑ animals' ability to communicate
- Ⓒ some differences in animal culture
- Ⓓ the emotions that animals have

Reading Skills Classification

 **Check-Up** The following are classified according to the article. Choose one characteristic to fill in the blank below.

Comparative Anatomy	Ethology
Researches bodies of animals Catalogs characteristics of animals Looks for similarities and differences in animals	Examines animal behavior ———————————— Looks at emotions of animals

- Ⓐ Looks at how humans talk
- Ⓑ Studies animal communication
- Ⓒ Examines animal and human emotions
- Ⓓ Looks at how animals get along with humans

• Exercise 2 •

Shellfish

Many animal species live at the bottoms of bodies of water. Scientists categorize the majority of them as shellfish. There are two different types of shellfish: mollusks and crustaceans.

Like all shellfish, mollusks lack backbones and fins, and their bodies reside in shells. Mollusks' bodies typically live entirely in their shells. However, some mollusks only partially live in their shells. Most mollusks live in shallow water although very few may live deep underwater. Clams, scallops, and oysters are three kinds of mollusks. Octopi and squids are also considered mollusks. Altogether, there are more than 250,000 species of mollusks known to man.

Crustaceans are related to mollusks but have some differences. Their bodies are typically elongated and are divided into segments. This is evident in animals like crabs and lobsters, the two best-known crustaceans. Crustaceans also have eyes on stalks on their heads instead of in their bodies. Their bodies are also not always symmetrical, thus occasionally giving them unique shapes.

lack v not to have; to be without
elongated adj extended; stretched out
symmetrical adj balanced; even

Q1 In paragraph 1, why does the author mention "shellfish"?
- Ⓐ To note that mollusks make up most of them
- Ⓑ To argue that there are more crustaceans than mollusks
- Ⓒ To agree that there are at least two different kinds
- Ⓓ To state that they comprise most ocean bottom-dwellers

Q2 The author discusses mollusks' shells in paragraph 2 in order to
- Ⓐ prove that they all live inside their shells
- Ⓑ explain why some mollusks do not live in them
- Ⓒ show how much mollusks live in them
- Ⓓ mention that the shells are used for defense

Q3 In paragraph 3, the author uses "lobsters" as an example of
- Ⓐ the most common type of mollusk
- Ⓑ a shellfish that many people enjoy eating
- Ⓒ a crustacean that many people know about
- Ⓓ a crustacean that has its eyes on stalks

Reading Skills | Classification

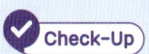 **Check-Up** The following are classified according to the article. Choose one characteristic to fill in the blank below.

Mollusks	Crustaceans
_____ Can live in shallow or deep water Are over 250,000 species	Have elongated, segmented bodies Have eyes on stalks on their heads May not have symmetrical bodies

- Ⓐ Live entirely in their shells
- Ⓑ Live most of their lives out of their shells
- Ⓒ May only live partially in their shells
- Ⓓ Use their shells only for defense

Exercise 3

Primates

Primates are a group of mammals that include humans, monkeys, apes, chimpanzees, and tarsiers. They tend to be omnivorous, so they eat both meat and vegetation. There are more than 300 species of primates. Two prominent ones are monkeys and apes.

Many people consider monkeys and apes to be the same, but they are incorrect. They have numerous differences. For instance, most monkeys have tails while apes never do. Likewise, apes tend to be larger than monkeys. Their chests are broader than those of monkeys as well. These help apes swing on vines through trees. Monkeys, in general, do not swing. Instead, they run or jump from branch to branch in trees.

Another difference is intelligence. As a general rule, apes are smarter than monkeys. Some captive apes have learned to communicate with humans by using sign language. Many species of apes also use tools.

omnivorous adj eating both meat and plant matter
prominent adj noticeable; standing out
vine n a plant with a long, slim stem and which often grows on trees

Q1 In paragraph 1, the author uses "meat and vegetation" as examples of
  Ⓐ the most common foods in the jungle
  Ⓑ two nutritious types of food
  Ⓒ the favorite foods of monkeys
  Ⓓ foods that are eaten by primates

Q2 In paragraph 2, why does the author mention "tails"?

- Ⓐ To state that all primates have them and use them
- Ⓑ To point out that monkeys rarely have them
- Ⓒ To claim monkeys have them while apes do not
- Ⓓ To show the ways that primates can use their tails

Q3 The author discusses "intelligence" in paragraph 3 in order to

- Ⓐ show how apes are smarter than monkeys
- Ⓑ note that monkeys are highly intelligent
- Ⓒ argue that monkeys are as intelligent as apes
- Ⓓ dispute the idea that apes are intelligent

Reading Skills Classification

Check-Up The following are classified according to the article. Choose one characteristic to fill in the blank below.

Monkeys	Apes
Mostly have tails Run from branch to branch in trees Are not as intelligent as apes	Never have tails _____ Are intelligent enough to learn sign language

- Ⓐ Do not often eat much meat
- Ⓑ Can be hostile to humans and other animals
- Ⓒ Have broad chests good for swinging on vines
- Ⓓ Live in large groups in the middle of forests

Exercise 4

Vertebrates and Invertebrates

Classifying all animals into two categories is virtually impossible. However, it can be done in the case of vertebrates and invertebrates. These are animals with backbones and those without them.

There are five members of the animal kingdom that are vertebrates: mammals, reptiles, amphibians, birds, and fish. Every member of these groups has a backbone. Backbones serve to protect the nerve cord in the animal's body. Vertebrates also share some other characteristics. Their brains are fairly well developed, and they typically have complex eyes, too.

Invertebrates, meanwhile, are animals that lack a backbone. Annelids, mollusks, arthropods, and echinoderms are all groups of animals without backbones. These animals typically have very soft bodies. Their bodies may also be divided into segments. Interestingly, more than ninety percent of the Earth's animals are invertebrates. These animals are often lower on the evolutionary scale and are much less complex than vertebrates are.

---

virtually adv practically; nearly
serve v to act

evolutionary adj related to evolution

Q1 In paragraph 1, why does the author mention "backbones"?

- Ⓐ To show the importance of having one
- Ⓑ To say that most animals require one
- Ⓒ To compare vertebrates with invertebrates
- Ⓓ To describe what they look like

Q2 In paragraph 2, why does the author mention the eyes of vertebrates?

- Ⓐ To point out they can see various colors
- Ⓑ To make a note of their complexity
- Ⓒ To mention their connection to the nerve cord
- Ⓓ To explain that only vertebrates possess them

Q3 In paragraph 3, the author uses "arthropods" as an example of

- Ⓐ animals with well-developed brains
- Ⓑ animals that have evolved little
- Ⓒ animals that lack backbones
- Ⓓ animals without segmented bodies

Reading Skills Classification

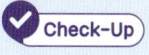 The following are classified according to the article. Choose one characteristic to fill in the blank below.

Vertebrates	Invertebrates
Have backbones Include mammals, reptiles, amphibians, birds, and fish --------	Lack backbones Include annelids, mollusks, arthropods, and echinoderms Are low on the evolutionary scale

- Ⓐ Have well-developed brains and eyes
- Ⓑ Have well-developed eyes and ears
- Ⓒ Have well-developed brains and backs
- Ⓓ Have well-developed nerves and brains

• Exercise 5 •

Native and Invasive Species

The world has countless ecosystems, which are specific areas and the animals and plants living there. The animals in an ecosystem are called its native species. However, sometimes animals from one ecosystem move to another one. People refer to them as invasive, or foreign, species.

Native species are the animals belonging to one particular ecosystem. They have generally reached a state of harmony with the other animals in their region. Therefore, there are neither too many nor too few of these animals. There are just the right numbers to achieve a perfect balance. For example, forest ecosystems usually have rabbits, squirrels, deer, bears, and other forest dwellers living together relatively harmoniously.

Unfortunately, invasive species usually disrupt the balance of an ecosystem. People may introduce these animals accidentally, or the animals may move to a new area by themselves. Invasive species usually harm their new region. They may devour the region's food supply or even kill all of one species of animal. An example is wolves moving into a forest which once had none. The wolves might then eat large numbers of animals, such as deer, squirrels, and rabbits. The effect would be to upset the balance of the ecosystem.

invasive [adj] coming in from outside somewhere
harmony [n] peace; concord
disrupt [v] to upset
devour [v] to eat all of something

Q1 The author discusses "native species" in paragraph 1 in order to
  Ⓐ note they are better than invasive species
  Ⓑ describe some of their ecosystems
  Ⓒ explain exactly what they are
  Ⓓ claim that there are many of them

Q2 In paragraph 2, why does the author mention "forest ecosystems"?
  Ⓐ To name some animals that live harmoniously in them
  Ⓑ To show how the animals in them never have problems
  Ⓒ To point out that they always have a perfect balance
  Ⓓ To argue that invasive species never go to them to live

Q3 The author discusses "invasive species" in paragraph 3 in order to

- Ⓐ describe some negative effects they have
- Ⓑ compare them with native species
- Ⓒ give several examples of them
- Ⓓ state why an area's food supply may run out

Q4 In paragraph 3, the author uses "wolves" as an example of

- Ⓐ the most dangerous invasive species
- Ⓑ a fearsome forest predator
- Ⓒ the reason a forest ecosystem was upset
- Ⓓ a species that may invade a forest

Reading Skills Classification

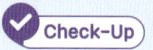 **Check-Up** The following are classified according to the article. Choose two characteristics to fill in the blanks below.

Native Species	Invasive Species
Belong in ecosystem Live harmoniously with other species ①	Move into new ecosystem ② Can kill all of a species living there

- Ⓐ Live in just one region - Are always wolves
- Ⓑ Have relatively small numbers - Often cause problems in forests
- Ⓒ Have perfect number of animals - Can disrupt new ecosystem
- Ⓓ Can live together with other animals - Have no permanent ecosystem

• Exercise 6 •

Predators and Prey

While the Earth has many different kinds of animals, they can all be divided into two large categories: predators and prey. Predators are animals that hunt other animals for food, and prey animals are those that get hunted. Interestingly, these animals have numerous differences.

In order to catch their prey, predators must have aggressive natures. Without a killer instinct, an animal cannot be a successful hunter at all. Predators also tend to have eyes in the front of their heads. This enables them to focus better on their objectives. Predators are, naturally, carnivorous animals that eat other animals' flesh. Some well-known predators are polar bears, lions, tigers, and the most feared of all: men.

Prey animals have developed certain characteristics that allow them to escape or elude predators. So they often possess defense mechanisms such as camouflage and the ability to change colors. Some, like gazelles, can run very fast to avoid predators. Prey animals usually have eyes on the sides of their head. This lets them watch out for attacking predators much better. While prey animals often just eat plants, this is not always the case. Deer, squirrels, and rabbits are common North American prey animals.

aggressive adj hostile; attacking
tend v to be likely to
elude v to avoid
mechanism n a method; a system

Q1 The author discusses "prey animals" in paragraph 1 in order to

Ⓐ explain how they are hunted
Ⓑ name several different kinds of them
Ⓒ give a definition of what they are
Ⓓ point out that there are many categories of them

Q2 In paragraph 2, why does the author mention "a killer instinct"?

- Ⓐ To explain why animals have eyes in the front of their heads
- Ⓑ To claim that animals need one to be good predators
- Ⓒ To portray all predators as fearsome animals
- Ⓓ To note that it gives animals their aggressive natures

Q3 In paragraph 2, why does the author mention "men"?

- Ⓐ To compare their hunting methods with those of tigers
- Ⓑ To claim that they are the most dangerous predator
- Ⓒ To say that all men are carnivorous animals
- Ⓓ To state that men are very successful hunters

Q4 In paragraph 3, the author uses "gazelles" as an example of

- Ⓐ animals that use camouflage as protection
- Ⓑ animals which run faster than all others
- Ⓒ animals that possess a defense mechanism
- Ⓓ animals with eyes on the sides of their heads

Reading Skills | Classification

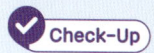 **Check-Up** The following are classified according to the article. Choose two characteristics to fill in the blanks below.

Predators	Prey
①	Can escape and elude predators
Need a killer instinct	Use defenses like camouflage
Have eyes in the front of their heads	Have eyes on the sides of their heads
Polar bears, lions, tigers, and men	②

- Ⓐ Are often herbivores - Are often carnivores
- Ⓑ Have aggressive natures - Deer, squirrels, and rabbits
- Ⓒ Mostly hunt at night - Often just eat plants
- Ⓓ Are not always successful hunters - Commonly live in North America

• **Exercise 7** •

Cetaceans

🎧 03-08

Countless large creatures—a large number of which belong to the Cetacea order—inhabit the undersea world of the oceans. The three types of cetaceans are whales, dolphins, and porpoises.

Whales grow to enormous sizes with some blue whales reaching over 110 feet in length. They are also mammals so require air, not water, to breathe. Scientists have subdivided them into baleen whales and toothed whales. Baleen whales strain minuscule animals like shrimp and kelp through their mouths to serve as food. Toothed whales hunt prey and swallow it whole. Most whales are baleen whales while a small number are toothed.

Dolphins, meanwhile, grow to much smaller sizes than whales, typically being six to fifteen feet in length. Their smaller sizes enable people to differentiate dolphins from whales. Furthermore, all dolphins are toothed whales; therefore, they consume their prey whole. Dolphins are known for their playful attitudes, often swimming with humans and sometimes even saving people from shark attacks.

Porpoises look very similar to dolphins and share some of their characteristics. They are toothed whales and somewhat playful as well. But they often live near the shore. They also have teeth that are flat while dolphins' teeth are conical in shape.

---

inhabit v to live in; to dwell in
subdivide v to divide into smaller groups
kelp n a kind of seaweed found in oceans
differentiate v to be able to tell the difference between two or more things

---

Q1 In paragraph 1, the author uses "porpoises" as an example of

Ⓐ baleen whales
Ⓑ dolphins
Ⓒ cetaceans
Ⓓ sharks

Q2 The author discusses "Baleen whales" in paragraph 2 in order to

Ⓐ demonstrate how their size is important
Ⓑ explain their unique hunting methods
Ⓒ show what kind of food they eat
Ⓓ describe how they need to breathe

Q3 In paragraph 3, why does the author mention the typical sizes of dolphins?

Ⓐ To explain why they are all toothed whales
Ⓑ To compare their sizes with those of whales
Ⓒ To give the reason they can prevent shark attacks
Ⓓ To state why they are comfortable with humans

Q4 The author discusses "teeth" in paragraph 4 in order to

Ⓐ explain how dolphins and porpoises can eat fish
Ⓑ state the reason why porpoises live near shore
Ⓒ note the main difference between dolphins and porpoises
Ⓓ show how dolphins' and porpoises' teeth differ

Reading Skills | Classification

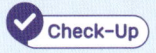 **Check-Up** The following are classified according to the article. Choose two characteristics to fill in the blanks below.

Whales	Dolphins
① _____ Are baleen and toothed whales Most eat small animals like shrimp and kelp	Are often six to fifteen feet long Are all toothed whales Have playful attitudes

Porpoises
Are toothed whales   Are somewhat playful   ②

Ⓐ Are all over 110 feet long - Live near the shore
Ⓑ Must breathe air - Are bigger than dolphins
Ⓒ Need to breathe water - Are similar to dolphins
Ⓓ Can grow to enormous sizes - Have flat teeth

Exercise 8

Animal Evolution

The creatures in the animal kingdom constantly undergo various changes. Most of these changes happen over time in a process called natural selection. However, there is another kind of change called artificial selection. Here, humans play a role in making animals evolve.

Under natural selection, animals with traits that are desirable in their species reproduce faster or more successfully than animals without these traits. This allows the superior animals to dominate their species. These traits are most often genetic changes in nature. The changes also always help the animals in some way. These transformations can be major or minor. They may also occur quickly—in just one generation—or over the course of several generations.

Artificial selection, on the other hand, is something humans cause. Humans may breed animals for certain characteristics. They have done this with horses and dogs for hundreds of years. Another method is inbreeding, which mates closely related animals to one another. The results of this, however, are not always positive. Nowadays, scientists even use gene therapy to alter the genetic structures of animals.

The result of both natural and artificial selection is to make animals change or evolve. These can happen naturally or intentionally.

---

trait n a characteristic
dominate v to rule over; to control
over the course of phr throughout; during
inbreed v to mate with one's close relatives

Q1 In paragraph 1, why does the author mention "the animal kingdom"?

Ⓐ To prove humans are involved in its changes
Ⓑ To comment that its changes happen slowly
Ⓒ To state that most of its changes are artificial
Ⓓ To note that it is always changing somehow

Q2 In paragraph 2, the author uses "genetic changes" as an example of

Ⓐ a form of inbreeding
Ⓑ the most successful changes
Ⓒ a way that makes only big changes
Ⓓ one type of natural selection

Q3 In paragraph 3, why does the author mention "Artificial selection"?

- Ⓐ To claim it is less effective than natural selection
- Ⓑ To explain how it can use gene therapy
- Ⓒ To show how humans can change animals
- Ⓓ To comment that it is usually successful

Q4 The author discusses "inbreeding" in paragraph 3 in order to

- Ⓐ describe a form of artificial selection that is not always effective
- Ⓑ mention that it may only be done by people in laboratories
- Ⓒ say that it usually results in very special characteristics
- Ⓓ produce animals that are closely related to one another

Reading Skills Classification

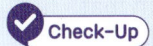 **Check-Up** The following are classified according to the article. Choose two characteristics to fill in the blanks below.

Natural Selection	Artificial Selection
Develop desirable traits ① May be major or minor changes Can happen quickly or over generations	Is caused by humans Breed animals to get certain characteristics ② Use gene therapy today

- Ⓐ Reproduce faster than others - Always mate related animals
- Ⓑ Undergo genetic changes - Can use inbreeding
- Ⓒ Changes not always helpful - Is relatively new method
- Ⓓ Not always genetic changes - Do with dogs and horses

Grammar Point

Punctuation

Punctuation Mark	Uses	Example Sentences
period (.)	ends a sentence	• But they often live near the shore. • Some are reptiles while others are amphibians.
comma (,)	joins two independent clauses	• Reptiles and amphibians are both cold blooded, and they can all survive either on land or in water.
	joins an independent clause and a dependent clause	• As they work though, zoologists take many different approaches to studying animals.
	is used after an introductory phrase	• Additionally, flightless birds are frequently larger than average.
	is used in a list of three or more things	• People visiting lakes can typically see frogs, toads, turtles, lizards, and even snakes.
	separates two adjectives modifying the same noun	• Amphibians also have smooth, moist skin.
semicolon (;)	joins two independent clauses	• But reptile eggs hatch on land; amphibian eggs hatch underwater. • Furthermore, all dolphins are toothed whales; therefore, they consume their prey whole.
colon (:)	introduces something explained in the preceding sentence	• Flying birds use their wings for several purposes: Wings are beneficial when hunting prey. • There are five members of the animal kingdom that are vertebrates: mammals, reptiles, amphibians, birds, and fish.
hyphen (-)	makes compound words	• They are the two best-known crustaceans.
dash (—)	inserts comments that are related to the sentence but are apart from it	• Countless large creatures—a large number of which belong to the Cetacea order—inhabit the undersea world of the oceans.

Grammar Check-Up

A Check (✓) the underlined parts that have the correct punctuation.

1. ☐ Some animals have one cell<u>;</u> others have many.
2. ☐ There are more than twenty-two dolphins living in the aquarium<u>.</u>
3. ☐ There are three kinds of cetaceans: dolphins<u>—</u>whales<u>—</u>and porpoises.
4. ☐ In addition<u>;</u> most predators are very aggressive animals.
5. ☐ Natural selection<u>—</u>which Darwin discussed<u>—</u>happens in many species.
6. ☐ Ethology is a field of zoology<u>.</u> and so is comparative biology.

B Complete the story with the correct punctuation.

Dolphins, some of nature's most playful animals _____ are cetaceans. Their feeding habits are similar to those of porpoises _____ Eating their food whole. Some people even go swimming with dolphins _____ the dolphins enjoy swimming around them. However, when sharks _____ some of nature's most fearsome animals—come, the dolphins often protect the humans and drive away the sharks _____

C Choose the correct punctuation marks for the blanks.

1. Rabbits, squirrels _____ and deer are all animals that live in forest ecosystems.
   ⓐ ;   ⓑ :   ⓒ ,   ⓓ -

2. Five species of animals have backbones _____ mammals, birds, reptiles, amphibians, and fish.
   ⓐ :   ⓑ ;   ⓒ ,   ⓓ -

3. Birds like ostriches—and also emus and penguins _____ can no longer fly.
   ⓐ ,   ⓑ .   ⓒ :   ⓓ —

4. Shellfish are bottom _____ dwellers that often live in shallow water.
   ⓐ ,   ⓑ -   ⓒ .   ⓓ ;

5. Natural selection is common _____ some scientists are using artificial selection now.
   ⓐ .   ⓑ :   ⓒ ;   ⓓ ,

Chapter ❸ 85

Vocabulary Review

A Circle the words that best complete the sentences.

1 Some animals are able to live (harmony / **harmoniously**) with one another.
2 This (herbivorous / **omnivorous**) animal eats all kinds of meat as well as plants.
3 (**Carnivorous** / Aggressive) animals eat the flesh of others.
4 Amphibians such as frogs and toads have (**moist** / dry) skin.
5 Some people use (genetic / **artificial**) selection to breed the species they desire.

B Choose the best words to complete the sentences.

1 The appearance of the shark in the area _____ all the sea life in the water.
  Ⓐ underwent
  Ⓑ disrupted
  Ⓒ enabled
  Ⓓ divided

2 Invertebrates have _____ much less than animals that have backbones.
  Ⓐ bred
  Ⓑ balanced
  Ⓒ evolved
  Ⓓ lacked

3 Some animals, such as fish, have _____, so they can breathe underwater.
  Ⓐ scales
  Ⓑ stalks
  Ⓒ gills
  Ⓓ segments

4 The eagle is one of the most _____ hunters out of all the birds on the Earth.
  Ⓐ successful
  Ⓑ flightless
  Ⓒ evolutionary
  Ⓓ playful

5 Some zoologists want to know how animals _____ with one another.
  Ⓐ differentiate
  Ⓑ elect
  Ⓒ communicate
  Ⓓ possess

C Choose the words with the closest meanings to the highlighted words.

1. There are many different fields of zoology for people to study.
   - Ⓐ species
   - Ⓑ catalogs
   - Ⓒ characteristics
   - Ⓓ branches

2. Some invasive species moved to the lake and killed many fish.
   - Ⓐ native
   - Ⓑ foreign
   - Ⓒ aggressive
   - Ⓓ predator

3. Some animals can reside in places where humans could never survive.
   - Ⓐ swallow
   - Ⓑ inhabit
   - Ⓒ require
   - Ⓓ utilize

4. The shark devoured many of the smaller fish as fast as it could.
   - Ⓐ ate
   - Ⓑ hatched
   - Ⓒ possessed
   - Ⓓ hunted

5. Many animals are hunters that search for other animals to kill and eat.
   - Ⓐ prey
   - Ⓑ carnivorous
   - Ⓒ invasive
   - Ⓓ predators

D Complete the sentences by filling in the blanks with the best words from the list. Change the forms of the words if necessary. Use each word only once.

> swing   breathe   ecosystem   transformation   hatch

1. Very few animals can survive in a desert _____.
2. As soon as an alligator _____ from its egg, it starts looking for food.
3. Evolution causes some animals to undergo various _____.
4. Some primates _____ on vines in order to move from tree to tree.
5. Since whales cannot _____ underwater, they must surface every few minutes.

Practice Test

Waterfowl

    Around the world, waterfowl can be found living in or near rivers, lakes, streams, and oceans. Waterfowl are birds such as ducks, geese, and swans. Many waterfowl have similar characteristics. For instance, they have webbed feet and waterproof feathers. These feathers help keep the birds dry even when they dive beneath the water.

    Of ducks, geese, and swans, ducks are the most colorful. Males can be a variety of colors. Mandarin ducks, which are native to East Asia, can be blue, green, red, orange, and purple in color. Males of other species may be somewhat less colorful. Females tend to be brown or white. Male and female geese and swans are typically white or gray.

    Waterfowl are mostly omnivores, so they have varied diets. One exception is Canadian geese, which are herbivores that only eat plant matter such as aquatic vegetation. Other types of geese consume plants but also eat insects, shells, and even small fish they catch. The same is true of swans and most species of ducks.

    Another feature of waterfowl is that they often migrate. **1** A common sight in North America in autumn is flocks of geese migrating south while flying in a V pattern. **2** Some waterfowl can fly at great speeds—even exceeding 100 kilometers per hour. **3** This enables those birds to fly hundreds of kilometers in just a few hours. **4** For instance, mallards, a type of duck, can fly more than 800 kilometers in half a day.

---

herbivore [n] an animal that only eats plant matter
autumn [n] fall

1. In paragraph 1, the author uses "webbed feet" as an example of
   - Ⓐ something that lets waterfowl swim fast
   - Ⓑ the most unique characteristic of all waterfowl
   - Ⓒ a feature that all waterfowl have
   - Ⓓ a colorful aspect of waterfowl

2. According to paragraph 1, which of the following is NOT true of waterfowl?
   - Ⓐ They include ducks and geese.
   - Ⓑ Their feathers keep water out.
   - Ⓒ They live around various bodies of water.
   - Ⓓ They are not always able to fly.

3. The word "somewhat" in the passage is closest in meaning to
   - Ⓐ slightly
   - Ⓑ sufficiently
   - Ⓒ incredibly
   - Ⓓ variously

4. In paragraph 2, the author implies that male ducks
   - Ⓐ build nests before females lay eggs
   - Ⓑ are more colorful than female ducks
   - Ⓒ always have at least two colors
   - Ⓓ can fly faster than female ducks

5. Which of the following best expresses the essential information in the highlighted sentence? *Incorrect* answer choices change the meaning in important ways or leave out essential information.
   - Ⓐ Only Canadian geese are able to consume aquatic vegetation.
   - Ⓑ Aquatic vegetation is the primary food herbivorous Canadian geese eat.
   - Ⓒ Canadian geese, which are strictly herbivores, are an exception.
   - Ⓓ It is true that Canadian geese are herbivores and eat plants growing in the water.

6. The word "they" in the passage refers to
   - Ⓐ Canadian geese
   - Ⓑ other types of geese
   - Ⓒ plants
   - Ⓓ insects, shells, and even small fish

7 The word "flocks" in the passage is closest in meaning to

- Ⓐ groups
- Ⓑ species
- Ⓒ males
- Ⓓ couples

8 According to paragraph 4, which of the following is true of waterfowl?

- Ⓐ They are all capable of flying very quickly.
- Ⓑ They fly high in the sky whenever they migrate.
- Ⓒ Many of them fly to other lands at times.
- Ⓓ Many of them fly farther than mallards do.

9 Look at the four squares [■] that indicate where the following sentence could be added to the passage.

They do this in order to find food sources as well as to reach their mating grounds.

Where would the sentence best fit?

Click on a square [■] to add the sentence to the passage.

10 *Directions:* An introductory sentence for a brief summary of the passage is provided below. Complete the summary by selecting the THREE answer choices that express the most important ideas in the passage.

Waterfowl include ducks, geese, and swans, and these birds share certain characteristics.

-
-
-

Answer Choices

① Many waterfowl migrate during fall to fly to other lands.	④ The majority of waterfowl are able to eat both vegetation and animals.
② Waterfowl have feathers that help them dive beneath the water.	⑤ Only ducks, geese, and swans are considered to be waterfowl.
③ Male waterfowl can be colorful while females tend to be less colorful.	⑥ There are hundreds of species of waterfowl around the world.

CHAPTER 04

Art
(Cause and Effect)

❶ Art Deco
❷ Leonardo da Vinci
❸ Impressionism
❹ The Dutch Golden Age
❺ Michelangelo
❻ Ansel Adams
❼ Cave Paintings
❽ Perspective in the Renaissance

CHAPTER 4　Art (Cause and Effect)

Understanding TOEFL Question Types & Reading Skills

1 Question Types — Inference Questions

Inference questions ask about arguments or ideas that the passage does not mention. The author implies these things but does not actually include them in the passage. Pay attention to the causes and effects of different arguments or ideas. Think about why something happened or why something will happen in the future.

- **Example Inference Questions**
    - Which of the following can be inferred about X?
    - The author of the passage implies that X ~
    - Which of the following can be inferred from paragraph 1 about X?

- **Useful Tips for Your Success**
    - Pay attention to → causes and effects.
        → suggestions and results.
    - Don't → pick answers that contradict the main idea.
        → choose answers just because they look right.

Sample Question

Illuminated Manuscripts

Some of the most beautiful artwork from the Middle Ages does not come from paintings but is instead found in books. Illuminated manuscripts from this time had pictures in them.

Centuries ago, books were incredibly expensive, so only wealthy individuals purchased them. They typically ordered books specially made. If the books had been plain, they would not have been pleased. So bookmakers commonly illustrated the texts.

The Bible was the most common book in medieval times, so many illuminated manuscripts depicted scenes from the Bible. In addition, other books—usually religious texts—were illustrated. Even today, the pictures in these books remain brilliant. The reason is the paints the artists used; they included various herbs, and some even had real gold and silver.

illuminated adj illustrated
plain adj ordinary
remain v to stay; not to change

Q In paragraph 2, the author implies that wealthy individuals

Ⓐ only wanted books that looked nice
Ⓑ enjoyed reading books without pictures
Ⓒ always purchased books on religious topics
Ⓓ liked plain books more than any others

2 Reading Skills — Cause and Effect

The cause is the reason something happened. The effect is the result of that action. By using cause and effect, writers can show how one action caused another. Writers often use words and phrases like *so*, *because*, *therefore*, *due to*, and *thanks to* to connect a cause and its effect.

Check-Up

▶ For the pair of sentences below, mark "C" for cause and "E" for effect.

_____ If the books were plain, they would not have been pleased.
_____ So bookmakers commonly illustrated the texts.

Exercise 1

Art Deco

In the 1920s, the world was recovering from the damage caused by World War I. People wanted a new style to show the prosperity and glamour of the time. As a result, Art Deco was created. It was a highly decorative art style.

Art Deco had many influences. They included Cubism and Futurism. Ancient Egyptian, Greek, and Roman styles also influenced Art Deco artists. Art Deco focused on creating geometric shapes as well as natural forms that were stylized. It stressed lavish decorations. It was not just an art movement though. It also influenced architects, interior designers, and fashion designers.

In the United States, architects were fascinated by Art Deco. So they often designed buildings in that style. In New York City, the Chrysler Building was made in the Art Deco style. So was the Empire State Building. Art Deco was popular in Miami, Florida. Today, that city has the largest number of Art Deco buildings in the world.

glamour n the quality of being attractive
stress v to emphasize
lavish adj extravagant; excessive

Q1 Which of the following can be inferred from paragraph 1 about the 1920s?
- Ⓐ There was not much special about that time.
- Ⓑ There was only one style of art in it.
- Ⓒ World War I was fought during it.
- Ⓓ It was a time when people made a lot of money.

Q2 In paragraph 2, the author implies that Art Deco
- Ⓐ was only popular with artists
- Ⓑ was influenced by styles from the past
- Ⓒ was a very simple style of art
- Ⓓ was the result of a group of European artists

Q3 In paragraph 3, which of the following can be inferred about Miami, Florida?
- Ⓐ Most of its Art Deco buildings were destroyed.
- Ⓑ Art Deco never became popular there.
- Ⓒ Architects influenced by Art Deco worked there.
- Ⓓ The Chrysler Building is located there.

Reading Skills Cause and Effect

Check-Up For each pair of sentences below, mark "C" for cause and "E" for effect.

1. _____ As a result, Art Deco was created.
   _____ People wanted a new style to show the prosperity and glamour of the time.
2. _____ In the United States, architects were fascinated by Art Deco.
   _____ So they often designed buildings in that style.

• **Exercise 2** •

Leonardo da Vinci

Leonardo da Vinci was the ideal Renaissance man. He was a man of countless talents, including art, engineering, science, and naturalism. This enabled him to make amazing accomplishments during his life. While people know Leonardo for many things, his skills as a painter have brought him the most renown.

Early in his life, Leonardo spent considerable time working in Milan. There, he created some of his most famous works. One of these was *The Last Supper*, a mural depicting the last supper of Jesus Christ and his apostles. Leonardo painted this for his patron Duke Ludovico Sforza, who commissioned this work.

Leonardo later moved to Florence. There, a wealthy merchant desired a painting of his wife, so he paid Leonardo to create one. Although it took him many years, Leonardo finally produced the *Mona Lisa* near the end of his life. This is arguably the most famous painting in the world; surely it is one of the most recognizable.

---

renown n fame
mural n a wall painting; a fresco
commission v to order; to pay for

Q1 In paragraph 1, the author implies that a Renaissance man

Ⓐ lived a long time ago
Ⓑ has many different skills
Ⓒ is usually Italian
Ⓓ has to be able to paint

Q2 Which of the following can be inferred from paragraph 2 about *The Last Supper*?

Ⓐ It is Leonardo's best painting.
Ⓑ It is very large.
Ⓒ It is located in Rome.
Ⓓ Many people have seen it.

Q3 Which of the following can be inferred from paragraph 3 about the *Mona Lisa*?

Ⓐ It is now kept in a French museum.
Ⓑ Leonardo never actually finished it.
Ⓒ Leonardo completed it in a short time.
Ⓓ Leonardo painted it in Florence.

Reading Skills Cause and Effect

Check-Up For each pair of sentences below, mark "C" for cause and "E" for effect.

1 _____ Leonardo was a man of countless talents, including art, engineering, science, and naturalism.
   _____ This enabled him to make amazing accomplishments during his life.

2 _____ So he paid Leonardo to create one.
   _____ A wealthy merchant desired a painting of his wife.

• Exercise 3 •

Impressionism

At times, many artists begin painting in similar styles. The result is that a new art movement is born. There have been many different art movements throughout history, but perhaps the most famous is the Impressionism movement.

Impressionism began in the 1860s and took its name from the painting *Impression, Sunrise*, which was painted by Claude Monet. Impressionism began as a reaction against the present trends in art. During the nineteenth century, religious images and historical themes were very popular. But the impressionists were not particularly interested in these subjects. So they often painted everyday objects such as people or even just bowls of fruit.

Likewise, pre-Impressionist artists often used dark colors. The Impressionists, however, were interested in the effect of sunlight on the objects they painted; accordingly, they used brighter colors in their paintings.

Some of the world's most famous Impressionists were Paul Cezanne, Pierre Auguste Renoir, and Edouard Manet. Today, their paintings often sell for millions of dollars.

---

to be born phr to begin
trend n a fad; a fashion

accordingly conj therefore; so

Q1 Which of the following can be inferred from paragraph 1 about Impressionism?

Ⓐ It developed when many painters used the same style.
Ⓑ It was the first art movement ever to develop.
Ⓒ The world's most famous painters were all Impressionists.
Ⓓ It was born at a very important time in world history.

Q2 In paragraph 2, the author implies that *Impression, Sunrise*

- Ⓐ was a painting many Impressionists copied
- Ⓑ was Claude Monet's best-known painting
- Ⓒ was one of the first Impressionist paintings
- Ⓓ was created in the early nineteenth century

Q3 Which of the following can be inferred from paragraph 2 about the Impressionists' subject matter?

- Ⓐ It often featured important people from history.
- Ⓑ It used only things the sun shined on.
- Ⓒ It often had people doing various activities.
- Ⓓ It was often of things people regularly saw.

Reading Skills Cause and Effect

Check-Up For each pair of sentences below, mark "C" for cause and "E" for effect.

1. _____ At times, many artists begin painting in similar styles.
   _____ The result is that a new art movement is born.

2. _____ Accordingly, they used brighter colors in their paintings.
   _____ The Impressionists, however, were interested in the effect of sunlight on the objects they painted.

Exercise 4

The Dutch Golden Age

In the seventeenth century, the Netherlands was a leading European country. The Netherlands engaged in global trade, and its scientists made great discoveries and inventions. Because of its immense wealth, its citizens dedicated considerable time to creating artwork. This resulted in the Dutch Golden Age, which lasted for about a century.

Interestingly, Dutch painters did not all have identical styles. They instead made all sorts of paintings, including landscapes, historical scenes, and portraits. This made the Dutch Golden Age a very diverse art period.

Rembrandt and Peter Paul Rubens were the two most famous Dutch painters of this age. Still, they had very different styles. Rembrandt often painted self-portraits and biblical scenes. He also instructed many Dutch painters, so he had a more lasting influence even after his death. Meanwhile, Rubens stressed movement and color in his works. Together, their works show how brilliant this age was for works of art.

immense adj huge; enormous
identical adj same; similar
landscape n a picture of outdoor scenery

Q1 In paragraph 1, the author implies the Dutch Golden Age
- Ⓐ was a time when everyone in the Netherlands was rich
- Ⓑ made the Dutch the masters of Europe
- Ⓒ was a very good period of time in the Netherlands
- Ⓓ saw the Dutch make Europe's best artwork

Q2 Which of the following can be inferred from paragraph 1 about trade in the Netherlands during the Dutch Golden Age?

- Ⓐ It dealt mostly with machines and inventions.
- Ⓑ It involved people on other continents.
- Ⓒ It was mainly done in gold and silver.
- Ⓓ It was organized by the Dutch navy.

Q3 Which of the following can be inferred from paragraphs 2 and 3 about Dutch painters?

- Ⓐ They were all taught by Rembrandt.
- Ⓑ They often used different methods.
- Ⓒ They preferred to use bright colors.
- Ⓓ They were not interested in fame.

Reading Skills Cause and Effect

Check-Up For each pair of sentences below, mark "C" for cause and "E" for effect.

1. _____ Because of its immense wealth, its citizens dedicated considerable time to creating artwork.
   _____ This resulted in the Dutch Golden Age, which lasted for about a century.
2. _____ This made the Dutch Golden Age a very diverse art period.
   _____ Interestingly, Dutch painters did not all have identical styles.

Exercise 5

Michelangelo

The Renaissance was a period in Europe when there was a rebirth in knowledge thanks to its many brilliant men. One of the greatest was Michelangelo. A sculptor born in 1475 in Caprese, Italy, he would become one of the greatest artists of all time.

When he was twelve, Michelangelo became a painter's apprentice. However, he preferred to learn sculpture, so he began studying that instead. Early in his teenage years, one of the Medici rulers of Florence noticed Michelangelo and thus became his patron. If Michelangelo had not met the Medici ruler, his life would have been very different.

As a young man, Michelangelo rapidly began producing great works. He finished *Pieta* when he was only twenty-three. Two years later, he began sculpting *David*. He wanted to give *David* a look different from that of other sculptors. Therefore, he sculpted *David* as a young boy, not an old man.

But Michelangelo's greatest work was painting the ceiling of the Sistine Chapel in the Vatican. He considered himself a sculptor, not a painter, so he had no interest in the project at first. The pope, however, persuaded him to start and complete it. So Michelangelo worked from 1508 to 1512 to complete his masterpiece.

---

rebirth n a renewal; a renaissance
apprentice n a learner; a trainee
sculpt v to make a statue from stone
persuade v to convince

Q1 In paragraph 1, the author implies that the Renaissance
  Ⓐ was a time when one of the best artists lived
  Ⓑ was the period that saw the most learning in history
  Ⓒ started in Italy and then moved to the rest of Europe
  Ⓓ had just a few intelligent people who did great things

Q2 Which of the following can be inferred from paragraph 2 about Michelangelo's youth?

Ⓐ He made several well-known sculptures then.
Ⓑ He had no real skills at that time.
Ⓒ He began working during this time.
Ⓓ He helped change the Medici ruler's life.

Q3 Which of the following can be inferred from paragraph 3 about *David*?

Ⓐ It was made before *Pieta*.
Ⓑ It was a sculpture.
Ⓒ It was very expensive.
Ⓓ It was finished quickly.

Q4 Which of the following can be inferred from paragraph 4 about Michelangelo?

Ⓐ He had to get paid a lot to do any work.
Ⓑ He did not enjoy working in the Vatican.
Ⓒ People thought he was a better painter than sculptor.
Ⓓ It was possible to make him change his mind.

Reading Skills Cause and Effect

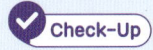 Which sentence group below does NOT show cause and effect?

Ⓐ However, he preferred to learn sculpture, so he began studying that instead.
Ⓑ The pope, however, persuaded him to start and complete it. So Michelangelo worked from 1508 to 1512 to complete his masterpiece.
Ⓒ One of the greatest was Michelangelo. A sculptor born in 1475 in Caprese, Italy, he would become one of the greatest artists of all time.
Ⓓ He wanted to give *David* a look different from that of other sculptors. Therefore, he sculpted *David* as a young boy, not an old man.

• Exercise 6 •

Ansel Adams

People typically think of art as paintings and drawings, yet there are many other kinds of art. Photography is one. And one of the greatest photographers ever was Ansel Adams.

Adams had a solitary life growing up, so he spent considerable time outdoors. This turned him into a great nature lover, which would inspire his entire career. Adams grew up in northern California, so his nature walks often included visits to Yosemite National Park. When he first visited Yosemite in 1916, it changed him by making him dedicate his life to nature. He also decided to visit the park at least once annually. He did this until his death in 1984.

Adams joined the Sierra Club in 1919. This organization was interested in preserving the environment. Within a couple of years, he began publishing his photographs and drawings in the Sierra Club's bulletin. People began noticing his work, so this brought him a great amount of fame. He soon began making a living just from his photography work. Adams continually improved the quality of his photographs throughout his life. This made people recognize his technical genius as a photographer. When he died, he was arguably the most famous photographer in the world.

solitary adj lonely; private
dedicate v to devote
bulletin n an announcement; a statement; a report
arguably adv possibly; perhaps

Q1 Which of the following can be inferred from paragraph 2 about Ansel Adams's youth?
- Ⓐ His family was quite wealthy.
- Ⓑ He did not have many friends.
- Ⓒ He was often very sick.
- Ⓓ He had many pets in his house.

Q2 In paragraph 2, the author implies that Yosemite National Park

- Ⓐ was established in the twentieth century
- Ⓑ was a place where Adams took many pictures
- Ⓒ was located near Ansel Adams's home
- Ⓓ was where Adams worked in his youth

Q3 In paragraph 3, the author implies that the Sierra Club

- Ⓐ sponsored some of Adams's work
- Ⓑ helped Adams to become famous
- Ⓒ published pictures in color
- Ⓓ was a fairly large organization

Q4 Which of the following can be inferred from paragraph 3 about Ansel Adams?

- Ⓐ He worked other jobs besides doing photography.
- Ⓑ He traveled to places all around the world.
- Ⓒ He became the president of the Sierra Club.
- Ⓓ He had a lot of skill as a photographer.

Reading Skills | Cause and Effect

Check-Up Which sentence group below does NOT show cause and effect?

- Ⓐ Adams grew up in northern California, so his nature walks often included visits to Yosemite National Park.
- Ⓑ Adams continually improved the quality of his photographs throughout his life. This made people recognize his technical genius as a photographer.
- Ⓒ Adams joined the Sierra Club in 1919. This organization was interested in preserving the environment.
- Ⓓ Adams had a solitary life growing up, so he spent considerable time outdoors.

Exercise 7

Cave Paintings

04-08

In 1879, Marcelino Sautuola and his daughter found some drawings in a cave. After much research, Sautuola publicly announced his findings. Most people believed the paintings were fakes, so they refused to believe Sautuola's find was legitimate. However, Europeans soon began finding more cave paintings. The result was that people realized the cave paintings were actually real.

Cave paintings are anywhere from 32,000 to 10,000 years old. They are typically simple depictions of various objects, including animals such as bison, deer, and horses and traced drawings of people's hands. There are very few pictures of humans. The paintings are often very simplistic. However, some of the newest cave paintings discovered, like those at Lascaux, are more sophisticated. This has led people to focus their research on these caves.

No one knows why ancient people made these paintings. Some believe they were painted for religious purposes; others think they were attempts at communication. However, while simple, if these paintings did not exist, people's knowledge of the past would be different. For example, anthropologists have seen drawings of animals that do not live in Europe now. So now they realize these animals, like rhinoceroses and hyenas, actually once lived in parts of Europe.

---

publicly adv in public
legitimate adj real; authentic
bison n a buffalo
sophisticated adj complicated; difficult

Q1 In paragraph 1, the author implies that Marcelino Sautuola

Ⓐ did not often tell the truth
Ⓑ found paintings in many caves
Ⓒ sometimes explored caves
Ⓓ was trained in art history

Q2 Which of the following can be inferred from paragraph 2 about cave paintings?

Ⓐ They use many different colors.
Ⓑ They were made in prehistoric times.
Ⓒ They included humans hunting animals.
Ⓓ They were often quite complicated.

Q3 In paragraph 2, the author implies that the cave paintings at Lascaux

Ⓐ were discovered by Marcelino Sautuola
Ⓑ were found in the nineteenth century
Ⓒ are not the oldest ones in existence
Ⓓ show both humans and animals

Q4 Which of the following can be inferred from paragraph 3 about the reasons people made cave paintings?

Ⓐ There is no reason everyone agrees on.
Ⓑ They were primitive ways to record history.
Ⓒ They were ways people told stories.
Ⓓ There was always a religious reason for them.

Reading Skills Cause and Effect

 Which sentence group below does NOT show cause and effect?

Ⓐ However, Europeans soon began finding more cave paintings. The result was that people realized the cave paintings were actually real.

Ⓑ Cave paintings are anywhere from 32,000 to 10,000 years old. They are typically simple depictions of various objects, including animals such as bison, deer, and horses and traced drawings of people's hands.

Ⓒ Most people believed the paintings were fakes, so they refused to believe Sautuola's find was legitimate.

Ⓓ For example, anthropologists have seen drawings of animals that do not live in Europe now. So now they realize these animals, like rhinoceroses and hyenas, actually once lived in parts of Europe.

Exercise 8

Perspective in the Renaissance

During medieval times, most artists painted two-dimensional figures since they were unable to paint in three dimensions. However, during the Renaissance, artists learned new methods of painting, so they began introducing perspective into their works.

Perspective is the art of painting things as they appear in reality. This means that figures in the foreground are painted larger while those in the background look smaller. Artists in ancient Greece understood this method, but it was lost to the West for centuries. Later, Muslims reintroduced perspective to the West. Giotto, an Italian painter, was one of the first to try painting in perspective.

When the Renaissance began years after Giotto died, more painters attempted working with perspective. They began employing mathematical formulas in order to paint their paintings with perspective. Others simply practiced by drawing the reflections of various objects in mirrors. This way, they learned how to vary the sizes of different objects and to work with shadows.

Many painters in Florence began experimenting with perspective. Had it not been for them, Renaissance art would have looked much different. Their methods quickly spread throughout the rest of Europe, thereby helping change the way artists looked at and painted their works.

---

perspective (n) a viewpoint
foreground (n) the forefront; the front
employ (v) to use
vary (v) to change; to alter

Q1 In paragraph 1, the author implies that medieval artists

Ⓐ were rather sophisticated
Ⓑ were unable to use perspective
Ⓒ were better than Renaissance artists
Ⓓ painted in three dimensions

Q2 Which of the following can be inferred from paragraph 2 about perspective?

Ⓐ Artists today do not currently use it.
Ⓑ It was invented by the ancient Greeks.
Ⓒ The Muslims used it better than the Greeks.
Ⓓ It can make paintings look real.

Q3 Which of the following can be inferred from paragraphs 2 and 3 about Giotto?

Ⓐ He was influenced by Muslims.
Ⓑ He copied the ancient Greeks.
Ⓒ He used mathematical formulas.
Ⓓ He lived during the Renaissance.

Q4 Which of the following can be inferred from paragraph 4 about Renaissance art?

Ⓐ It was influenced by painters in Florence.
Ⓑ It affected only a few places in Europe.
Ⓒ Perspective was the most crucial aspect of it.
Ⓓ It had better topics than medieval art.

Reading Skills Cause and Effect

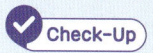 **Which sentence group below does NOT show cause and effect?**

Ⓐ Artists in ancient Greece understood this method, but it was lost to the West for centuries. Later, Muslims reintroduced perspective to the West.

Ⓑ However, during the Renaissance, artists learned new methods of painting, so they began introducing perspective into their works.

Ⓒ Many painters in Florence began experimenting with perspective. Had it not been for them, Renaissance art would have looked much different.

Ⓓ Others simply practiced by drawing the reflections of various objects in mirrors. This way, they learned how to vary the sizes of different objects and to work with shadows.

Grammar Point

Moods

1 **Mood** describes the speaker's attitude toward the verb he or she is using. There are only three moods: the **indicative**, the **imperative**, and the **subjunctive**.

2 Make statements or ask questions in the **indicative mood**. This is the most common mood in English. Almost all English sentences are written in the indicative mood.

- Many painters in Florence began experimenting with perspective.
- At times, many artists begin painting in similar styles.
- What did you think of the art exhibit?
- Are you going to sign up for the course on painting?

3 Make commands or requests in the **imperative mood**. The verbs in the imperative mood are in the second person. In addition, the subject of the sentence is "you," but do not say "you." It is understood to be there.

- Finish your essay right now.
- Please help me with this project.
- Go home as soon as you finish class.
- Remember to do your homework.

4 Make wishes or make statements that are not factual in the **subjunctive mood**. You can often express imaginary situations in the subjunctive. The words **if**, **though**, **lest**, **unless**, and **till** are all used in the subjunctive. **If** is the most common word used.

- If the books had been plain, they would not have been pleased.
- If Michelangelo had not met the Medici ruler, his life would have been very different.
- Had it not been for them, Renaissance art would have looked much different.
- Unless you try harder, you will not succeed.

Grammar Check-Up

A Indicate the correct moods (Indicative, Imperative, or Subjunctive) for the sentences.

1 Look at that book of paintings right now.
2 Michelangelo was one of history's greatest sculptors.
3 What kinds of animals were featured in the cave paintings?
4 Unless you are as talented as Leonardo, you cannot be a Renaissance man.
5 Please compare the works of Rubens and Rembrandt.
6 If the books were too expensive, no one would purchase them.

B Choose the sentence whose mood is different from that of the others.

1 ⓐ If you visit the art gallery, you can see many great works of art.
　ⓑ Had Art Deco not been popular, many buildings would have looked simpler.
　ⓒ The Dutch Golden Age was a time of great wealth in the Netherlands.
　ⓓ Unless you adopt a new painting style, your work will never improve.

2 ⓐ Take a look at the paintings in this exhibition.
　ⓑ Remember to use perspective when you paint.
　ⓒ Think about the influence of the Greeks on painting.
　ⓓ The Muslims helped introduce perspective to the West.

3 ⓐ Many people originally thought the cave paintings were fakes.
　ⓑ If the Impressionists had used darker colors, their paintings would have looked different.
　ⓒ Ansel Adams spent a great amount of his time in Yosemite National Park.
　ⓓ Manet and Monet are two Impressionists from the nineteenth century.

C Check (✔) the sentences that are written in the subjunctive mood.

1 ☐ Till someone purchases that painting, it will remain in the art gallery.
2 ☐ What kind of paint did the artist use to make that work over there?
3 ☐ If Picasso were alive today, he would still be making great art.
4 ☐ That was one of the most important periods for artwork.
5 ☐ Take a close look at the vase and then begin painting it.

Vocabulary Review

A Circle the words that best complete the sentences.

1. His skills at (engineer / engineering) enabled him to design a bridge over the river.
2. The cave paintings were not frauds but were actually (legitimate / fakes).
3. Ansel Adams was a (photography / photographer) who took pictures of nature scenes.
4. Many people are (fascinated / lavish) by the works of that artist.
5. Artists in the (Middle / Renaissance) Ages did not use perspective in their work.

B Choose the best words to complete the sentences.

1. Most cave paintings are _____ and have few details.
   - A understood
   - B sophisticated
   - C solitary
   - D simplistic

2. Some artists often paint _____ of various people.
   - A perspectives
   - B landscapes
   - C scenes
   - D portraits

3. Some painters capture the _____ from the sun very well in their work.
   - A herbs
   - B shadows
   - C depictions
   - D rebirth

4. There were many _____ set up in the room for the holiday season.
   - A influences
   - B styles
   - C architects
   - D decorations

5. The artist managed to _____ a beautiful scene in the landscape she painted.
   - A depict
   - B attempt
   - C accomplish
   - D inspire

C Choose the words with the closest meanings to the highlighted words.

1. The professor noticed the unknown artist and made him famous.
   - Ⓐ understood
   - Ⓑ found
   - Ⓒ brought
   - Ⓓ realized

2. There are many texts which describe the lives of various authors.
   - Ⓐ books
   - Ⓑ artworks
   - Ⓒ paintings
   - Ⓓ landscapes

3. Nobody recognized that the painting was a fake and not an original.
   - Ⓐ realized
   - Ⓑ illustrated
   - Ⓒ spent
   - Ⓓ improved

4. Some books from the Middle Ages were illuminated with many pictures.
   - Ⓐ legitimate
   - Ⓑ expensive
   - Ⓒ identical
   - Ⓓ illustrated

5. He desired to paint the most beautiful landscape possible.
   - Ⓐ ordered
   - Ⓑ made
   - Ⓒ wanted
   - Ⓓ traced

D Complete the sentences by filling in the blanks with the best words from the list. Change the forms of the words if necessary. Use each word only once.

| solitary | image | sculptor | bookmaker | quality |

1. Many artists lead _____ lives and do almost everything alone.
2. It once took years for a(n) _____ to create a single manuscript.
3. The _____ created his statues out of solid stone.
4. Many paintings from the past include religious _____ from the Bible.
5. The _____ of the artist's work improved as he gained more experience.

Practice Test

The Hudson River School

  The Hudson River runs through the state of New York from the northern region down to New York City. Part of it flows through the Adirondack Mountains. The area where the river goes is highly scenic as it passes through mountains, hills, fields, and forests. It was this area—as well as other parts of upstate New York—that inspired a group of artists in the nineteenth century. The movement they started would come to be known as the Hudson River School of Art.

  The artists in the Hudson River School were influenced by Romanticism. They mostly painted landscapes that frequently featured the Hudson River. Others showed natural scenery in the nearby Catskill and White mountains. The artist who started the movement was Thomas Cole. In 1825, he took a steamship on the Hudson River, hiked into the mountains, and began painting. Another artist, Asher Brown Durand, was friends with Cole. He too painted landscapes of the region. The popularity of the school rose, so more artists joined it. They focused on themes of nationalism, discovery, and nature.

  As the movement expanded, the subject matter began varying. Artists painted landscapes based in New England and parts of Canada. Some painted landscapes of the American West and places as far away as South America. **1** New artists in the movement, including Frederic Edwin Church and John Frederick Kensett, became famous. **2** Today, some artists still paint in that style. **3** The paintings of the original artists also remain in high demand. **4**

---

landscape n a picture that shows a natural environment
nationalism n patriotism; devotion to and love of one's country

1. In paragraph 1, why does the author mention "the Adirondack Mountains"?
   - Ⓐ To note that the Hudson River flows through them
   - Ⓑ To stress the natural beauty of the mountains
   - Ⓒ To claim they are the highest mountains in New York
   - Ⓓ To name one of the highest peaks in the mountains

2. The word "scenic" in the passage is closest in meaning to
   - Ⓐ beautiful
   - Ⓑ unique
   - Ⓒ natural
   - Ⓓ stylish

3. Which of the following can be inferred from paragraph 1 about the Hudson River?
   - Ⓐ It is the longest river located in New York.
   - Ⓑ The river only flows through the countryside.
   - Ⓒ Its source is located in New York City.
   - Ⓓ The geography of the area it flows in is varied.

4. The word "it" in the passage refers to
   - Ⓐ the region
   - Ⓑ the popularity
   - Ⓒ the school
   - Ⓓ nationalism

5. According to paragraph 2, which of the following is true of the artists in the Hudson River School?
   - Ⓐ Most of them were Americans.
   - Ⓑ They usually painted in the Realist style.
   - Ⓒ Landscapes were the pictures they mostly painted.
   - Ⓓ They attended schools to learn how to paint.

6. In paragraph 2, the author implies that Thomas Cole
   - Ⓐ spent much of his time painting in the Catskill Mountains
   - Ⓑ made the first paintings in the Hudson River School style
   - Ⓒ was originally from a town located near the Hudson River
   - Ⓓ preferred to paint pictures of people rather than landscapes

7 In paragraph 3, all of the following questions are answered EXCEPT:

- Ⓐ What type of paint did artists in the Hudson River School use?
- Ⓑ Who were some artists that joined the Hudson River School?
- Ⓒ What places did some Hudson River School artists paint?
- Ⓓ How do some people feel about paintings from the Hudson River School today?

8 In paragraph 3, the author implies that the Hudson River School

- Ⓐ only influenced artists for a few years
- Ⓑ has an influence on some modern painters
- Ⓒ is considered an outdated style nowadays
- Ⓓ was dominated by a small number of artists

9 Look at the four squares [■] that indicate where the following sentence could be added to the passage.

Paintings by these artists therefore show a wide range of outdoor scenes.

Where would the sentence best fit?
Click on a square [■] to add the sentence to the passage.

10 *Directions:* An introductory sentence for a brief summary of the passage is provided below. Complete the summary by selecting the THREE answer choices that express the most important ideas in the passage.

The Hudson River School was an art movement popular in the nineteenth century.

-
-
-

Answer Choices

① Most artists in the movement painted landscapes inspired by Romanticism.	④ Thomas Cole and Asher Brown Durand were two early artists in the movement.
② Artists today are sometimes influenced by the movement.	⑤ It was difficult for many artists to create paintings in the style of the school.
③ Later artists in the movement painted landscapes based in many different places.	⑥ Some paintings by Hudson River School artists were based in the Catskill Mountains.

CHAPTER

05

Physiology
(Guessing Unknown Words)

1. The Cavities of the Heart
2. Cancer
3. Aging
4. Reflexes
5. The Layers of the Skin
6. Teeth
7. The Composition of Blood
8. The Functions of the Bones

CHAPTER 5 **Physiology** (Guessing Unknown Words)

Understanding TOEFL Question Types & Reading Skills

1 Question Types — Vocabulary Questions

Vocabulary questions ask you to determine the meanings of words or phrases in the passage. Many times, a word may have several meanings. The meaning depends upon how the writer uses the word in the passage. Try to recognize how the writer is using a word or phrase. Then, you will be able to answer the question correctly.

- **Example Vocabulary Questions**
  - The word "X" in the passage is closest in meaning to ~
  - In stating "X", the author means that ~

- **Useful Tips for Your Success**
  - Remember that → one word may have many meanings.
    → you should be able to substitute the new word into the passage.
  - Don't → simply choose a word's most common meaning.
    → choose an answer just because it looks right.

Sample Question

The Digestive System

05-01

 Eating food allows people to live healthily, strongly, and happily. Without food, people could not survive. And without the body's digestive system, any food consumed could not be processed. Numerous body parts comprise the digestive system. These include the mouth, the esophagus, the stomach, the small and large intestines, the rectum, and the anus. Through these, food enters the body, gets converted into nutrients, and departs the body as waste.

 All the organs in the digestive system are hollow, which enables food to move through them. They also contain muscles that push the food through the body. Many of them contain mucosa, a lining that contains glands which digest the food. Thanks to these various body parts, people can digest food easily.

process v to handle; to treat
esophagus n the passage connecting the mouth and the stomach
nutrient n something that provides nutrition

Q The word "converted" in the passage is closest in meaning to
 Ⓐ moved   Ⓑ changed
 Ⓒ transported   Ⓓ covered

---

2 Reading Skills   Guessing Unknown Words

 Guessing unknown words is determining the meaning of a word from the context of the passage. Many times, you can guess the meaning of a word by looking at the other words in the same sentence or a sentence next to it. Look at these words carefully, and you should be able to guess the unknown word's meaning.

Check-Up

▶ Guess the meaning of the underlined word.

All the organs in the digestive system are <u>hollow</u>, which enables food to move through them.
 Ⓐ smooth   Ⓑ empty   Ⓒ wide   Ⓓ open

• **Exercise 1** •

The Cavities of the Heart

05-02

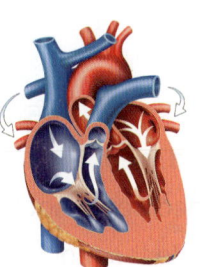

The heart is the body's most essential organ, for without it, no blood could be pumped anywhere in the body, thereby causing the person to die. The heart weighs approximately a pound, but it still contains four chambers, all of which serve important purposes.

The heart is split into four separate cavities. These are the left and right atria and the left and right ventricles. Blood enters the heart in the right atrium, which is in the top right-hand portion of the heart. From the right atrium, the blood next moves into the right ventricle, located directly beneath it. The right ventricle transports the blood into the lungs, where it can receive oxygen and get rid of carbon dioxide.

The blood in the lungs then reenters the heart through the left atrium. The blood finally moves down again to the left ventricle, where the aorta, the body's largest artery, proceeds to pump it throughout the body over and over again.

cavity n   a chamber
organ n   a part of a body, like the lungs, the heart, and the liver, that has a specific function
approximately adv   around; about

Q1 The word "essential" in the passage is closest in meaning to
 Ⓐ critical   Ⓑ impressive
 Ⓒ useless   Ⓓ replaceable

Q2 The word "split" in the passage is closest in meaning to
 Ⓐ halved   Ⓑ sliced
 Ⓒ divided   Ⓓ cut

Q3 The word "reenters" in the passage is closest in meaning to
 Ⓐ moves around   Ⓑ detours
 Ⓒ goes back in   Ⓓ remains in

Reading Skills   Guessing Unknown Words

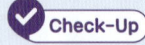 Guess the meaning of the underlined word.

The right ventricle transports the blood into the lungs, where it can receive oxygen and get rid of carbon dioxide.

 Ⓐ moves   Ⓑ pours   Ⓒ shoots   Ⓓ transmits

• Exercise 2 •

Cancer

🎧 05-03

A human body contains billions of cells. These cells often divide to create new cells; however, old cells continuously die, so the body never has an excess of cells. There are, however, some abnormal cells that never die, do not cease growing, and increase their numbers at tremendous rates: These are cancer cells.

There are several different types of cancer. But they all share one thing in common: They are cells growing in places where they do not belong. Cancer cells are also mutated, so they no longer resemble normal cells. Scientists are actually not sure what causes cancer.

Unfortunately, cancer cells often combine in various organs to form tumors, which are enormous clumps of cancer cells. Some tumors are benign, so they do not venture to other parts of the body, but other malignant tumors spread throughout the body. While many cancers eventually kill their sufferers, doctors have managed to discover cures for some.

continuously　adv　constantly; regularly　　　venture　v　to move; to go
resemble　v　to look like; to seem

Q1 The word "abnormal" in the passage is closest in meaning to
Ⓐ extreme　　　　　　　　　　Ⓑ unusual
Ⓒ additional　　　　　　　　　Ⓓ powerful

Q2 The word "mutated" in the passage is closest in meaning to
Ⓐ altered　　　　　　　　　　Ⓑ enhanced
Ⓒ replicated　　　　　　　　　Ⓓ assumed

Q3 The word "clumps" in the passage is closest in meaning to
Ⓐ attacks　　　　　　　　　　Ⓑ partitions
Ⓒ divisions　　　　　　　　　Ⓓ groups

Reading Skills　Guessing Unknown Words

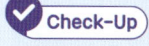 Guess the meaning of the underlined word.

These cells often divide to create new cells; however, old cells continuously die, so the body never has an excess of cells.

Ⓐ lack　　　　Ⓑ difference　　　　Ⓒ oversupply　　　　Ⓓ dying

• **Exercise 3** •

Aging

🎧 05-04

Aging is the process through which people become older. As adult humans reach middle age and then become elderly, aging can have many negative effects on them. These can be both physical and mental in nature.

As people age, they become more susceptible to illnesses. Sicknesses young adults easily recover from may kill elderly individuals. People's organs also undergo many changes. For instance, the performance of the heart declines over time. One result is that heart diseases are the primary killers of the elderly. People's eyesight usually worsens as they age. They suffer more digestive problems as well.

Mentally, the brain's functions decline due to aging, too. Responses to various stimuli slow down. In addition, elderly people frequently develop memory problems. Alzheimer's disease and dementia are two problems that affect the minds of the elderly. Older people often have trouble thinking as clearly as they did when they were younger.

---

elderly adj old
worsen v to become bad or poor
response n a reaction

Q1 The word "susceptible" in the passage is closest in meaning to
- Ⓐ objective
- Ⓑ vulnerable
- Ⓒ responsive
- Ⓓ arranged

Q2 The word "primary" in the passage is closest in meaning to
- Ⓐ main
- Ⓑ dangerous
- Ⓒ swift
- Ⓓ apparent

Q3 The word "stimuli" in the passage is closest in meaning to
- Ⓐ discussions
- Ⓑ questions
- Ⓒ impulses
- Ⓓ instincts

Reading Skills | Guessing Unknown Words

✅ **Check-Up** Guess the meaning of the underlined word.

For instance, the performance of the heart <u>declines</u> over time. One result is that heart diseases are the primary killers of the elderly.

- Ⓐ reveals
- Ⓑ stops
- Ⓒ drops
- Ⓓ varies

• **Exercise 4** •

Reflexes

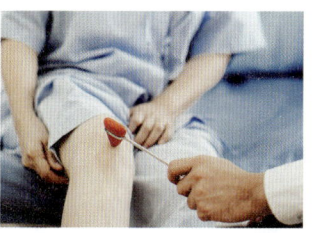
Occasionally, the body may involuntarily do something the individual does not intend or want to do. The most common example of this happens when a person visits the doctor, who then taps the patient's knee. Without meaning to, the person will kick his or her knee. Doctors call this a reflex.

The body has several different reflexes. These are intended either to prevent an individual from suffering harm or to protect a person somehow. Two common reflexes are sneezing and coughing. A person typically sneezes when something irritating is caught in his or her nasal passage. By sneezing, a person can rid the passage of that foreign object. The same is true of coughing. A person may have an obstruction or something annoying in the throat. Having to cough is a reflexive behavior that a person cannot control. The individual coughs only because the body tells the person to do so.

intend v to mean
irritating adj annoying
nasal adj relating to the nose

Q1 The word "involuntarily" in the passage is closest in meaning to
 Ⓐ suddenly   Ⓑ strangely
 Ⓒ accordingly   Ⓓ unwillingly

Q2 The word "rid" in the passage is closest in meaning to
 Ⓐ wipe   Ⓑ clean
 Ⓒ cut   Ⓓ free

Q3 The word "obstruction" in the passage is closest in meaning to
 Ⓐ impediment   Ⓑ garbage
 Ⓒ clot   Ⓓ scrap

Reading Skills Guessing Unknown Words

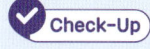 Guess the meaning of the underlined word.

The most common example of this happens when a person visits the doctor, who then taps the patient's knee. Without meaning to, the person will kick his or her knee.

 Ⓐ punches   Ⓑ strikes   Ⓒ hits   Ⓓ slaps

• **Exercise 5** •

The Layers of the Skin

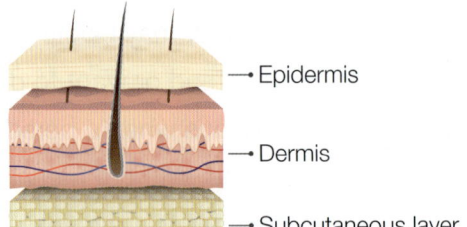

Skin covers virtually every exposed part of a person's body. While it does not appear complex, skin is actually composed of three different layers, which all have their own purposes.

The outer perceptible layer of skin is the epidermis, which is tough since it must protect the skin from being harmed. The epidermis contains melanin, the substance that gives people color. People with more melanin are darker in appearance than individuals with less melanin. Melanin shields the body from the sun's rays by causing the body to tan after overexposure to sunlight.

The dermis is the skin's second layer. It lies concealed from view underneath the epidermis. The dermis contains nerve endings and blood vessels as well as sweat and oil glands. The body's nerve endings allow a person to feel and sense things, and blood vessels bring oxygen and nutrients to the skin while disposing of waste products. The oil glands lubricate the body, and the sweat glands permit sweat to escape the body.

Subcutaneous fat is the third layer. It is, unsurprisingly, mostly comprised of fat. It keeps the body warm and enables the skin to remain connected to the rest of the body.

expose v to show in the open	lubricate v to oil; to apply oil to something
overexposure n getting too much of something	unsurprisingly adv naturally

Q1 The word "perceptible" in the passage is closest in meaning to

Ⓐ unique
Ⓑ visible
Ⓒ touchable
Ⓓ thin

Q2 The word "shields" in the passage is closest in meaning to

- Ⓐ spreads
- Ⓑ dehydrates
- Ⓒ protects
- Ⓓ uncovers

Q3 The phrase "disposing of" in the passage is closest in meaning to

- Ⓐ removing
- Ⓑ verifying
- Ⓒ cleansing
- Ⓓ altering

Q4 The word "permit" in the passage is closest in meaning to

- Ⓐ allow
- Ⓑ show
- Ⓒ release
- Ⓓ create

Reading Skills   Guessing Unknown Words

Check-Up Guess the meaning of the underlined word.

It lies concealed from view underneath the epidermis.

- Ⓐ apparent
- Ⓑ directly
- Ⓒ protected
- Ⓓ hidden

Exercise 6

Teeth

Whenever someone eats, the person's teeth must chop and chew food. Altogether, people may possess thirty-two permanent teeth, which can be partitioned into five separate categories.

Incisors are the four front teeth and are situated on the mouth's top and bottom. Incisors cut the food into smaller pieces; therefore, their ends are typically slightly sharp. Located immediately next to the incisors are canines, which account for four of the mouth's teeth. Utilized to cut food, canines are somewhat pointed like incisors.

There are two premolars, or bicuspids, found next to each canine tooth, giving people a total of eight. Premolars are relatively large, so they function to grind and mash the food. Next are molars, of which people have eight. Molars are larger than premolars and assist the tongue in swallowing by crushing food until it is small enough to be swallowed easily and safely.

The final teeth are called wisdom teeth. Each side of the mouth has one. However, they develop in people's late teenage years, and people often have these teeth extracted because they essentially serve no purpose. So although people's mouths are equipped for thirty-two teeth, most individuals only have twenty-eight.

---

chop [v] to cut into small pieces
account for [phr] to make up; to comprise
relatively [adv] somewhat; quite
equipped [adj] prepared; ready

Q1 The word "situated" in the passage is closest in meaning to
  Ⓐ determined
  Ⓑ scheduled
  Ⓒ located
  Ⓓ growing

Q2 The word "pointed" in the passage is closest in meaning to
  Ⓐ dangerous
  Ⓑ sharp
  Ⓒ important
  Ⓓ critical

Q3 The word "mash" in the passage is closest in meaning to

   Ⓐ slice
   Ⓑ chew
   Ⓒ swallowed
   Ⓓ pound

Q4 The word "extracted" in the passage is closest in meaning to

   Ⓐ shortened
   Ⓑ removed
   Ⓒ tightened
   Ⓓ drilled

Reading Skills Guessing Unknown Words

 Guess the meaning of the underlined word.

Altogether, people may possess thirty-two permanent teeth, which can be partitioned into five separate categories.

   Ⓐ gathered
   Ⓑ separated
   Ⓒ regrouped
   Ⓓ portioned

Exercise 7

The Composition of Blood

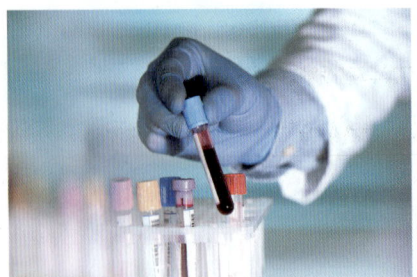

Human blood appears to be one type of substance, but it can be divided by doctors using a centrifuge. Scientists have broken down blood into two components: plasma and formed elements.

Once divided, about fifty-five percent of blood breaks down into plasma. Plasma is around ninety-percent water while the remainder is different proteins, minerals, carbohydrates, and fats. The role of the blood's plasma is to move both nutrients and waste throughout the body.

The formed elements in the blood are red blood cells, white blood cells, and platelets. Of these three, red blood cells are much more plentiful. Red blood cells mostly move oxygen, and some carbon dioxide, throughout the body. There are much fewer white blood cells in the blood. White blood cells primarily take care of the body and keep it healthy. They manufacture antibodies to fight diseases and help attack bacteria, germs, and other harmful organisms in the body. Platelets are small cell fragments that enable the blood to clot whenever a blood vessel breaks or gets damaged and the flow of blood needs to be stopped or slowed down. Together, they make blood one of the body's most powerful substances.

---

centrifuge (n) a machine that spins at high speeds and separates various objects
role (n) a purpose; a use
fragment (n) a small piece; a broken piece of something larger
flow (n) movement

Q1 The word "remainder" in the passage is closest in meaning to

Ⓐ results
Ⓑ composition
Ⓒ leftovers
Ⓓ product

Q2 The word "plentiful" in the passage is closest in meaning to

- Ⓐ abundant
- Ⓑ effective
- Ⓒ duplicated
- Ⓓ powerful

Q3 The word "manufacture" in the passage is closest in meaning to

- Ⓐ establish
- Ⓑ create
- Ⓒ capture
- Ⓓ eliminate

Q4 The word "clot" in the passage is closest in meaning to

- Ⓐ heal
- Ⓑ flow
- Ⓒ recover
- Ⓓ harden

Reading Skills Guessing Unknown Words

Check-Up Guess the meaning of the underlined word.

Scientists have broken down blood into two components: plasma and formed elements.

- Ⓐ parts
- Ⓑ formulas
- Ⓒ halves
- Ⓓ sections

• Exercise 8 •

The Functions of the Bones

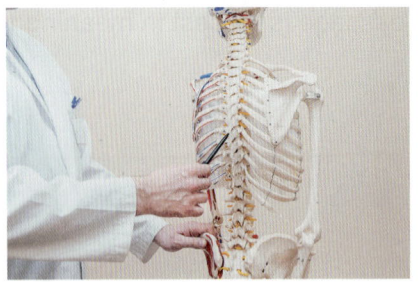

When people are born, they have approximately 350 bones in their bodies. By the time they reach adulthood, the number has shrunk to around 206 because some bones have combined with one another. Together, the bones form the body's skeletal system. Bones have five functions which they must execute for the body to be healthy and to work properly.

The bones' first function is the protection of the body's internal organs, which include the heart, the liver, the lungs, and the kidneys. To avoid being easily injured and to make protection simpler, many organs are located directly behind bones. One example is the heart, which rests immediately behind the rib cage.

Another function of bones is to support people's bodies by enabling them to move around. Bones also permit the body's muscles to attach themselves to them. Without muscles, people would lack the strength necessary to move.

Bones also make the body's blood cells. This occurs in the bone marrow, which is found in the middle of various bones. Finally, bones also store minerals, namely iron and calcium, which have been absorbed by the body.

Thanks to bones, people's lives are much easier, better, and more comfortable.

---

skeletal adj relating to the skeleton or bones
internal adj inside
rest v to lie; to be located
absorb v to soak up; to take in

Q1 The word "shrunk" in the passage is closest in meaning to

Ⓐ changed
Ⓑ switched
Ⓒ decreased
Ⓓ improved

Q2 The word "avoid" in the passage is closest in meaning to

- Ⓐ accept
- Ⓑ stop for
- Ⓒ keep from
- Ⓓ enhance

Q3 The word "enabling" in the passage is closest in meaning to

- Ⓐ allowing
- Ⓑ approving
- Ⓒ rewarding
- Ⓓ forcing

Q4 The word "namely" in the passage is closest in meaning to

- Ⓐ specifically
- Ⓑ especially
- Ⓒ possibly
- Ⓓ mostly

Reading Skills — Guessing Unknown Words

Check-Up Guess the meaning of the underlined word.

Bones have five functions which they must <u>execute</u> for the body to be healthy and to work properly.

- Ⓐ kill
- Ⓑ practice
- Ⓒ complete
- Ⓓ reconsider

Grammar Point

Parallel Construction

1 Use parallel construction to show that two or more ideas are equally important. You can use parallel construction with words, phrases, or clauses. In parallel construction, the forms of the words, phrases, or clauses must all be the same. There are many ways to use parallel construction.

2 Ways to Use Parallel Construction

Method	Example Sentences	
Words (Gerunds)	• People might endure swelling, numbness, and tingle. • Two common reflexes are sneezing and the cough.	X
Words (Gerunds)	• People might endure swelling, numbness, and tingling. • Two common reflexes are sneezing and coughing.	O
Phrases (Infinitives)	• These are intended to prevent an individual from suffering harm or for protecting a person.	X
Phrases (Infinitives)	• These are intended to prevent an individual from suffering harm or to protect a person.	O
Clauses	• There are some cells that never die, do not cease growing, and they increase their numbers. • White blood cells primarily take care of the body and are keeping it healthy.	X
Clauses	• There are some cells that never die, do not cease growing, and increase their numbers. • White blood cells primarily take care of the body and keep it healthy.	O
Lists	• Eating food allows people to live healthily, strongly, and be happy. • People's lives are much easier, better, and more comfortably.	X
Lists	• Eating food allows people to live healthily, strongly, and happily. • People's lives are much easier, better, and more comfortable.	O

Grammar Check-Up

A Check (✓) the sentences with correct parallel construction.

1. ☐ The layers of the skin are the epidermis, the dermis, and subcutaneous fat.
2. ☐ The bones protect the organs, support the body, and are making bone marrow.
3. ☐ Some of the teeth are premolars, bicuspids, and there are wisdom teeth.
4. ☐ Sneezing, kicking, and to cough are some involuntary reflexes.
5. ☐ The digestive system moves food through the body, processes it, and removes it from the body.

B Choose the correct words.

1. The digestive system includes the mouth, (intestines / the intestines), and the rectum.
2. Blood enters the heart, goes to the lungs, comes back to the heart, and then (goes / going) to the rest of the body.
3. Carpal tunnel syndrome can affect a person's wrists, hands, and (fingers / the fingers).
4. Plasma helps move waste and (move / to move) nutrients around the body.
5. Keeping the skin warm and (connecting / to connect) the skin to the body are the roles of subcutaneous fat.

C Choose the correct word for each blank.

1. As people get older, the _____ of the heart and the functions of the brain decline due to aging.
   ⓐ perform   ⓑ performance   ⓒ to perform   ⓓ performing

2. The number of bones in the body gets smaller and _____ as people get older and older.
   ⓐ small   ⓑ smaller   ⓒ smallest   ⓓ the smallest

3. Thanks to the heart, the blood can receive oxygen and _____ carbon dioxide.
   ⓐ getting rid of   ⓑ it gets rid of   ⓒ to get rid of   ⓓ can get rid of

4. Malignant cancer cells are mutated, dangerous, and _____.
   ⓐ harm   ⓑ harmful   ⓒ harming   ⓓ to harm

5. The teeth help the body with chewing, cutting food, and _____ it.
   ⓐ swallow   ⓑ swallowed   ⓒ swallowing   ⓓ to swallow

Chapter 5   133

Vocabulary Review

A Circle the words that best complete the sentences.

1. A (benign / malignant) tumor will not spread throughout the body.
2. Doctors use a (centrifuge / component) to separate particles from one another.
3. The heart (pushes / pumps) blood to the rest of the body.
4. Bones (enable / avoid) people to stand up and to move around.
5. (Epidermis / Melanin) gives people color and makes them appear light or dark.

B Choose the best words to complete the sentences.

1. His _____ on his tests improved because he studied more.
   - A function
   - B performance
   - C problem
   - D recovery

2. The _____ are some of the most important teeth in a person's mouth.
   - A canines
   - B organs
   - C dermis
   - D glands

3. Sneezing and coughing are two _____ that everyone has.
   - A reflexes
   - B components
   - C incisors
   - D nerves

4. The esophagus is _____ and is therefore not solid.
   - A skeletal
   - B plentiful
   - C hollow
   - D harmful

5. The woman was _____ to the sun for too long, so she got sunburned.
   - A concealed
   - B intended
   - C suffered
   - D exposed

C Choose the words with the closest meanings to the highlighted words.

1. One role of the muscles is to make various body parts move.
   - Ⓐ appearance
   - Ⓑ function
   - Ⓒ protection
   - Ⓓ strength

2. If the brain stops working, a person will not be able to do anything.
   - Ⓐ divides
   - Ⓑ digests
   - Ⓒ ceases
   - Ⓓ engages

3. Some teeth are quite sharp and are used for cutting up food.
   - Ⓐ healthy
   - Ⓑ hollow
   - Ⓒ large
   - Ⓓ pointed

4. The heart is made up of four chambers, all of which are important.
   - Ⓐ cavities
   - Ⓑ organs
   - Ⓒ ventricles
   - Ⓓ arteries

5. Many bones shield the organs that are hidden behind them.
   - Ⓐ protect
   - Ⓑ form
   - Ⓒ divide
   - Ⓓ damage

D Complete the sentences by filling in the blanks with the best words from the list. Change the forms of the words if necessary. Use each word only once.

| swallow | mutate | cell | organ | digestive |

1. The brain and the heart are two important _____ in the body.
2. People _____ their food after they chew it.
3. The body's _____ system processes all the food a person eats.
4. White blood _____ in the body have many important functions.
5. Cancer cells have _____ and no longer resemble anything normal.

Practice Test

Lactose Intolerance

Some people are unable to drink milk. They also cannot eat cheese, yogurt, and other products that contain milk. When they consume these dairy products, they may suffer various problems. They include diarrhea, nausea, stomach cramps, and vomiting. These people suffer from lactose intolerance.

Lactose is a sugar found in milk. In the small intestine, lactase, an enzyme, is produced. It is responsible for digesting lactose. Not everyone's body produces enough lactase though. This causes people to be lactose intolerant. When not enough lactase is produced, the body cannot process lactose. Instead, it moves to the colon, where it interacts with bacteria. There, the symptoms of lactose intolerance are created.

Researchers have determined that lactose intolerance is a problem that few infants and young children have. Instead, it typically develops in people during adulthood. In addition, people of African, Asian, Hispanic, and American Indian descent are more likely than Europeans to be lactose intolerant.

1 Many individuals with lactose intolerance are concerned about not getting enough calcium. **2** Fortunately for them, it is possible to take supplements. **3** Additionally, many foods nowadays are made for lactose-intolerant individuals. **4** There is even lactose-free milk available at many grocery stores. People also consume alternative foods, including almond milk and soy milk. As a result, major lifestyle changes due to lactose intolerance are not necessary.

enzyme [n] a protein in the body that can produce chemical changes
major [adj] important; main

1. The word "They" in the passage refers to
   A Some people
   B Cheese, yogurt, and other products that contain milk
   C These dairy products
   D Various problems

2. In paragraph 1, the author uses "stomach cramps" as an example of
   A a symptom of lactose intolerance
   B a problem caused by avoiding lactose
   C an issue that is worse than nausea
   D a life-threatening symptom of an illness

3. The word "process" in the passage is closest in meaning to
   A identify
   B reveal
   C accept
   D convert

4. In paragraph 2, the author's description of lactase mentions which of the following?
   A What it looks like
   B How it is created
   C Where it is made
   D Why some people do not have it

5. According to paragraph 2, people are lactose intolerant because
   A their bodies digest lactose too slowly
   B their bodies cannot break down lactose
   C their bodies lack some important bacteria
   D their bodies produce too much lactase

6. Which of the following best expresses the essential information in the highlighted sentence? *Incorrect* answer choices change the meaning in important ways or leave out essential information.
   A Scientists know that few young people are lactose intolerant.
   B Researchers do not know why infants and children are not lactose intolerant.
   C It is known that some infants and young children become lactose intolerant.
   D One problem few babies and children have is lactose intolerance.

7 In paragraph 3, the author implies that Europeans

- Ⓐ suffer from lactose intolerance as children
- Ⓑ are less likely to be lactose intolerant than Africans
- Ⓒ are never affected by lactose intolerance
- Ⓓ are working on ways to treat symptoms of lactose intolerance

8 According to paragraph 4, which of the following is NOT true of lactose-intolerant individuals?

- Ⓐ They can drink milk with no lactose in it.
- Ⓑ They must make major lifestyle changes.
- Ⓒ They may suffer from a lack of calcium.
- Ⓓ They have the ability to try alternative foods.

9 Look at the four squares [■] that indicate where the following sentence could be added to the passage.

This is a mineral that helps both bones and teeth.

Where would the sentence best fit?

Click on a square [■] to add the sentence to the passage.

10 *Directions:* An introductory sentence for a brief summary of the passage is provided below. Complete the summary by selecting the THREE answer choices that express the most important ideas in the passage.

Lactose intolerance is a problem that affects many people.

-
-
-

Answer Choices

① Adults are affected by it just as much as infants and young children are.	④ People affected by it can take supplements and enjoy lactose-free products.
② People with it suffer various symptoms, including nausea and diarrhea.	⑤ Alternative foods such as soy milk are available to people with this problem.
③ It is caused by the body's inability to process the lactose in dairy products.	⑥ People from Africa and Asia may often be lactose intolerant.

CHAPTER 06

Archaeology
(Mapping)

1. Mohenjo-Daro
2. The Construction of Stonehenge
3. The Ruins of Angkor
4. Underwater Archaeology
5. Archaeological Methods
6. Heinrich Schliemann
7. Pompeii
8. Archaeological Tools

CHAPTER 6 Archaeology (Mapping)

Understanding TOEFL Question Types & Reading Skills

1 Question Types — Reference Questions

Reference questions ask you to recognize how some words refer to others in the passage. These questions usually ask about a pronoun and the word or words it refers to. Sometimes the questions ask about other words like *which*, *that*, or *this*. The answer choices will always be a word or words from the passage.

- **Example Reference Questions**
    - The word "X" in the passage refers to ~

- **Useful Tips for Your Success**

    - Make sure
        → you don't confuse feminine and masculine pronouns.
        → you can substitute the answer choice for the pronoun.

    - Don't
        → match a singular pronoun with a plural answer.
        → match a plural pronoun with a singular answer.

Sample Question

Amateur Archaeologists

🎧 06-01

Professional archaeologists occasionally receive some amount of glamour and fame. However, almost as important as them are the unknown amateur archaeologists. For without amateurs, many archaeological digs could never happen.

Amateur archaeologists are often hobbyists. They may also be people who are just interested in archaeology. Perhaps they majored in it in college, or they might have picked **it** up some time later. But they often provide valuable assistance on various digs and excavations.

Funds for most archaeological digs are scarce. But archaeology is labor intensive. So many amateur archaeologists pay their own way to digs. They volunteer, so they work long hours for no money. Some become quite accomplished and knowledgeable, but they almost always remain anonymous.

amateur *adj* not professional; doing something as a pastime rather than a job

accomplished *adj* skilled; proficient

Q The word "it" in the passage refers to

Ⓐ hobbyists Ⓑ archaeology Ⓒ college Ⓓ valuable assistance

2 Reading Skills Mapping

Mapping is a way to organize information. You draw diagrams to show how all of the ideas in a paragraph or passage relate to one another. When you do this, you can easily notice the connection of each idea to the other.

Check-Up

▶ Which is the best answer for the blank below?

- Some are hobbyists
- Some are interested in archaeology

Provide valuable assistance on digs and excavations

Funds for archaeologists are scarce, and archaeology is labor-intensive work

Amateur Archaeologists

Become knowledgeable and accomplished yet remain _____

Volunteer long hours and make no money

Ⓐ scarce Ⓑ famous Ⓒ anonymous Ⓓ glamorous

Chapter **6** 141

Exercise 1

Mohenjo-Daro

   The four earliest human civilizations to arise were in Mesopotamia, Egypt, China, and the Indus River Valley. The civilization around the Indus River rose around 3300 B.C. It lasted until about 1300 B.C. Around 2500 B.C., the greatest city of that civilization was built. It was called Mohenjo-Daro.

   The first excavations of the ancient city took place in 1922. Since then, much has been learned about it. The city was laid out on a precise grid. It featured barriers protecting it from floodwaters of the Indus River. There was a citadel in the city. It was built higher than everywhere else. It is believed to have been the location of the city's government. It also may have served a religious function.

   Many houses had two floors and featured bathrooms. Drains and sewers for sanitation, something few places had until Roman times, have been excavated there. They indicate that the people of Mohenjo-Daro were highly advanced for their time.

---

excavation [n] a dig; the act of digging in the ground
precise [adj] exact
sewer [n] an underground passage that carries away human waste

Q1 The word "It" in paragraph 1 refers to
   Ⓐ The Indus River Valley
   Ⓑ The civilization
   Ⓒ The Indus River
   Ⓓ 3300 B.C.

Q2 The word "It" in paragraph 2 refers to

- Ⓐ A precise grid
- Ⓑ The Indus River
- Ⓒ A citadel
- Ⓓ The city

Q3 The word "They" in the passage refers to

- Ⓐ Two floors
- Ⓑ Bathrooms
- Ⓒ Drains and sewers for sanitation
- Ⓓ Roman times

Reading Skills Mapping

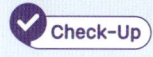 **Check-Up** What is the best answer for the blank below?

- Was in the Indus River Valley Civilization

Mohenjo-Daro

- Was first excavated in 1922
- Much has been learned about it since then

- Was built around the year 2500 B.C.

- Was laid out on a precise grid
- Had barriers protecting it from floodwaters
- Had a high citadel that was the location of the government

- Had houses with two floors and bathrooms

- Had drains and sewers for _____; showed how the people of the city were advanced

- Ⓐ sanitation
- Ⓑ warfare
- Ⓒ religion
- Ⓓ government

Exercise 2

The Construction of Stonehenge

In the past, ancient cultures achieved some remarkable feats of engineering. One of these remains today at Stonehenge, located near Salisbury, England. What remains of Stonehenge today is a large number of erect stones in a circle.

Construction on Stonehenge began around 3100 B.C. However, construction on the monument used wood, not the huge stones that exist today. Stones were used to rebuild Stonehenge around 2500 B.C. Some were enormous, weighing more than five tons. These stones came from a location in Wales almost 250 miles away, something that has amazed archaeologists.

Finally, in 2300 B.C., Stonehenge was once again renovated. The remains seen today are those from the third period. Even bigger stones—some weighing forty-five tons—were used. Amazingly, some of these stones have been placed on top of one another. How the ancient Briton people managed this, no one is sure. It is a mystery that must be solved in the future by archaeologists.

---

erect adj straight; upright
rebuild v to build again
renovate v to repair; to redo

Q1 The word "these" in the passage refers to
- Ⓐ ancient cultures
- Ⓑ remarkable feats
- Ⓒ engineering
- Ⓓ erect stones

Q2 The word "Some" in the passage refers to

Ⓐ Wood
Ⓑ Stones
Ⓒ Five tons
Ⓓ Archaeologists

Q3 The word "those" in the passage refers to

Ⓐ remains
Ⓑ bigger stones
Ⓒ forty-five tons
Ⓓ ancient Briton people

Reading Skills Mapping

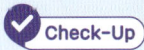 What is the best answer for the blank below?

- Located near Salisbury, England
- **Stonehenge**
- Are mysteries how people used the huge stones and how they moved them from miles away
- Around 3100 B.C., construction began, and wood was used
- Rebuilt around 2500 B.C.; enormous stones moved from 250 miles away in _____ were used
- In 2300 B.C., was renovated again, and even bigger stones were used and placed on top of one another

Ⓐ Salisbury   Ⓑ Wales   Ⓒ Briton   Ⓓ England

Exercise 3

The Ruins of Angkor

Most discoveries of ancient ruins come after months or years of careful research. However, sometimes people simply stumble upon them. This was the case of Angkor Wat, a huge temple complex in the jungles of Cambodia.

In the nineteenth century, the French had colonized Cambodia. They sometimes heard rumors about temples or buildings lost in the jungles, but most did not believe them. However, in 1860, some French missionaries found them near the city of Siem Reap. What was discovered were the incredibly well-preserved remains of the Khmer Empire, which had vanished by the fifteenth century.

Many buildings are still largely erect. The most impressive is Angkor Wat, a huge pyramid-shaped structure about 4,900 by 4,200 feet in size. It is the greatest example of Khmer architecture.

Today, archaeologists continue to explore the Angkor region, which covers an area over 1,100 square miles. Through their research, they continue to learn about both the long-gone Khmer Empire and the buildings.

---

stumble upon phr to find by accident
missionary n a person who tries to spread a religion to others
vanish v to disappear

Q1 The word "them" in the passage refers to
  Ⓐ discoveries
  Ⓑ ancient ruins
  Ⓒ months
  Ⓓ years

Q2 The word "most" in the passage refers to

Ⓐ the French
Ⓑ rumors
Ⓒ temples
Ⓓ jungles

Q3 The word "It" in the passage refers to

Ⓐ Khmer Empire
Ⓑ Fifteenth century
Ⓒ Angkor Wat
Ⓓ Khmer architecture

Reading Skills Mapping

Check-Up What is the best answer for the blank below?

- A huge temple complex in the jungles of Cambodia
- Well-preserved remains of the Khmer Empire
- Archaeologists
  - continue to explore the Angkor region
  - learn about both the buildings and the long-gone Khmer Empire

The Ruins of Angkor

- In 1860, some French .... found them near the city of Siem Reap
- Angkor Wat
  - Huge pyramid-shaped structure about 4,900 by 4,200 feet in size
  - The greatest example of Khmer architecture

Ⓐ archaeologists　　Ⓑ priests　　Ⓒ colonists　　Ⓓ missionaries

• Exercise 4 •

Underwater Archaeology

People often imagine archaeologists conducting their digs in deserts or jungles. These, of course, often happen, but there is another place archaeologists look for relics from the past: under the water.

Shipwrecks are important sites to conduct underwater archaeology. The most famous of them is the *Titanic*, located deep under the North Atlantic. But there are many other significant sites. By exploring ancient shipwrecks, archaeologists can learn about the cultures of the times the ships sailed. In addition, the ships themselves are sometimes quite valuable. For example, the *Hunley*, an early submarine, was recovered and examined by historians.

Sometimes buildings are even found buried underwater. They may have disappeared under the water because of earthquakes or even from changes in the courses of rivers. In fact, some of the ruins of the storied Library of Alexandria, located in Egypt, have been found in the Mediterranean Sea. Many more buildings like it also have watery graves waiting to be dug up.

relic [n] an artifact; an historical object
shipwreck [n] the underwater remains of a ship that sank

storied [adj] famous

Q1 The word "These" in the passage refers to
- Ⓐ People
- Ⓑ Archaeologists
- Ⓒ Digs
- Ⓓ Deserts

Q2 The word "them" in the passage refers to

- Ⓐ shipwrecks
- Ⓑ important sites
- Ⓒ the *Titanic*
- Ⓓ the North Atlantic

Q3 The word "They" in the passage refers to

- Ⓐ Historians
- Ⓑ Buildings
- Ⓒ Earthquakes
- Ⓓ The courses of rivers

Reading Skills | **Mapping**

Check-Up What is the best answer for the blank below?

Underwater Archaeology

Shipwrecks
- The *Titanic* is the most famous one, located deep under the North Atlantic
- Many other significant sites

Can learn about cultures during the times the ships sailed

Buildings buried underwater

Disappeared under the water because of earthquakes or changes in the courses of _____

- Library of Alexandria, located in Egypt, have been found in the Mediterranean Sea
- Many more buildings waiting to be dug up

Ⓐ oceans Ⓑ lakes Ⓒ streams Ⓓ rivers

Exercise 5

Archaeological Methods

Modern-day movies show courageous archaeologists such as Indiana Jones and Allan Quartermain traveling the world, fighting villains, and looking for and locating treasures in less than two hours. However, real archaeologists use much different methods when searching for these.

First, archaeologists must spend many hours conducting research prior to going out in the field. This can be done in libraries, churches, and other places where records are kept. Archaeologists typically must learn ancient languages. They must know several if they are doing research in language-intensive areas like the Mediterranean Sea.

Once they know what they are looking for, archaeologists must decide where to excavate. In a way, they must think like ancient people. The archaeologists need to consider where they would have built their cities or other places. Then, they can begin digging.

Once archaeologists discover something during their digs, they must be extremely cautious. While doing fieldwork, there must be care taken not to destroy the relics they excavate. After returning to their laboratories and offices, they must analyze the ones they have found. Through careful analysis, the significances of these items may be discovered or at least guessed at. So while their lives are not glamorous, archaeologists have extremely busy occupations.

---

courageous adj brave
villain n a criminal; a bad person
analyze v to examine
significance n importance

Q1 The word "these" in the passage refers to

Ⓐ modern-day movies
Ⓑ Indiana Jones and Allan Quartermain
Ⓒ villains
Ⓓ treasures

Q2 The word "This" in the passage refers to
- Ⓐ Archaeologists
- Ⓑ Hours
- Ⓒ Research
- Ⓓ Field

Q3 The word "they" in the passage refers to
- Ⓐ archaeologists
- Ⓑ ancient people
- Ⓒ scientists
- Ⓓ cities

Q4 The word "ones" in the passage refers to
- Ⓐ archaeologists
- Ⓑ digs
- Ⓒ relics
- Ⓓ laboratories and offices

Reading Skills Mapping

Check-Up What is the best answer for the blank below?

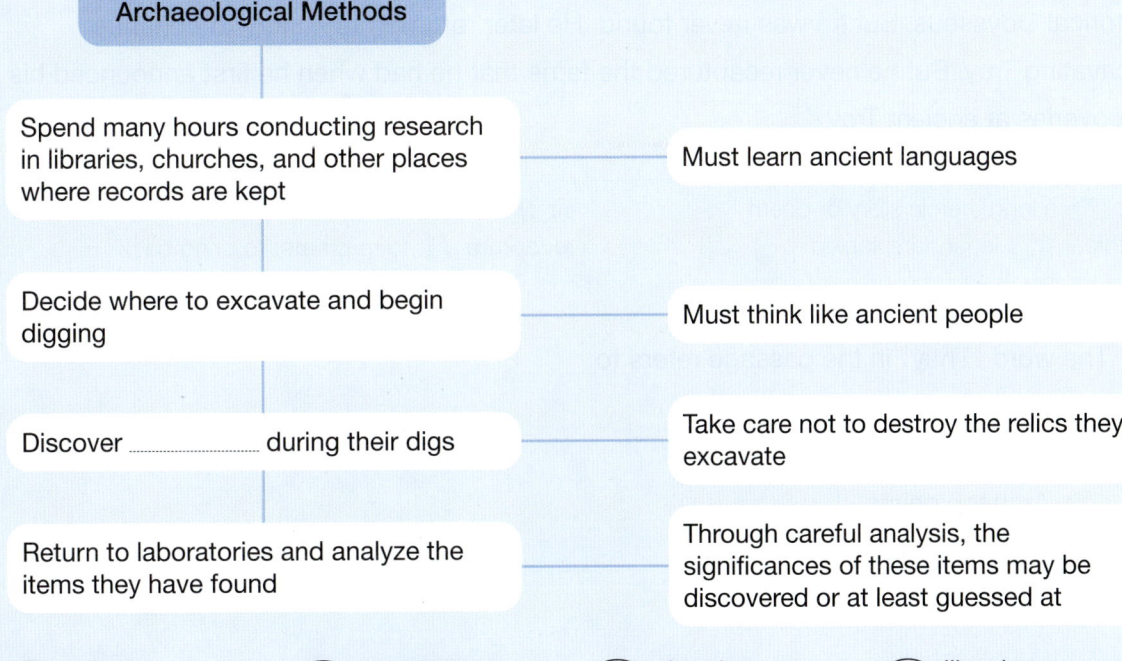

- Ⓐ relics
- Ⓑ treasures
- Ⓒ churches
- Ⓓ libraries

• Exercise 6 •

Heinrich Schliemann

Generally, people know the names of very few archaeologists. They often work hard but remain unknown. Heinrich Schliemann, however, is a name many people have heard of in archaeology.

While not exactly a professional archaeologist, Schliemann accomplished much in the field. He was actually more of a treasure hunter. He also had a great interest in Homer, the Greek poet who wrote the *Iliad* and the *Odyssey*, two great epics about the Trojan War and the ten-year voyage of Odysseus to return home from Troy. Most people assumed these described Troy as a mythical place. Schliemann thought differently.

In 1868, he became convinced that the Turkish city of Hissarlik sat on top of the site of Homer's Troy. In 1871, he began digging there, and in 1873, he found a huge amount of treasure. So pleased was he that he called this "Priam's Treasure" after King Priam, the legendary ruler of Troy. This brought him enormous fame throughout the world.

Schliemann would later conduct more digs in Greece. He was interested in finding the historical Odysseus. But he was never found. He later returned to Turkey to continue excavating Troy. But he never recaptured the fame that he had when he first announced his discoveries at ancient Troy.

---

epic n a long, heroic story or poem
mythical adj legendary; fabled
sit v to rest upon
recapture v to re-create; to bring back

Q1 The word "They" in the passage refers to

Ⓐ People
Ⓑ Names
Ⓒ Archaeologists
Ⓓ Heinrich Schliemann

Q2 The word "these" in the passage refers to

- Ⓐ the Greek poet
- Ⓑ the *Iliad* and the *Odyssey*
- Ⓒ the Trojan War and the ten-year voyage
- Ⓓ people

Q3 The word "there" in the passage refers to

- Ⓐ Troy
- Ⓑ a mythical place
- Ⓒ Hissarlik
- Ⓓ Homer's Troy

Q4 The word "he" in the passage refers to

- Ⓐ King Priam
- Ⓑ the legendary ruler of Troy
- Ⓒ Schliemann
- Ⓓ the historical Odysseus

Reading Skills | Mapping

Check-Up What is the best answer for the blank below?

- Not exactly a professional archaeologist
- Was actually a treasure hunter

Had a great interest in Homer

Heinrich Schliemann

In 1873, found a huge amount of treasure from Homer's _____ on the Turkish city of Hissarlik

Accomplished much in the field

Conducted more digs in Greece and Turkey to find the historical Odysseus and Troy

Brought him enormous fame throughout the world

- Ⓐ Priam
- Ⓑ *Iliad*
- Ⓒ Troy
- Ⓓ *Odyssey*

• **Exercise 7** •

Pompeii

On August 24, 79 A.D. occurred a momentous event in the city of Pompeii: It disappeared. Pompeii was a city in the Roman Empire. It was located near present-day Naples, Italy. Unfortunately, it also rested at the bottom of Mount Vesuvius, which was a volcano. When Vesuvius suddenly came to life for two days, it utterly destroyed the city. For almost 1,700 years, Pompeii was forgotten.

Then, in 1748, it was accidentally rediscovered. This was a tremendous event for archaeologists. The reason was that Vesuvius erupted so quickly that the people of Pompeii had no time to escape. Many of them were killed right where they stood. The volcano also covered the city with so much ash that it preserved Pompeii almost completely.

Thanks to its preservation, archaeologists have been able to study what a real Roman city once looked like. Indeed, many buildings are completely intact. Even today, archaeologists still dig them up so that they can learn more about the Roman Empire. Pompeii is also a popular tourist destination, with about 2.5 million visitors coming each year to see the remains of this once peaceful city.

---

momentous adj important; huge; historic
utterly adv completely; entirely
preserve v to save
intact adj in one piece; whole

Q1 The word "it" in paragraph 1 refers to

Ⓐ Pompeii
Ⓑ the Roman Empire
Ⓒ present-day Naples, Italy
Ⓓ Mount Vesuvius

Q2 The word "them" in paragraph 2 refers to
- Ⓐ a tremendous event
- Ⓑ archaeologists
- Ⓒ Vesuvius
- Ⓓ the people

Q3 The word "it" in paragraph 2 refers to
- Ⓐ Pompeii
- Ⓑ the volcano
- Ⓒ the city
- Ⓓ ash

Q4 The word "them" in paragraph 3 refers to
- Ⓐ buildings
- Ⓑ archaeologists
- Ⓒ visitors
- Ⓓ the remains

Reading Skills | Mapping

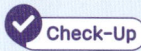 **What is the best answer for the blank below?**

- Located near present-day Naples, Italy
- On August 24, 79 A.D., was destroyed by Vesuvius
- Even today, archaeologists still dig up buildings so that they can learn more about _____
- A popular tourist destination now
- Vesuvius erupted so quickly that Pompeii was almost completely preserved
- Archaeologists have been able to study what a real Roman city once looked like
- Was a tremendous event for archaeologists
- In 1748, was rediscovered accidentally

Pompeii

- Ⓐ Vesuvius
- Ⓑ the Roman Empire
- Ⓒ Naples
- Ⓓ Italy

• **Exercise 8** •

Archaeological Tools

When digging for artifacts, archaeologists must be as precise as possible. For this reason, they almost never use anything bigger than a shovel. Above all, an archaeologist should be interested in excavating a site as precisely as possible while damaging it as little as possible. So a digger will use a number of different tools at an excavation site.

When digging in an area where there are no artifacts to damage, archaeologists use shovels. These allow them to get to important areas as quickly as possible. However, once they get to a certain layer of soil, they slow down their digging to become more exact. This requires different tools.

The most common one is the trowel. A small tool, it allows diggers to excavate tiny amounts of earth while seeing what they are doing. By using trowels, archaeologists will not upset the earth too much. When there are relics found, archaeologists will switch to even smaller instruments so as not to damage them. These instruments include spoons, brushes, and even dental picks. Naturally, this slows down the rate of digging considerably. However, by doing so, archaeologists can reconstruct sites much more accurately than if they started digging everything with shovels.

| tiny adj very small | instrument n a tool |
| upset v to disturb | reconstruct v to rebuild |

Q1 The word "it" in paragraph 1 refers to

- Ⓐ a shovel
- Ⓑ an archaeologist
- Ⓒ a site
- Ⓓ a digger

Q2 The word "These" in the passage refers to

Ⓐ Artifacts
Ⓑ Archaeologists
Ⓒ Shovels
Ⓓ Important areas

Q3 The word "it" in paragraph 3 refers to

Ⓐ soil
Ⓑ the trowel
Ⓒ earth
Ⓓ the rate of digging

Q4 The word "them" in the passage refers to

Ⓐ trowels
Ⓑ archaeologists
Ⓒ relics
Ⓓ smaller instruments

Reading Skills Mapping

Check-Up What is the best answer for the blank below?

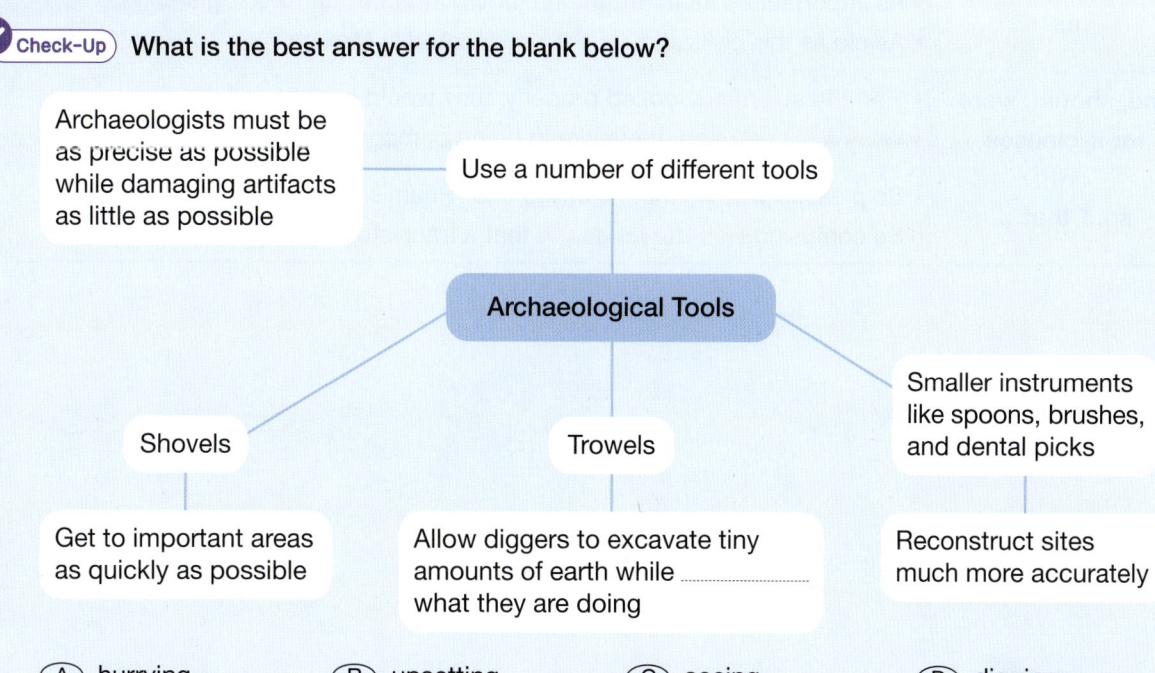

Ⓐ hurrying   Ⓑ upsetting   Ⓒ seeing   Ⓓ digging

Grammar Point

Inversion

Inversion occurs when the verb comes before the subject in the sentence. There are numerous ways to use inversion in English.

Method	Example Sentences
questions	• What is the answer to the question? • Did you visit the museum last week?
there is / are	• There were rumors heard by people of an ancient Incan city. • But there are many other significant sites.
here is / are	• Here is the relic you were looking for. • Here are the remains of an ancient civilization.
introduction -ed	• Discovered in the tomb was a treasure of gold. • Lost for hundreds of years were the buildings near Siem Reap.
introducing -ing	• Burying the city was the volcano Vesuvius. • Studying in the library were the students.
speech	• "This book is really great," said Minho. • "Where did they find the shipwreck?" asked Hyoju.
comparatives	• Archaeologists are less well known than are athletes. • The *Titanic* is in much deeper water than is the *Hunley*.
as	• As important as them are the unknown amateur archaeologists. • As old as this civilization is the one located in Mexico.
had, should, were for if-clauses	• Had the scientists looked properly, they would have found the item. • Were a trowel used, there would be no damage.
so… that…	• So pleased was he that he called this "Priam's Treasure." • So confusing was the language that a translator had to be used.

Grammar Check-Up

A Underline the parts of the sentences that use inversion.

1 In the forest, there are many sites of interest to local archaeologists.

2 <u>So deadly was Vesuvius</u> that almost no one escaped from Pompeii.

3 <u>Found by Heinrich Schliemann were</u> golden treasures from Troy.

4 <u>Did the archaeologist learn</u> enough foreign languages to do good research?

5 <u>Learning their areas of interest well are</u> some hobbyists who are just amateurs.

B Choose the sentences which use inversion.

1 ⓐ Schliemann went looking for the remains of Odysseus's kingdom.
　ⓑ Indiana Jones is a famous, but fictional, archaeologist.
　ⓒ Using a trowel to dig is the preferred method of archaeologists.
　ⓓ There is a strong likelihood that an ancient site is buried here.

2 ⓐ So many people are interested in learning about the past.
　ⓑ So well-hidden was Machu Picchu that no one could see it from below.
　ⓒ So the amateurs often remain unknown to most of the world.
　ⓓ So being precise is an important ability when digging at a site.

3 ⓐ Once the shipwreck is found, divers must explore it.
　ⓑ Doing research in libraries takes up most of his time.
　ⓒ Learning foreign languages is more important than is making contacts.
　ⓓ The tomb was buried in the desert so was not found for hundreds of years.

C Check (✓) the sentences that use inversion.

1 ☐ So many shipwrecks remain hidden deep under the water.

2 ☐ Looking for Troy was the lifelong goal of Heinrich Schliemann.

3 ☐ As brave as Indiana Jones was Allan Quartermain.

4 ☐ So amazing is Stonehenge that people are still not sure how it was built.

5 ☐ Had Machu Picchu been found earlier, many of its buildings might have been looted by treasure hunters.

Vocabulary Review

A Circle the words that best complete the sentences.

1 Archaeologists must (recover / **examine**) items before they can take them to their labs.
2 The volcano (accidentally / **utterly**) destroyed the island and buried the entire culture.
3 The archaeologists took back many (**relics** / ruins) they had gathered from the dig site.
4 Good (**sanitation** / barrier) is important for removing waste and for keeping people healthy.
5 Some treasure (villains / **hunters**) are only interested in finding valuable items.

B Choose the best words to complete the sentences.

1 A trowel is a small _____ archaeologists often use to dig with.
   - A pick
   - B tool
   - C spoon
   - D brush

2 Conducting _____ is an important part of an archaeologist's job.
   - A languages
   - B dig
   - C research
   - D assistance

3 Nobody knows what the _____ of this ancient artifact was.
   - A function
   - B sewer
   - C excavation
   - D barrier

4 They are impressed by the engineering _____ of some ancient cultures.
   - A labor
   - B treasures
   - C feats
   - D hunters

5 _____ a site is important since it shows people what it once looked like.
   - A Digging
   - B Reconstructing
   - C Conducting
   - D Discovering

C Choose the words with the closest meanings to the highlighted words.

1. A lot of ancient buildings remain standing, showing how well designed they were.
   - Ⓐ scarce
   - Ⓑ erect
   - Ⓒ careful
   - Ⓓ convinced

2. They are amateurs and simply work because they enjoy it.
   - Ⓐ hunters
   - Ⓑ unknowns
   - Ⓒ hobbyists
   - Ⓓ professionals

3. The archaeologists began digging up the temple buried underground.
   - Ⓐ excavating
   - Ⓑ reconstructing
   - Ⓒ shoveling
   - Ⓓ fighting

4. Some cultures completely vanish until archaeologists find their ruins.
   - Ⓐ pick
   - Ⓑ preserve
   - Ⓒ colonize
   - Ⓓ disappear

5. There is a lot of labor involved in digging up an entire site.
   - Ⓐ work
   - Ⓑ damage
   - Ⓒ artifacts
   - Ⓓ feats

D Complete the sentences by filling in the blanks with the best words from the list. Change the forms of the words if necessary. Use each word only once.

| ancient | precise | momentous | shipwreck | grave |

1. It was a(n) _____ event when King Tut's tomb was discovered.
2. The archaeologist found the _____ location of the lost temple.
3. Some people dig up the _____ of dead people to find important artifacts.
4. A good archaeologist knows many _____ languages.
5. Some people look underwater for _____ from the past.

Chapter ❻   161

Practice Test

The Valley of the Kings

06-10

The ancient Egyptian city of Thebes was located in southern Egypt. Today, the modern city Luxor stands in the same area. West of the Nile River, which flows by the city, is the Valley of the Kings. It was the resting place of many pharaohs and nobles for more than 500 years.

Around 1500 B.C., the Egyptians stopped building pyramids. Previously, they had been used as tombs. However, they were easy to find, so bandits frequently looted them and stole their treasures. As a result, the Egyptians began digging tombs into the sides of mountains in the Valley of the King.

1 More than sixty tombs have been found thus far. **2** Some are small, but others extend hundreds of feet and have numerous corridors and chambers. **3** The tomb of Queen Hatshepsut is found more than 700 feet from the entrance. **4** Pharaohs Ramses I, Ramses II, and Amenhotep I were buried there. Unfortunately, most of the tombs there were robbed of their valuables. However, in 1992, Howard Carter found the tomb of Pharaoh Tutankhamen, otherwise known as King Tut. His tomb was mostly intact and contained vast amounts of treasure.

Despite the lack of treasure, many tombs contained paintings on the walls. These have helped archaeologists understand events that happened in ancient Egypt. The treasures of King Tut have also taught archaeologists a great deal. These items also made more people become interested in ancient Egypt, thereby encouraging more excavations to take place.

tomb n a place where a person is buried
chamber n a room

1. In paragraph 1, why does the author mention "the modern city Luxor"?
   - Ⓐ To stress the importance of the Nile to it
   - Ⓑ To point out its location
   - Ⓒ To give the time when it was founded
   - Ⓓ To compare it with Thebes

2. In paragraph 1, the author's description of the Valley of the Kings mentions which of the following?
   - Ⓐ How large it is
   - Ⓑ When the first tombs were made there
   - Ⓒ The names of people buried there
   - Ⓓ The importance of the place

3. The word "them" in the passage refers to
   - Ⓐ the Egyptians
   - Ⓑ pyramids
   - Ⓒ bandits
   - Ⓓ their treasures

4. According to paragraph 2, the Egyptians began digging tombs in the Valley of the Kings because
   - Ⓐ pyramids were expensive to built
   - Ⓑ it took too long to construct pyramids
   - Ⓒ too many pyramids were being robbed
   - Ⓓ construction materials for pyramids were hard to find

5. The word "corridors" in the passage is closest in meaning to
   - Ⓐ rooms
   - Ⓑ passageways
   - Ⓒ entrances
   - Ⓓ columns

6. In paragraph 3, the author implies that many tombs in the Valley of the Kings
   - Ⓐ were not well hidden
   - Ⓑ took a short time to make
   - Ⓒ were at the tops of mountains
   - Ⓓ have not been found yet

7 According to paragraphs 3 and 4, which of the following is NOT true about King Tut?

   Ⓐ He became the pharaoh after Amenhotep I died.
   Ⓑ Archaeologists have learned a lot from his tomb.
   Ⓒ His tomb was discovered by Howard Carter.
   Ⓓ Many treasures were found in his tomb.

8 According to paragraph 4, archaeologists have learned about ancient Egypt by

   Ⓐ searching for the treasures of King Tut
   Ⓑ studying paintings on the walls of tombs
   Ⓒ doing research on the mummies of pharaohs
   Ⓓ learning to read ancient Egyptian writing

9 Look at the four squares [■] that indicate where the following sentence could be added to the passage.

   Hers is the longest ever to have been found.

   Where would the sentence best fit?
   Click on a square [■] to add the sentence to the passage.

10 *Directions:* An introductory sentence for a brief summary of the passage is provided below. Complete the summary by selecting the THREE answer choices that express the most important ideas in the passage.

   The Egyptians built many tombs for pharaohs in the Valley of the Kings in the past.

   -
   -
   -

   ### Answer Choices

   1 Archaeologists believe there are many tombs that have not been found yet.
   2 Many tombs were looted, but King Tut's tomb had a large amount of treasure.
   3 The Valley of the Kings is located near the ancient city of Luxor, Egypt.
   4 There are some tombs that have pictures drawn on the walls.
   5 Around sixty tombs have been discovered in the Valley of the Kings.
   6 Pyramids were getting looted, so the Egyptians built tombs in the Valley of the Kings.

CHAPTER 07

Physics
(Identifying Cohesive Devices)

1. Simple Machines
2. Gravity
3. Escape Velocity
4. Practical Applications from Physics
5. Sir Isaac Newton
6. The Manhattan Project
7. Time Travel
8. Albert Einstein

CHAPTER 7 **Physics** (Identifying Cohesive Devices)

Understanding TOEFL Question Types & Reading Skills

1 Question Types — Sentence Simplification & Insert Text Questions

- *Sentence Simplification questions* ask you to look at a sentence from the passage. Then, you must choose a shorter version of the sentence that has the same meaning. You need to recognize which words are important and which ones you can omit from the sentence.
- *Insert Text questions* ask you to look at a sentence not in the passage. You must then decide where in the passage you could include the new sentence. For this question, you should be able to understand how ideas logically connect to each other.

● Example Sentence Simplification & Insert Text Questions

- Which of the following best expresses the essential information in the highlighted sentence? *Incorrect* answer choices change the meaning in important ways or leave out essential information.
- Look at the four squares [■] that indicate where the following sentence could be added to the passage.

[You will see a sentence in bold.]

Where would the sentence best fit?

Click on a square [■] to add the sentence to the passage.

● Useful Tips for Your Success

- Learn to → identify synonyms of various words.
  → recognize important connector words.
- Don't → choose answers that only provide half of a sentence's meaning.
  → insert sentences where they make no sense logically.

Sample Question

Benjamin Franklin

Most people do not associate Benjamin Franklin, who was one of America's Founding Fathers, with physics. Yet in addition to his many contributions to the U.S., Franklin was also the first American physicist.

In the 1750s, Franklin began thinking about lightning. He once famously flew a kite in the middle of a thunderstorm. Franklin attached a metal key to the kite string and then ran a metal wire from the key to a jar. When lightning struck the kite, he then touched the key, which gave him a shock. ==From this experiment, Franklin proved that his suspicions about lightning's nature were correct and that it was really static electricity.== He also proved with his experiment that electricity is both positively and negatively charged.

strike *v* to hit, often hard or violently   **suspicion** *n* a belief for which there is little or no evidence

Q Which of the following best expresses the essential information in the highlighted sentence? *Incorrect* answer choices change the meaning in important ways or leave out essential information.

- Ⓐ Franklin did not know lightning was electricity until he did his experiment.
- Ⓑ Franklin's experiment proved he was right that lightning was static electricity.
- Ⓒ Without doing an experiment, Franklin knew that lightning was static electricity.
- Ⓓ Because lightning was electricity, Franklin had to conduct his experiment.

2 Reading Skills — Identifying Cohesive Devices

Identifying cohesive devices is an important skill that shows how writers connect different ideas. These cohesive devices allow readers to understand how one idea leads to another. When writers use these ideas, they make their passages more logical and easier to understand.

Check-Up

▸ Choose the best conjunction in the box below to complete the sentence.

| because   so   if   when |

_____ lightning struck the kite, he then touched the key, which gave him a shock.

Chapter 7

Exercise 1

Simple Machines

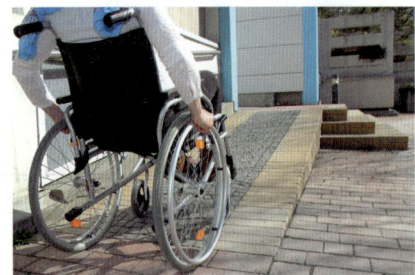

  Physicists are primarily concerned with both the direct and indirect effects that each object in the universe has on other objects. People also often use machines directly to affect other objects. Practically all machines are complex versions of the six types of simple machines, which are the lever, the inclined plane, the wedge, the screw, the wheel and axle, and the pulley.

  Simple machines act in various ways to make work simpler and less difficult. Simple machines have either very few or no moving parts as well but instead rely upon energy to do work. Looking at the machines being used throughout the world, one can see numerous simple machines.

  The wheelchair ramps in front of most buildings are inclined planes. **1** People roller-skating are using a wheel and axle. **2** Even children on the seesaw on a playground are making use of a lever. **3** Thanks to these simple machines and the more complex creations that come from them, people's lives have become much less complicated. **4**

---

primarily adv   mostly
inclined adj   leaning; angled

creation n   an invention

Q1 Which of the following best expresses the essential information in the highlighted sentence in paragraph 1? *Incorrect* answer choices change the meaning in important ways or leave out essential information.

Ⓐ Not every object in the universe has an effect on each other one.
Ⓑ The direct and indirect effects of objects are all different.
Ⓒ Physicists know all about the indirect and direct effects of objects.
Ⓓ The effects of objects on one another are what physicists study.

Q2 Which of the following best expresses the essential information in the highlighted sentence in paragraph 2? *Incorrect* answer choices change the meaning in important ways or leave out essential information.

Ⓐ The only machines most people use are simple ones.
Ⓑ There are many simple machines in use around the world.
Ⓒ In most of the world, there are only simple machines.
Ⓓ The majority of the world has a need for simple machines.

Q3 Look at the four squares [■] that indicate where the following sentence could be added to the passage.

The elevators people ride in daily also rely upon the wheel and axle to transport them up and down.

Where would the sentence best fit?

Reading Skills — Identifying Cohesive Devices

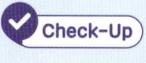 In the passage, the pronoun "them" in the sentence, "Thanks to these simple machines and the more complex creations that come from them, people's lives have become much less complicated," refers to _____.

Ⓐ children
Ⓑ simple machines
Ⓒ complex creations
Ⓓ people's lives

• Exercise 2 •

Gravity

■1 When a person throws something into the air, it goes up but then falls back to the ground. ■2 Likewise, if a person drops something from a high structure, it will continue falling until it reaches the ground. ■3 The reason this occurs is gravity. ■4

Gravity was first explained by Sir Isaac Newton, who came up with the law of universal gravitation. ■1 Essentially, he believed that every object in the universe attracted every other object. ■2 However, the strength of the attraction depended upon how large the object was and how near the other object it was. ■3 This meant that while the sun might have a strong gravitational force on Earth, its gravitational attraction is weaker on Saturn, which is farther away. ■4

Unfortunately, scientists have not yet determined why each atom attracts every other atom. There are some theories on this, but none of them has been completely acceptable to the scientific community. Therefore, physicists continue to search for the answer to this question.

structure n a building; a place
gravitational adj relating to gravity
acceptable adj satisfactory

Q1 Look at the four squares [■] in paragraph 1 that indicate where the following sentence could be added to the passage.

No matter how high up that object goes, it is still eventually going to come back down.

Where would the sentence best fit?

Q2 Look at the four squares [■] in paragraph 2 that indicate where the following sentence could be added to the passage.

According to legend, he came up with the law of gravity when an apple fell off a tree he was under and hit him on the head.

Where would the sentence best fit?

Q3 Which of the following best expresses the essential information in the highlighted sentence? *Incorrect* answer choices change the meaning in important ways or leave out essential information.

- Ⓐ The scientific community never agrees on any theories.
- Ⓑ There are some theories that explain everything for scientists.
- Ⓒ Not every scientist agrees with the proposed theories.
- Ⓓ Scientists have completely accepted some of the theories.

Reading Skills Identifying Cohesive Devices

Check-Up Choose the best conjunctions in the box below to complete the sentences.

> if   before   but   and

1 Likewise, _____ a person drops something from a high structure, it will continue falling until it reaches the ground.

2 There are some theories on this, _____ none of them have been completely acceptable to the scientific community.

• **Exercise 3** •

Escape Velocity

When a person tosses a ball into the air, it rises to a certain height, stops, and then falls to the ground. The reason for this is the Earth's gravity, which pulls on objects in the air and causes them to fall. When countries began looking to send rockets into outer space, they had to concern themselves with gravity.

1 To escape from the Earth's gravitational pull, an object must attain a speed of 11.2 kilometers per second. **2** This is known as escape velocity. **3** An object that achieves this will no longer fall to the ground but can fly into outer space. **4**

Achieving such a speed requires a tremendous amount of fuel, which is the primary reason rockets are so large. They must carry enough fuel to allow them to achieve escape velocity. The Saturn V rocket, which transported astronauts to the moon, was enormous. Thanks to its great size, it attained escape velocity while also carrying a large payload.

---

gravity [n] the force of attraction that causes objects to fall to the ground

attain [v] to reach; to achieve

tremendous [adj] great; very large

Q1 Which of the following best expresses the essential information in the highlighted sentence in paragraph 1? *Incorrect* answer choices change the meaning in important ways or leave out essential information.

Ⓐ Gravity prevented most countries from sending rockets into outer space.
Ⓑ In order to send a rocket into out space, the force of gravity must be defeated.
Ⓒ Countries had to consider gravity when they wanted to send rockets to space.
Ⓓ Going to space requires rockets that can escape the force of gravity.

Q2 Look at the four squares [■] that indicate where the following sentence could be added to the passage.

That is more than thirty times the speed of sound.

Where would the sentence best fit?

Q3 Which of the following best expresses the essential information in the highlighted sentence in paragraph 3? *Incorrect* answer choices change the meaning in important ways or leave out essential information.

- Ⓐ When rockets are full of fuel, they are able to attain very high speeds.
- Ⓑ Rockets are so big because they need very much fuel to attain a high speed.
- Ⓒ Rocket cannot travel fast unless they are large and have a lot of fuel.
- Ⓓ Because rockets are so large, they have to be filled with a great amount of fuel.

Reading Skills Identifying Cohesive Devices

Check-Up In the passage, the pronoun "it" in the sentence, "Thanks to its great size, it attained escape velocity while also carrying a large payload," refers to _____.

- Ⓐ the Saturn V rocket
- Ⓑ the moon
- Ⓒ its great size
- Ⓓ escape velocity

• **Exercise 4** •

Practical Applications from Physics

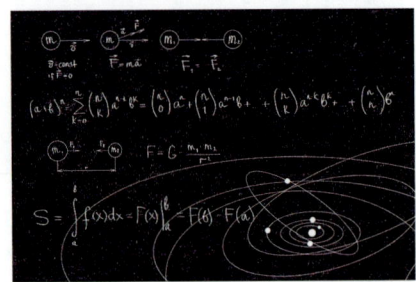

🎧 07-05

The field of physics covers a very wide range of topics. It includes light, electricity, magnetism, and even outer space. The research done by many physicists is quite complex and is usually beyond most people's comprehension. However, their research and discoveries have helped the modern world to become as advanced as it is today.

1 For one thing, without developments in physics, there would be no televisions, radios, computers, or refrigerators. **2** Nor would there be any other home appliances that people own. **3** The reason is that these machines all operate with electricity, which physicists have made many discoveries on. **4**

Likewise, the space programs that send both satellites and men into outer space would not exist without physics. **1** With no satellites, modern telecommunications would be incredibly different. **2** These are just some of the advances that have been made possible through physics. **3** In the future, there will surely be even more improvements in people's quality of life thanks to physicists. **4**

---

comprehension n understanding
appliance n a machine that makes work easier
incredibly adv very; greatly

Q1 Which of the following best expresses the essential information in the highlighted sentence? *Incorrect* answer choices change the meaning in important ways or leave out essential information.

Ⓐ Many people are unaware of what physicists really do.
Ⓑ Physicists often do not even understand their own complex work.
Ⓒ Physicists do difficult work many people cannot understand.
Ⓓ It is nearly impossible for anyone to understand a physicist's work.

Q2 Look at the four squares [■] in paragraph 2 that indicate where the following sentence could be added to the passage.

These include toasters, irons, and microwave ovens.

Where would the sentence best fit?

Q3 Look at the four squares [■] in paragraph 3 that indicate where the following sentence could be added to the passage.

For one thing, nobody would be able to communicate with wireless tools such as cell phones.

Where would the sentence best fit?

Reading Skills Identifying Cohesive Devices

Check-Up Choose the best conjunctions in the box below to complete the sentences.

> or   nor   so   however

1 The research done by many physicists is quite complex and is usually beyond most people's comprehension. _____, their research and discoveries have helped the modern world to become as advanced as it is today.

2 For one thing, without developments in physics, there would be no televisions, radios, computers, or refrigerators. _____ would there be any other home appliances that people own.

Chapter 7   175

• Exercise 5 •

Sir Isaac Newton

Living in the seventeenth and eighteenth centuries, Sir Isaac Newton was the greatest physicist of the early modern age. ■1 In fact, many people call him the father of modern physical science. ■2 Among his achievements, of which there were many, one especially stands out. ■3 This was his declaration of the three laws of motion. ■4

Newton's first law of motion, which is called the Law of Inertia, states that an object at rest will remain at rest until it is acted upon by an outside force. ■1 It merely means that objects do not move by themselves but need something to cause them to move. ■2 The second law is his most important because it allows people to calculate the dynamics of various objects. ■3 In mathematical terms, it states that the force of an object is equal to its mass multiplied by its acceleration. ■4 Finally, the third law states that for every action, there is an equal and opposite reaction. Thanks to this law, physicists can explain numerous phenomena, one of which is how airplanes can fly.

These three laws of motion helped explain much about the world. Because of Newton's discovery, the world became much clearer to the people living in it.

---

achievement (n) an accomplishment
stand out (phr) to be exceptional; to be noticeable
inertia (n) inactivity
dynamics (n) energy

Q1 Look at the four squares [■] in paragraph 1 that indicate where the following sentence could be added to the passage.

He was even greater than scientists such as Copernicus and Galileo.

Where would the sentence best fit?

Q2 Which of the following best expresses the essential information in the first highlighted sentence in paragraph 2? *Incorrect* answer choices change the meaning in important ways or leave out essential information.

- Ⓐ The first law of motion states that something not moving will not be able to move at all no matter what.
- Ⓑ According to the first law, something stationary will remain that way until something else makes it move.
- Ⓒ Newton's first law states that moving objects continue to move until something causes them to stop.
- Ⓓ The Law of Inertia mentions that moving objects will stop whenever they encounter some nonmoving objects.

Q3 Look at the four squares [■] in paragraph 2 that indicate where the following sentence could be added to the passage.

There is even a relatively simple math equation that lets people figure out how much force an object has.

Where would the sentence best fit?

Q4 Which of the following best expresses the essential information in the second highlighted sentence in paragraph 2? *Incorrect* answer choices change the meaning in important ways or leave out essential information.

- Ⓐ This law helps people understand many things, including what lets airplanes fly.
- Ⓑ Without this law, airplanes would never be able to get off the ground and fly.
- Ⓒ Physicists use this law to do many things, including helping make airplanes fly.
- Ⓓ The explanation of many things, including flight, is not possible thanks to this law.

Reading Skills Identifying Cohesive Devices

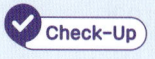 In the passage, the pronoun "there" in the sentence, "Among his achievements, of which there were many, one especially stands out," refers to _____.

- Ⓐ people
- Ⓑ father
- Ⓒ modern physical science
- Ⓓ achievements

• **Exercise 6** •

The Manhattan Project

🎧 07-07

In the 1930s, the world was heading toward war. Oppressive regimes in Germany, Italy, and Japan were trying to expand their territory. **1** In addition, in 1939, there were rumors that Nazi Germany was looking to discover how to create an atomic bomb. **2** This bomb would use the power of the atom to create an enormously powerful explosion. **3** To counter the Nazis, the United States began working on the top-secret Manhattan Project. **4**

The Manhattan Project was America's attempt to create an atomic bomb of its own. Under the direction of Leslie Groves, who was a general in the U.S. Army, some of the most brilliant minds in the world began to work on the project. These people included J. Robert Oppenheimer, who led the project, Enrico Fermi, Glenn Seaborg, and Richard Feynman. There were many research facilities, but the ones at the University of Chicago, Oak Ridge, Tennessee, and Los Alamos, New Mexico were the most crucial.

In 1942, some physicists in Chicago achieved the first nuclear reaction. **1** After that, they learned a lot about uranium and plutonium, which were the keys to the bomb. **2** Then, on July 16, they exploded an A-bomb at Alamogordo, New Mexico. **3** The nuclear age had begun. **4**

---

oppressive *adj* harsh; cruel
regime *n* a government
counter *v* to act against
key *n* an answer; an explanation

Q1 Which of the following best expresses the essential information in the highlighted sentence in paragraph 1? *Incorrect* answer choices change the meaning in important ways or leave out essential information.

Ⓐ The first atomic bomb was rumored to have been made by the Germans in 1939.
Ⓑ People had heard that the Germans were trying to build an atomic bomb in 1939.
Ⓒ By 1939, it was believed that Nazi Germany was succeeding at making an atomic bomb.
Ⓓ According to rumors, the Germans discovered the secret of the atomic bomb in 1939.

Q2 Look at the four squares [■] in paragraph 1 that indicate where the following sentence could be added to the passage.

This would eventually become the most expensive project that man had ever attempted.

Where would the sentence best fit?

Q3 Which of the following best expresses the essential information in the highlighted sentence in paragraph 2? *Incorrect* answer choices change the meaning in important ways or leave out essential information.

- Ⓐ Leslie Groves, a brilliant general, led the project while working for the U.S. Army.
- Ⓑ The American general who led the very brilliant people was also working on the project.
- Ⓒ The project, despite having very smart people, needed the U.S. Army in order to succeed.
- Ⓓ An American general was in charge of the incredibly intelligent people doing the research.

Q4 Look at the four squares [■] in paragraph 3 that indicate where the following sentence could be added to the passage.

One month later, the United States would drop two atomic bombs on Japan, which would end World War II.

Where would the sentence best fit?

Reading Skills Identifying Cohesive Devices

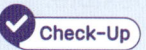 **Check-Up** Choose the best conjunctions in the box below to complete the sentences.

> unless   because   but   after

1 There were many research facilities, _____ the ones at the University of Chicago, Oak Ridge, Tennessee, and Los Alamos, New Mexico were the most crucial.

2 In 1942, some physicists in Chicago achieved the first nuclear reaction. _____ that, they learned a lot about uranium and plutonium, which were the keys to the bomb.

Chapter 7   179

• Exercise 7 •

Time Travel

■ Time travel commonly appears in many science-fiction novels and movies. ■ However, physicists cannot agree as to whether or not it is possible. ■ Many argue that time travel is impossible simply because people in the present have not met anyone from the future. ■ They claim that if it were possible, tourists from the future should be overrunning modern-day society.

On the other hand, some physicists claim that time travel is theoretically possible. ■ They note several different ways in which it could be done. ■ One way is for someone to travel faster than the speed of light, which moves at around 300,000 meters per second. ■ By achieving speeds this fast, a person should be able to go back in time. ■ At present, though, no one has invented a machine capable of even a fraction of the speed of light.

Some physicists believe traveling through a black hole, which is an enormous region in space with incredibly strong gravity, will let people travel in time. Likewise, others postulate the existence of wormholes, which are essentially shortcuts in space that should let people travel from star system to star system. For the time being, these ideas are all theoretical and remain but dreams.

---

overrun [v] to flood; to swarm
theoretically [adv] in theory; hypothetically
fraction [n] a part; a portion
postulate [v] to believe; to state; to declare

Q1 Look at the four squares [■] in paragraph 1 that indicate where the following sentence could be added to the passage.

Some say that it will happen while others argue that it will never become possible.

Where would the sentence best fit?

Q2 Look at the four squares [■] in paragraph 2 that indicate where the following sentence could be added to the passage.

Unfortunately, while the ideas show it is possible, modern technology cannot create the machines needed.

Where would the sentence best fit?

Q3 Which of the following best expresses the essential information in the highlighted sentence in paragraph 2? *Incorrect* answer choices change the meaning in important ways or leave out essential information.

- Ⓐ People are working on inventing machines that move at light speed.
- Ⓑ Nothing that can travel even remotely near light speed exists yet.
- Ⓒ Machines that can move at fractions of light speed currently exist.
- Ⓓ The speed of light will never be approached by a machine.

Q4 Which of the following best expresses the essential information in the highlighted sentence in paragraph 3? *Incorrect* answer choices change the meaning in important ways or leave out essential information.

- Ⓐ Wormholes, which would let people travel to the stars quickly, might possibly exist.
- Ⓑ Scientists have located some wormholes, so people can now travel from star to star.
- Ⓒ Traveling from star to star will not be possible unless wormholes actually exist.
- Ⓓ A shortcut in space called a wormhole allows people to move easily to star systems.

Reading Skills | **Identifying Cohesive Devices**

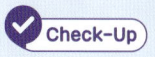 **Check-Up** In the passage, the pronoun "They" in the sentence, "They claim that if it were possible, tourists from the future should be overrunning modern-day society," refers to _____ .

- Ⓐ science-fiction novels and movies
- Ⓑ physicists
- Ⓒ time travel
- Ⓓ tourists

• Exercise 8 •

Albert Einstein

There have been many brilliant physicists throughout history, yet almost none was as bright as Albert Einstein. **1** Born in Germany in 1879, his early life did not show that he was destined for greatness. **2** He took a job in the Swiss Patent Office in 1901, and it seemed as though he would spend the rest of his life there. **3** However, Einstein simultaneously worked on his doctorate, which he received in 1905. **4** After that, he made a lot of discoveries that astounded the world in general.

Working in a number of fields in physics, Einstein produced many crucial papers that revolutionized the physics world. **1** The first was his paper on the special theory of relativity, which covered space and time, in 1905. **2** He followed this in 1916 with his work on the general theory of relativity. **3** Einstein also worked in the fields of mechanics and electromagnetics. **4** Another area of physics he covered was light.

An avowed pacifist, Einstein fled Germany when the Nazis took over. Despite his dislike of war, it was Einstein's letter to American President Franklin D. Roosevelt that convinced him to begin the research that would lead to the creation of the atomic bomb.

---

bright *adj* intelligent; clever
simultaneously *adv* at the same time

pacifist *n* a person who does not believe in fighting; an antiwar person

---

Q1 Which of the following best expresses the essential information in the highlighted sentence in paragraph 1? *Incorrect* answer choices change the meaning in important ways or leave out essential information.

Ⓐ Albert Einstein became the greatest physicist in the world.
Ⓑ There has never been a smarter physicist than Einstein.
Ⓒ Albert Einstein was one of the smartest physicists ever.
Ⓓ In all history, Einstein was one of the top ten physicists.

Q2 Look at the four squares [■] in paragraph 1 that indicate where the following sentence could be added to the passage.

As a matter of fact, Einstein famously got a very poor grade in a physics class once.

Where would the sentence best fit?

Q3 Look at the four squares [■] in paragraph 2 that indicate where the following sentence could be added to the passage.

It was this ability to work in several different areas that helped make him famous.

Where would the sentence best fit?

Q4 Which of the following best expresses the essential information in the highlighted sentence in paragraph 3? *Incorrect* answer choices change the meaning in important ways or leave out essential information.

- Ⓐ Even though he hated war, Einstein got the American president to start working on making an atomic bomb.
- Ⓑ President Roosevelt, despite Einstein's opposition to war, started researching how to make an atomic bomb.
- Ⓒ Albert Einstein described how to make an atomic bomb in a letter he wrote to President Franklin Roosevelt.
- Ⓓ Einstein would not work on the atomic bomb project, but he explained the method to President Roosevelt.

Reading Skills — Identifying Cohesive Devices

Check-Up Choose the best conjunctions in the box below to complete the sentences.

> yet   so   and   since

1. There have been many brilliant physicists throughout history, _____ almost none was as bright as Albert Einstein.
2. He took a job in the Swiss Patent Office in 1901, _____ it seemed as though he would spend the rest of his life there.

Chapter 7   183

Grammar **Point**

Relative Clauses

1 **Relative clauses** are clauses that modify the noun coming before them. They begin with relative pronouns such as which, that, who, whom, and whose. People often use relative clauses to combine two sentences into a single longer one.

2 Types of Relative Clauses

1. Use the relative pronouns who, which, and that as the subjects of relative clauses.

   - The project was under the direction of Leslie Groves, who was a general.
   - They learned a lot about uranium and plutonium, which were the keys to the bomb.
   - Many movies feature characters that use lasers as weapons.

2. Use the relative pronoun whose to express possession. In the relative clause, whose takes the place of a noun and acts like a possessive noun.

   - Wormholes, whose existence has not been proven, may allow fast interstellar transportation.
   - Einstein, whose work has been studied much, was a brilliant man.

3. Use the relative pronouns whom and which as the objects of a relative clause. Another noun acts as the subject, and one of these pronouns is the object.

   - Franklin, of whom much has been written, was the first American physicist.
   - Isaac Newton, to whom many people owe their success, wrote the three laws of gravity.

4. Use the relative pronoun what to create a relative clause that does not modify another noun. It stands alone and acts as either the subject or object of a sentence.

   - At first, only a few people knew what Newton was talking about.
   - Research at the University of Chicago is what allowed the atomic bomb to be made.
   - Gravity is what causes objects to fall to the ground.

Grammar Check-Up

A Choose the correct relative pronouns.

1 Albert Einstein was the man (who / whom) got Roosevelt to start working on the A-bomb.

2 Lasers, (that / which) are focused light, are becoming more advanced nowadays.

3 Gravity, (whose / which) effects were explained by Newton, is an important force.

4 The person to (who / whom) you are speaking won a Nobel Prize in Physics.

5 The reason (that / what) wormholes may exist is that scientists can prove them mathematically.

B Choose the correct words for the blanks.

1 The atomic bomb, _____ took many years to develop, was used twice on Japan.
   ⓐ that   ⓑ who   ⓒ which   ⓓ whose

2 The televisions _____ people watch were invented because of modern physics.
   ⓐ that   ⓑ whose   ⓒ whom   ⓓ what

3 Benjamin Franklin, _____ flew a kite in a storm, did important work on lightning.
   ⓐ which   ⓑ who   ⓒ that   ⓓ whose

4 Going through a black hole, _____ has never been done, would be a new experience.
   ⓐ what   ⓑ which   ⓒ that   ⓓ who

C Read the following story and fill in the blanks. Use each word only once.

> who   whose   that   which   whom

Albert Einstein, _____ was born in the nineteenth century, was one of the world's smartest men. He first became famous for his work on relativity, _____ is a field of physics. Einstein, _____ theories on relativity were proven correct, won a Nobel Prize for this work. He also studied other fields _____ had confused many intelligent men. Although he was a pacifist, he helped begin work on the atomic bomb. He sent a letter to President Roosevelt, to _____ he explained the importance of creating the atomic bomb before the Nazis could.

Vocabulary Review

A Circle the words that best complete the sentences.

1. They took a (shortcut / system) to reach their destination faster.
2. Wormholes are (simply / theoretically) possible but have not been found yet.
3. The wheel and (pulley / axle) is one kind of simple machine.
4. The student got his (patent / doctorate) after several years of graduate study.
5. Jason (dropped / fell) the ball from the ninth floor of the building.

B Choose the best words to complete the sentences.

1. _____ is the force that causes things to fall to the ground.
   - A Time travel
   - B Electricity
   - C Gravity
   - D Magnetism

2. She was one of the most _____ students in the class.
   - A static
   - B indirect
   - C complex
   - D brilliant

3. There was a large amount of lightning during the _____.
   - A regime
   - B thunderstorm
   - C fraction
   - D general

4. Thanks to the _____ of the professor, the project was a success.
   - A appliance
   - B universe
   - C direction
   - D explosion

5. Use math to determine the _____ of the moving vehicle.
   - A velocity
   - B fuel
   - C appearance
   - D rocket

C Choose the words with the closest meanings to the highlighted words.

1. The rocket that transported the astronauts is now in a museum.
   - A orbited
   - B recovered
   - C carried
   - D trained

2. Some machines physicists use can be very complicated.
   - A complex
   - B direct
   - C capable
   - D oppressive

3. You must work hard in order to attain your goals.
   - A report
   - B bypass
   - C consider
   - D achieve

4. It is not always easy to create new machines.
   - A postulate
   - B calculate
   - C invent
   - D operate

5. Sir Isaac Newton stated there were three different laws of motion.
   - A thought
   - B claimed
   - C produced
   - D learned

D Complete the sentences by filling in the blanks with the best words from the list. Change the forms of the words if necessary. Use each word only once.

| prove | regime | key | calculate | telecommunications |

1. The _____ to solving the answer was using an effective computer.
2. Modern _____ are very effective because of the many satellites in space.
3. The physicist used his computer to _____ the answer to the problem.
4. Benjamin Franklin _____ he was correct when his experiment was successful.
5. Because of the Nazi _____ in Germany, Einstein moved to the United States.

Practice Test

Kinetic and Potential Energy

07-10

Energy refers to the capacity to do work. There are two main types of energy: kinetic and potential energy. Kinetic energy refers to the energy created by the motion of a thing. Potential energy refers to the energy associated with the position of a thing.

There are numerous examples of both types of energy. For instance, a dam that blocks a river creates a reservoir behind it. This stored water has a huge amount of potential energy. When the floodgates of the dam are opened, the water begins to flow. In this instance, the potential energy of the water is converted into kinetic energy because it is moving. The water can then be used to create electricity, which can be stored as potential energy and used later.

A rollercoaster is another example. Rollercoasters are known for rolling up to great heights and then descending quickly. When a rollercoaster reaches its highest point on the tracks, it has very much potential energy. This energy comes from the height of the rollercoaster as well as its weight and the weight of the people in it. As the rollercoaster heads down the track, the potential energy becomes kinetic energy.

A third example is the food that people eat. ■1 Food contains nutrients that can be digested and used by the body. ■2 This means that food contains potential energy. ■3 When the body digests food, it is essentially changed into energy. ■4 This allows people to move, speak, think, and do other activities.

dam n a barrier that blocks a moving body of water
reservoir n a manmade lake where water is collected
descend v to go down

1. In paragraph 1, all of the following questions are answered EXCEPT:
   - (A) How is kinetic energy used?
   - (B) What is potential energy?
   - (C) What does the word energy refer to?
   - (D) What are two types of energy?

2. The word "it" in the passage refers to
   - (A) the dam
   - (B) the potential energy
   - (C) the water
   - (D) kinetic energy

3. Which of the following best expresses the essential information in the highlighted sentence? *Incorrect* answer choices change the meaning in important ways or leave out essential information.
   - (A) The water creates electricity, which is stored as potential energy.
   - (B) Electricity stored as potential energy can be created from water.
   - (C) The best way to create potential energy is to make electricity from flowing water.
   - (D) Water from a dam can be used in the creation of potential energy.

4. In paragraph 2, the author implies that dams
   - (A) produce less energy than is required to build them
   - (B) are efficient at changing potential energy into kinetic energy
   - (C) can create a large amount of kinetic energy
   - (D) are almost always used to create electricity

5. The author discusses "Rollercoasters" in paragraph 3 in order to
   - (A) show how they move on tracks
   - (B) describe the types of energy they have
   - (C) compare them with dams
   - (D) prove that they can create their own energy

6. The word "heads" in the passages is closest in meaning to
   - (A) moves
   - (B) transfers
   - (C) approaches
   - (D) thinks

7 According to paragraph 3, a rollercoaster has a lot of potential energy when

- (A) it is going down the tracks
- (B) it reaches the bottom of the tracks
- (C) it is climbing up the tracks
- (D) it is at the top of the tracks

8 According to paragraph 4, which of the following is true of food?

- (A) It creates energy in the same way that a dam does.
- (B) It can have both potential and kinetic energy.
- (C) It has more potential energy than a rollercoaster.
- (D) It can convert kinetic energy into potential energy.

9 Look at the four squares [■] that indicate where the following sentence could be added to the passage.

In this form, it is considered kinetic energy.

Where would the sentence best fit?

Click on a square [■] to add the sentence to the passage.

10 *Directions:* Complete the table below to summarize information about kinetic and potential energy discussed in the passage. Match the appropriate statements to the type of energy which they are associated.

TYPE OF ENERGY	STATEMENTS
Kinetic energy	Select 2 • •
Potential energy	Select 3 • • •

Statements

1. Exists in food before it is eaten
2. Forms when water is released from a dam
3. Is in a rollercoaster at the moment it stops moving
4. Is considered harder to create than the other
5. Is the type that can be used in people's homes
6. Can be found in the stored water of a dam
7. Is associated with energy created by motion

CHAPTER 08

Political Science
(Outlining)

1. The Magna Carta
2. Niccolo Machiavelli
3. The Bill of Rights
4. The Divine Right of Kings
5. Thomas Jefferson and the Declaration of Independence
6. Dictatorships
7. Plato's *Republic*
8. The American Electoral System

CHAPTER 8 Political Science (Outlining)

Understanding TOEFL Question Types & Reading Skills

1 Question Types — Prose Summary & Fill in a Table Questions

- *Prose Summary questions* test your ability to detect the major ideas in the passage. You must be able to find the major ideas and ignore the minor ideas.
- *Fill in a Table questions* ask you to complete a table that classifies various parts of the passage. You must be able to find the major ideas in the passage and then classify them according to the topic.

● Example Prose Summary & Fill in a Table Questions

- An introductory sentence for a brief summary of the passage is provided below. Complete the summary by selecting the THREE answer choices that express the most important ideas in the passage.
- Complete the table below to summarize information about X discussed in the passage. Match the appropriate statements to X with which they are associated.

● Useful Tips for Your Success

- Learn to
  → find the main ideas in the passage.
  → recognize the facts associated with the main ideas.

- Don't
  → pay attention to the minor ideas.
  → become confused between major and minor ideas.

Sample Question

Communism and Capitalism

🎧 08-01

In the twentieth century, two political systems competed for power. They were communism and capitalism.

Under communism, everything is owned by the people. There is no private property. People, in theory, work for the good of the community, not for themselves. Meanwhile, under capitalism, there is private ownership of products and land. People work to earn profits, which they may keep for themselves. In addition, communist governments tend to be oppressive, but capitalist countries often practice democracy and respect people's freedom.

In the twentieth century, the Soviet Union had a communist government while the United States practiced capitalism. Due to the numerous flaws in communism, the Soviet Union crumbled. But the U.S. showed capitalism's superiority and became the world's only superpower.

Q An introductory sentence for a brief summary of the passage is provided below. Complete the summary by selecting the THREE answer choices that express the most important ideas in the passage.

Communism and capitalism are two different political systems that competed against each other in the twentieth century.

- Ⓐ The United States practiced democracy in addition to capitalism.
- Ⓑ The goal of capitalism is for people to make money for themselves.
- Ⓒ The Soviet Union's use of communism resulted in failure.
- Ⓓ Capitalism will always be more successful than communism.
- Ⓔ Under communism, there is supposed to be no private property.

2 Reading Skills Outlining

Outlining can identify both the major and minor ideas in a passage. Use outlines to organize all of the ideas in the passage. Then, you can show the relationships between all of these ideas.

Check-Up

▶ **Complete the following outline.**

I Communism
  A. All property owned by the people together
  B. People work for good of community
  C. Are often oppressive governments

II Capitalism
  A. Private ownership of products and _____
  B. People try to make profits
  C. Are often free governments practicing democracy

Chapter ❽ 193

• Exercise 1 •

The Magna Carta

08-02

Many people consider the American Constitution to be one of the most vital political documents in history. However, without the Magna Carta, the American Founding Fathers never would have written the Constitution.

The Magna Carta—Latin for "Great Charter"—was signed in 1215. It helped develop British common law. It later influenced American law as well. The Magna Carta basically restricted the limits of the British king's power by stating exactly which powers he had and which he did not.

In the thirteenth century, King John of England often abused his powers. His nobles essentially joined forces, wrote the Magna Carta, and forced the king to sign it. It not only limited the king's powers, but it also gave certain powers and protections to both the nobles and the British people. While it was not always enforced, people still respect it today as one of the world's most important political documents.

---

vital [adj] important; crucial
restrict [v] to limit

abuse [v] to mistreat; to make improper use of

Q1 An introductory sentence for a brief summary of the passage is provided below. Complete the summary by selecting the THREE answer choices that express the most important ideas in the passage.

The Magna Carta helped limit the king's powers and strongly influenced British and American law.

- Ⓐ British nobles forced King John to sign the Magna Carta to reduce his control.
- Ⓑ The British kings did not always respect the words of the Magna Carta.
- Ⓒ The American Constitution is based on some ideas from the Magna Carta.
- Ⓓ People today still refer to the Magna Carta for help running governments.
- Ⓔ The Magna Carta described what the king's powers were and were not.

Q2 Complete the table below to summarize information about the Magna Carta discussed in the passage. Match the appropriate statements to the reasons for the Magna Carta's signing and the effects of the Magna Carta's signing with which they are associated.

MAGNA CARTA

Reasons for its signing

STATEMENTS

Select 2
-
-

Effects of its signing

Select 3
-
-
-

Statements

Ⓐ King John was not treating his nobles properly.
Ⓑ British common law became further developed.
Ⓒ The government sometimes did not enforce the Magna Carta.
Ⓓ The British people wanted protection under the law.
Ⓔ The American Constitution was able to be written.
Ⓕ The British people became more powerful than the king.
Ⓖ American law was greatly influenced by the Magna Carta.

Reading Skills Outlining

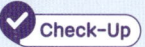 **Check-Up** Complete the following outline.

I Magna Carta
   A. Signed in 1215
   B. Influenced British common law and _____ _____
   C. Stated powers of king

II Reasons for signing Magna Carta
   A. King John was abusing his powers
   B. Nobles joined forces to make king sign it
   C. Gave power and protection to nobles and people

Chapter ❽   195

Exercise 2

Niccolo Machiavelli

08-03

Niccolo Machiavelli lived during the Renaissance. Born in Florence, Italy, in 1469, Machiavelli wrote *The Prince*, a treatise on how a ruler should govern.

Machiavelli lived in a time of political upheaval in northern Italy. The powerful city-states of Florence, Milan, and Venice were constantly competing for power. They were also interfered with by Spain, the Holy Roman Empire, France, and the Roman Catholic Pope. With this in mind, Machiavelli described his ideal ruler in *The Prince*.

He felt it was acceptable for a ruler to use violence. However, it should be done in extreme situations. Likewise, a good ruler should respect private property and people's possessions, which would lead to the enhancement of the wealth of the state. Finally, Machiavelli thought the ruler did not have to follow an absolute set of rules. Sometimes, a ruler could act immorally if the state's best interests were in mind. This idea has given rise to the concept of a "Machiavellian" individual.

upheaval n turmoil; a disturbance
enhancement n improvement; increasing
concept n an idea; a thought; a notion

Q1 An introductory sentence for a brief summary of the passage is provided below. Complete the summary by selecting the THREE answer choices that express the most important ideas in the passage.

Machiavelli wrote *The Prince*, a book which describes how a leader should act.

Ⓐ According to Machiavelli, a good ruler was not always moral.
Ⓑ Machiavelli lived in Florence, a city-state in Italy.
Ⓒ *The Prince* stated that good rulers made their lands richer.
Ⓓ There were many political problems during Machiavelli's lifetime.
Ⓔ Machiavelli thought that a leader must sometimes use violence.

Q2 Complete the table below to summarize information about *The Prince* discussed in the passage. Match the appropriate statements to the political situation during the writing of *The Prince* and the description of the ideal ruler in *The Prince* with which they are associated.

THE PRINCE

Political situation	**Select 2** • •
Ideal ruler	**Select 3** • • •

STATEMENTS

Statements

Ⓐ A ruler could occasionally use violence to do something.
Ⓑ People nowadays sometimes call politicians "Machiavellian."
Ⓒ Machiavelli wrote *The Prince* while he was living in Florence.
Ⓓ The leader of a city was supposed to make it much wealthier.
Ⓔ Many city-states tried to become more powerful than the others.
Ⓕ It was not always important to follow the laws.
Ⓖ Countries such as Spain and France interfered with Florence.

Reading Skills Outlining

 **Complete the following outline.**

I Italy in Machiavelli's time
   A. Was political upheaval in northern Italy
   B. City-states there competing for power
   C. Spain, France, HRE, and others interfering in Italy

II Machiavelli's ideal ruler in *The Prince*
   A. Should avoid violence except in extreme situations
   B. Should respect private property and possessions
      1. Will make the state wealthier
   C. Can act _____ if state's interests are in mind

Chapter ❽ 197

• **Exercise 3** •

The Bill of Rights

08-04

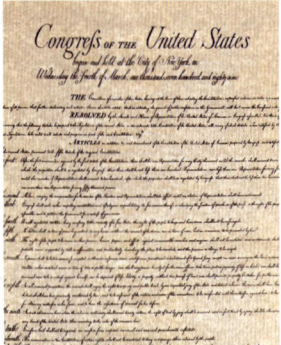

In 1789, the American states were considering the ratification of the Constitution. Doing so would result in the creation of the United States. However, many Americans were concerned about the Constitution. They believed the rights of the people were not stated well enough. In their minds, the government could possibly later abuse its powers. They worried the U.S. government would become oppressive, just like Britain's had. Therefore, ten amendments were added to the Constitution. These are now called the Bill of Rights.

These are some of the most important rights for American citizens. The First Amendment gives citizens freedom of religion, speech, and the press. The Second Amendment gives them the right to own their own weapons. Most Americans cherish these two rights. The other eight amendments include the right to a trial by jury and protection from excess bail. The Tenth Amendment also limits the power of the federal government, giving more power to the states and citizens.

ratification [n] approval; acceptance
the press [n] the media
cherish [v] to hold dear; to have affection for

Q1 An introductory sentence for a brief summary of the passage is provided below. Complete the summary by selecting the THREE answer choices that express the most important ideas in the passage.

The Bill of Rights is the first ten amendments to the Constitution and gives important rights to the American people.

- Ⓐ The Constitution and the Bill of Rights were ratified in 1789.
- Ⓑ The First Amendment gives Americans freedom of speech.
- Ⓒ Many Americans were afraid the government would get too much power.
- Ⓓ Americans can have their own weapons thanks to the Second Amendment.
- Ⓔ The Bill of Rights gives Americans the right to a trial by a jury.

Q2 Complete the table below to summarize information about the Bill of Rights discussed in the passage. Match the appropriate statements to the reasons the Bill of Rights was created and the rights it gives with which they are associated.

THE BILL OF RIGHTS

Reasons for its creation
•
•

Rights it gives
•
•
•

STATEMENTS

Select 2
-
-

Select 3
-
-
-

Statements

Ⓐ People are allowed freedom of speech, religion, and the press.

Ⓑ The Constitution contains the Bill of Rights, which has ten amendments.

Ⓒ Many Americans thought the government would abuse its power.

Ⓓ Americans do not have to pay a very large amount of bail.

Ⓔ America became a country after the Constitution was ratified.

Ⓕ Americans did not want the government to become like Britain's.

Ⓖ The federal government has some limits on its power.

Reading Skills | Outlining

Check-Up Complete the following outline.

I Constitution
    A. Americans considered ratifying in 1789
    B. Worried government would get too much power
    C. Made ten amendments to it called the Bill of Rights

II Bill of Rights
    A. Gives important rights to people
        1. First Amendment gives freedom of religion, speech, and press
        2. Second Amendment gives right to own weapons
        3. Others give right to trial by 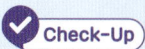 and no excessive bail
    B. Limits power of federal government
    C. Gives more power to states and people

Exercise 4

The Divine Right of Kings

Centuries ago in Europe, many countries were led by monarchs. In most cases, these kings had absolute power. They could therefore do anything they desired in their realms. The reason for this was a concept called the divine right of kings.

This notion stated that the king had been chosen to rule by God. As a result, the king answered only to God. His word was law in his land, and he could do what he liked. The king's subjects were expected to obey and be obedient to him.

In the West, divine right existed during the Middle Ages and afterward. In the 1600s, it reached its peak. The rulers of England and France believed in divine right. However, over time, people began opposing the absolute rule of kings. There were revolutions in both countries resulting in kings being deprived of power—and even their lives—and more power given to the people.

monarch [n] a king or queen
absolute [adj] total; complete
peak [n] the highest point

Q1 An introductory sentence for a brief summary of the passage is provided below. Complete the summary by selecting the THREE answer choices that express the most important ideas in the passage.

Monarchs in Europe once based their rule on the divine right of kings.

- Ⓐ Divine right started in the Middle Ages and went through the 1600s.
- Ⓑ The notion of the divine right of kings existed in ancient Egypt and other places.
- Ⓒ Kings in France and England were often absolute monarchs.
- Ⓓ According to divine right, kings could do anything that they wanted.
- Ⓔ Most people did not want to be ruled by absolute monarchs.

Q2 Complete the table below to summarize information about the divine right of kings discussed in the passage. Match the appropriate statements to the cause and effect of the divine right of kings with which they are associated.

THE DIVINE RIGHT OF KINGS

Cause	**STATEMENTS** Select 2 • •
Effect	Select 3 • • •

Statements

Ⓐ The king's subjects were supposed to obey him.

Ⓑ Revolutions in some places happened when people opposed divine right.

Ⓒ The king was said to have been given power by God.

Ⓓ The divine right of kings began as a concept in the 1600s.

Ⓔ The only one a king had to answer to was God.

Ⓕ The king could choose the person who would become king after him.

Ⓖ The king had the power to do anything he wanted to.

Reading Skills Outlining

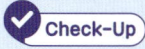 **Complete the following outline.**

I   Kings in Europe
   A. Led many countries centuries ago
   B. Had absolute power
   C. Could do anything they wanted

II The Divine Right of Kings
   A. King had been chosen to rule by God
   B. Word was law and could do what he liked
   C. Subjects had to obey and be obedient

III The Results of Divine Right
   A. Existed in Europe from the Middle Ages and afterward
   B. Reached its peak in the 1600s
   C. Were _____ against kings that made kings lose power and their lives

• Exercise 5 •

Thomas Jefferson and the Declaration of Independence

In colonial America in the eighteenth century, there were many men of amazing political skills. They helped start the American Revolution and caused the country to declare its independence from Great Britain. On July 4, 1776, America did this when several state delegates signed the Declaration of Independence. The author of this work was Thomas Jefferson.

The Declaration of Independence listed the reasons why America was declaring its independence. It mentioned the abuses of King George III of England. It also stated that all men had the right to "life, liberty, and the pursuit of happiness." Finally, it stated that no men should be subject to life under the rule of a king.

Jefferson was influenced by many individuals in writing this work. Much of his writing was inspired by the philosopher John Locke, who wrote many books, including the *Treatise on Government*. The works of Thomas Paine, the author of *Common Sense*, also helped give Jefferson his ideas. Jefferson even used part of the English Bill of Rights from 1689 to complete the Declaration of Independence. Altogether, Jefferson wrote one of the most powerful and influential works in modern times.

pursuit n a search; a hunt   philosopher n a person who studies philosophy

Q1 An introductory sentence for a brief summary of the passage is provided below. Complete the summary by selecting the THREE answer choices that express the most important ideas in the passage.

Thomas Jefferson was inspired by many different people when he wrote the Declaration of Independence.

- Ⓐ The American colonists thought King George III was a terrible ruler.
- Ⓑ Some of John Locke's ideas helped Jefferson to develop his own.
- Ⓒ The American Revolution began after the signing of the declaration.
- Ⓓ Thomas Paine was the author of *Common Sense*, an influential text.
- Ⓔ Jefferson wrote the declaration to explain why America disliked British rule.
- Ⓕ The English Bill of Rights was a source of knowledge for Jefferson.

Q2 Complete the table below to summarize information about the Declaration of Independence discussed in the passage. Match the appropriate statements to the reasons for writing and the influences on Declaration of Independence with which they are associated.

THE DECLARATION OF INDEPENDENCE

Reasons for writing

STATEMENTS

Select 2
-
-

Influences on its writing

Select 3
-
-
-

Statements

Ⓐ The work *Treatise on Government* had many ideas Jefferson used.
Ⓑ Thomas Jefferson used some of the writings of Thomas Paine.
Ⓒ The Declaration of Independence was signed on July 4, 1776.
Ⓓ The 1689 English Bill of Rights was one of Jefferson's sources.
Ⓔ The American colonists wrote the declaration to describe King George III's abuses.
Ⓕ The American colonists had many brilliant Founding Fathers.
Ⓖ A list of reasons why America declared independence was included.

Reading Skills — Outlining

✓ **Check-Up** Complete the following outline.

I America in the eighteenth century
   A. Had men with great political skills
   B. Helped start American Revolution
      1. Declared independence from Great Britain
      2. Signed Declaration of Independence on _____, _____

II Declaration of Independence
   A. Listed reasons America was becoming _____
   B. Mentioned abuses by King George III
   C. Said people had right to "life, liberty, and the pursuit of happiness"
   D. Said no men should be ruled by king

III Jefferson's influences
   A. Work of John Locke
      1. Wrote *Treatise on Government*
   B. 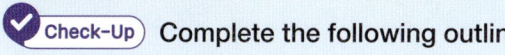 work *Common Sense*
   C. 1689 English Bill of Rights

Exercise 6

Dictatorships

One person may sometimes attain power over an entire country and all of its citizens. This person is known as a dictator, and the person's period of rule is called a dictatorship.

The most important feature of a dictatorship is that the dictator has unlimited and uncontrolled power. The dictator's word is law. There might be some sort of parliament or congress. But it has no real power over the dictator.

Unfortunately, dictatorships are usually oppressive in nature. The majority of dictators come from the army. In recent times, they include Saddam Hussein of Iraq, Kim Il-sung of North Korea, and Fidel Castro in Cuba. In all cases, they had the support of their country's military, so they were able to impose their will on the people. While there are benevolent dictators, they are very rare.

Fortunately, due to international pressure and the chance of revolution by the country's citizens, most dictatorships are short lasting. In recent years, the citizens in many eastern European countries rose up against their own dictators. In some cases, like in East Germany, the transition to democracy was peaceful. However, in Romania in 1989, the country's dictator was executed by his own citizens.

unlimited adj having no boundaries or limits   **benevolent** adj kind

Q1 An introductory sentence for a brief summary of the passage is provided below. Complete the summary by selecting the THREE answer choices that express the most important ideas in the passage.

Dictators often rise to absolute power through the military, but many dictatorships do not last a very long time.

Ⓐ There are occasionally benevolent dictators who rule over a country.
Ⓑ Sometimes people revolt against dictators and cause them to fall.
Ⓒ There is no limit to the amount of power a dictator has in his country.
Ⓓ Fidel Castro of Cuba was one of the longest-lasting dictators in the world.
Ⓔ Other countries sometimes put pressure on a ruler to end his dictatorship.
Ⓕ Dictatorships often rely upon a parliament or congress to pass laws.

Q2 Complete the table below to summarize information about dictatorships discussed in the passage. Match the appropriate statements to the rise and fall of dictators with which they are associated.

DICTATORS	STATEMENTS
Rise to power	**Select 2** • •
Fall from power	**Select 3** • • •

Statements

Ⓐ The military often helps a dictator gain power.
Ⓑ Sometimes people rise up in revolt against dictators.
Ⓒ The congress in a dictatorship has no real power.
Ⓓ Saddam Hussein was the longtime dictator of Iraq.
Ⓔ The Romanian people executed their own dictator in 1989.
Ⓕ International pressure can often help end dictatorships.
Ⓖ A dictator is able to gain power over the entire country.

Reading Skills Outlining

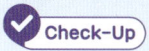 **Complete the following outline.**

I Dictators
  A. Have complete rule over country
     1. Word of dictator is law   2. Have _____ and uncontrolled power
  B. May have congress but has no power

II Dictatorships
  A. Are usually oppressive
  B. Are many dictators in recent times
     1. Saddam Hussein of Iraq   2. Kim Il-sung of North Korea   3. Fidel Castro of _____
  C. Are supported by military
  D. Can impose will on people

III Fall of dictatorships
  A. International pressure can make them short lasting   B. People may rise in rebellion
  C. Eastern European citizens rose up against dictators
     1. East Germany had peaceful revolution   2. _____ people executed their dictator

• **Exercise 7** •

Plato's *Republic*

Over 2,300 years ago, the Greek philosopher Plato recorded his thoughts on government in *The Republic*. A controversial text, it has been debated for centuries. Plato covered an enormous amount of information in *The Republic*, but two of the most important things he described were the bad forms of government and the ideal form.

Plato greatly disliked democracy. He felt it would cause too much pressure between the various social classes. He also disapproved of giving so much power to the people. Oligarchies, where the rich rule, were another form of government he urged to be avoided. He felt that being rich did not necessarily make a man a good leader. Plato also despised tyranny, which would lead to tension between the members of different classes.

Plato focused on describing the forms of government he disliked. He also described his ideal form. This was a government led by a philosopher-king. According to Plato, philosophers were the only people in society who could recognize good. Therefore, they must rule the people to instruct them. The rulers would also focus on helping the state since they would not be greedy or harsh. Instead, they would rule as enlightened individuals.

---

controversial *adj* divisive   **oligarchy** *n* a form of government where the rich rule

Q1 An introductory sentence for a brief summary of the passage is provided below. Complete the summary by selecting the THREE answer choices that express the most important ideas in the passage.

Plato wrote about the kinds of government he both disliked and liked in his work *The Republic*.

- Ⓐ According to Plato, democracy would cause many kinds of problems.
- Ⓑ A philosopher-king would rule the people in Plato's ideal government.
- Ⓒ Plato described a number of important theories in his work *The Republic*.
- Ⓓ The Greek philosopher Plato wrote *The Republic* around 2,300 years ago.
- Ⓔ Plato did not believe that oligarchies were good forms of government.
- Ⓕ Even though *The Republic* is very old, people continue to debate it today.

Q2 Complete the table below to summarize information about governments discussed in the passage. Match the appropriate statements to governments Plato liked and those he disliked with which they are associated.

PLATO

Governments liked
Select 2 • •

Governments disliked
Select 3 • • •

STATEMENTS

Statements

Ⓐ Democracy would result in problems between different social classes.
Ⓑ Plato thought philosophers were best able to rule the people.
Ⓒ Tyranny would involve too many problems between classes of people.
Ⓓ A person who is not greedy would be an effective ruler.
Ⓔ *The Republic* remains a controversial text even nowadays.
Ⓕ Rich people did not always have the skills to lead well.
Ⓖ Plato described several different forms of government in his work.

Reading Skills   Outlining

Check-Up Complete the following outline.

I *The Republic*
  A. Written by _____ 2,300 years ago   B. Describes bad and ideal forms of government

II Bad forms of government
  A. _____ is bad
    1. Creates pressure between social classes   2. Gives too much power to people
  B. Oligarchies are to be avoided
    1. Are government by rich   2. Rich do not make good rulers
  C. Despised tyranny
    1. Has tension between different classes of people

III Ideal form of government
  A. Government led by _____-_____   B. Philosophers are only ones to recognize good
  C. Must be able to instruct people   D. Will be enlightened individuals

• **Exercise 8** •

The American Electoral System

Many democracies directly elect their leaders, so the victor of the popular vote becomes president. This is not true of the United States of America since the USA is a republic. Instead, the USA relies upon the Electoral College to elect its president.

The Electoral College has 538 members. Each state has a different number of members. The number of members in the college is equal to the state's representation in Congress. Each state has two senators and a different number of members of the House of Representatives. Some states, such as Wyoming, have just one member of the House. Others have very many. California, for example, has fifty-two.

In most American states, all of the state's electors are given to the winner in each state. Therefore, a candidate must win 270 electors to become president. In most cases, the winner of the popular vote has won the Electoral College vote as well. However, on rare occasions, the popular vote winner lost the Electoral College vote so did not become president. This happened most recently in 2016, when Donald Trump lost the popular vote to Hillary Clinton but won more electors, making him the president.

---

republic [n] a form of government where elected officials represent the people

elector [n] a voting member

rare [adj] uncommon; unusual

Q1 An introductory sentence for a brief summary of the passage is provided below. Complete the summary by selecting the THREE answer choices that express the most important ideas in the passage.

The winner of the Electoral College, not the popular vote, becomes the president of the United States.

Ⓐ There are 538 members of the Electoral College.
Ⓑ A person needs 270 votes in the Electoral College to become president.
Ⓒ Donald Trump became president of the United States in 2016.
Ⓓ Some men have become president despite losing the popular vote.
Ⓔ Since America is a republic, not a democracy, it uses the Electoral College.
Ⓕ The state of Wyoming has only three electors, but other states have many.

Q2 Complete the table below to summarize information about the Electoral College discussed in the passage. Match the appropriate statements to how a person uses the Electoral College to win and the Electoral College's makeup with which they are associated.

THE ELECTORAL COLLEGE	STATEMENTS
How it is needed to win	Select 2 • •
Makeup of the Electoral College	Select 3 • • •

Statements

Ⓐ The United States is a republic, not a democracy.
Ⓑ There are 538 members of the Electoral College.
Ⓒ Most states give all their electors to the winner in that state.
Ⓓ Most presidents win the popular vote and Electoral College vote.
Ⓔ States all have different numbers of electors.
Ⓕ It takes 270 votes for a person to become president.
Ⓖ The number of electors equals the states representation in Congress.

Reading Skills Outlining

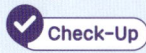 **Check-Up** Complete the following outline.

I Electoral College
   A. Responsible for electing American president
   B. Has 538 members
      1. Members determined by state representation in Congress
      2. Is 2 senators plus number of members of House of Representatives
      3. _____ has 1 member of the House   4. California has 52 members of the House

II Winning the Electoral College
   A. Most states give all electors to winner of the vote in that state
   B. Need _____ votes to win
   C. Usually popular vote winner becomes _____
      1. May have president lose popular vote but win Electoral College
      2. Donald Trump lost popular vote but became president in 2016

Grammar Point — Voice

1 The voice of a sentence or question indicates the importance of the subject. It tells if the subject is doing the action or if the subject is receiving the action. There are two voices in English: the **active** and the **passive**.

2 The subject is doing the action in the active voice. Most sentences and questions in English use the active voice.

- Many democracies directly *elect* their leaders.
- Plato greatly *disliked* democracy.
- People *work* to earn profits.
- Some programs still *exist* today.

3 The subject receives the action in the passive voice. The passive voice is less common than the active. It is often used to report information, such as in reports, essays, and newspaper articles. It is also used when the person or thing doing the action is not important. There are many ways to form the passive voice.

Types of Passive Voice	Formation	Example Sentences
Present Passive	be verb + p.p.	• These *are* now *called* the Bill of Rights. • Under communism, everything *is owned* by the people.
Past Passive	was / were + p.p.	• Many of Roosevelt's programs *were declared* unconstitutional. • The Magna Carta—Latin for "Great Charter"—*was signed* in 1215.
Future Passive	will + be + p.p.	• The winner *will be determined* by an election. • In the future, people *will* still *be influenced* by the works of Thomas Jefferson.
Present Perfect Passive	have / has been + p.p.	• It *has been debated* for centuries. • The dictators *have been executed* by their own people.

Grammar Check-Up

A Indicate whether the following sentences are in the active or passive voice.

1 Unfortunately, dictatorships are usually oppressive in nature. _____
2 Jefferson was influenced by many individuals in writing this work. _____
3 The person's period of rule is called a dictatorship. _____
4 Capitalist countries often practice democracy and respect people's freedom. _____
5 The subjects of kings were expected to be obedient to them. _____

B Choose the correct words for the blanks.

1 The winner of the election _____ by the people next week.
   ⓐ decides   ⓑ will decide   ⓒ be decided   ⓓ will be decided

2 *The Republic* _____ by Plato more than 2,000 years ago.
   ⓐ was wrote   ⓑ was written   ⓒ wrote   ⓓ will be written

3 Saddam Hussein _____ as the dictator of Iraq for a long time.
   ⓐ ruled   ⓑ was ruled   ⓒ ruling   ⓓ is ruled

4 For more than 200 years, the American people _____ many rights in the Constitution.
   ⓐ gave   ⓑ were given   ⓒ have been given   ⓓ will be given

5 Today, communism _____ by some countries, all of which have failing economies.
   ⓐ practices   ⓑ is practicing   ⓒ is practiced   ⓓ was practiced

C Read the following story and fill in the blanks. Use each word only once.

| added   ratified   given   founded   written   pleased |

In the 1780s, there was a debate in America about the Constitution. Many Americans thought they were not _____ enough rights. So they thought the Constitution was _____ badly. However, the representatives of the people changed the Constitution. The Bill of Rights was _____ to it. This gave the people more rights, so they were _____ by it. Finally, in 1789, the Constitution was _____ by the thirteen colonies, and the United States was _____.

Vocabulary Review

A Circle the words that best complete the sentences.

1 An (absolute / absolutely) monarch has total power over a country.
2 Capitalism encourages people to earn (profits / products) for themselves.
3 The executive branch of government must (enforce / focus) the country's laws.
4 A (senate / dictator) is a person with total control of the government.
5 The rights of kings have been (restricted / abused) by legislatures over the years.

B Choose the best words to complete the sentences.

1 He _____ the rights the Constitution gave him and the other citizens.
   A cherished
   B competed
   C despised
   D urged

2 People still _____ many books because they have different opinions of them.
   A elect
   B respect
   C encourage
   D debate

3 Today, the United States is the only _____ in the world.
   A democracy
   B superpower
   C republic
   D legislature

4 Eric was too _____ and wanted to keep everything for himself.
   A oppressive
   B greedy
   C repressive
   D harsh

5 Some countries today still have a _____ as the head of their government.
   A realm
   B subject
   C monarch
   D power

C Choose the words with the closest meanings to the highlighted words.

1. There were too many flaws in the politician's solution.
   - Ⓐ electors
   - Ⓑ depressions
   - Ⓒ natures
   - Ⓓ problems

2. The delegates all voted on the proposal made by the president.
   - Ⓐ dictators
   - Ⓑ kings
   - Ⓒ representatives
   - Ⓓ treatises

3. The dictator was despised by most of the people who lived in his country.
   - Ⓐ disapproved
   - Ⓑ described
   - Ⓒ disliked
   - Ⓓ debated

4. He considered John's idea to be the best one they had.
   - Ⓐ elected
   - Ⓑ believed
   - Ⓒ attained
   - Ⓓ respected

5. Thomas Jefferson was one of the most important men in American history.
   - Ⓐ influential
   - Ⓑ controversial
   - Ⓒ restricted
   - Ⓓ unlimited

D Complete the sentences by filling in the blanks with the best words from the list. Change the forms of the words if necessary. Use each word only once.

| treatise | private | subject | transition | deprive |

1. The _____ he wrote on politics became very influential.
2. The president was convicted of a crime and _____ of power.
3. The country's _____ to democracy happened very quickly.
4. Communism does not allow people to have any _____ property.
5. The people in that country are considered _____ of the king.

Practice Test

The Three Branches of Government

Many countries divide their governments into three parts. This division of powers enables them to function at relatively smooth and efficient levels. The three branches are the executive, legislative, and judicial branches.

The executive branch enforces a country's laws. Typically, a president or prime minister leads the executive branch. In the United States, the president's cabinet, a group of advisors, is in the executive branch. So are organizations such as, the Federal Bureau of Investigation (FBI).

The legislative branch makes the country's laws. Most countries have a congress or parliament made up of many representatives. ■1 Some, such as the United States and Great Britain, have bicameral legislatures, so their legislative branches have two parts. ■2 In the United States, the upper house is the Senate, and the lower house is the House of Representatives. ■3 The Senate has two members per state while the House gives all fifty states a different number of representatives depending upon their populations. ■4

The judicial branch interprets laws and determines whether they are legal. It comprises a country's entire court system. In the United States, at the top is the Supreme Court, which has nine members. There are also federal courts, state courts, and city and county courts.

These three branches often work well together. They operate on a system called "checks and balances." Each branch has equal power, so they balance the others to keep them from becoming too powerful. It is a seemingly complicated system yet works due to its simplicity.

enforce v to impose; to put into effect   **bicameral** adj having two parts

1. The word "them" in the passage refers to
   - Ⓐ their governments
   - Ⓑ three separate parts
   - Ⓒ powers
   - Ⓓ smooth and efficient levels

2   The word "efficient" in the passage is closest in meaning to
    Ⓐ speedy
    Ⓑ sufficient
    Ⓒ effective
    Ⓓ inexpensive

3   According to paragraph 2, which of the following is true of the executive branch?
    Ⓐ There is only one person who is a member of it.
    Ⓑ The most powerful people in it belong to the cabinet.
    Ⓒ The FBI is one of its most important members.
    Ⓓ It includes the cabinet and various organizations.

4   In paragraph 2, why does the author mention "the Federal Bureau of Investigation"?
    Ⓐ To name it as a member of the executive branch
    Ⓑ To claim it is the largest organization in the executive branch
    Ⓒ To describe the duties its members must carry out
    Ⓓ To note that it handles all federal law enforcement

5   According to paragraph 3, which of the following is NOT true of the legislative branch?
    Ⓐ The U.S. Senate has two members from each state.
    Ⓑ It is the branch that makes a country's laws.
    Ⓒ Most of the world's countries have bicameral legislatures.
    Ⓓ The legislative branch in Great Britain has two houses.

6   In paragraph 3, the author implies that the U.S. House of Representatives
    Ⓐ is more powerful than the Senate
    Ⓑ has more members than the Senate
    Ⓒ passes most of the country's laws
    Ⓓ has fewer responsibilities than the Senate

7   In paragraph 4, the author's description of the judicial branch mentions which of the following?
    Ⓐ The number of members of the Supreme Court
    Ⓑ The manner in which it makes the country's laws
    Ⓒ The reason some countries have weak judicial branches
    Ⓓ The problems caused when it misinterprets the law

8 The word "seemingly" in the passage is closest in meaning to

- Ⓐ comparably
- Ⓑ apparently
- Ⓒ accidentally
- Ⓓ justifiably

9 Look at the four squares [■] that indicate where the following sentence could be added to the passage.

This gives the states equal representation in the Senate and unequal representation in the House.

Where would the sentence best fit?

Click on a square [■] to add the sentence to the passage.

10 *Directions:* Complete the table below to summarize information about the executive, legislative, and judicial branches discussed in the passage. Match the appropriate statements to the branch of government with which they are associated.

BRANCHES OF GOVERNMENT	STATEMENTS
Executive	Select 2 • •
Legislative	Select 3 • • •
Judicial	Select 2 • •

Statements

1. This branch of government is led by the Supreme Court.
2. The president is the head of this branch of government.
3. It is responsible for enforcing the laws of a country.
4. The capital of the United States is in Washington, D.C.
5. This branch is divided into two parts in many countries.
6. This branch of government makes a country's laws.
7. Many countries have this branch in the form of a parliament.
8. The policy of "checks and balances" was made for this.
9. Interpreting the laws is the job of this branch of government.

Actual Test

Actual Test 1

Ancient Rome

According to legend, Rome was founded in 753 B.C. Over the course of its existence, it changed governments at various times. For around 500 years, Rome was a republic. Later, after the republican form of government failed, it became an empire. It would exist as an empire until the year 476 A.D.

The Roman Republic was established in 509 B.C. It had a complex form of government that basically enabled Roman citizens to elect officials who would rule over them. There were also highly detailed laws covering a wide variety of topics.

The highest position in the republic was that of consul. There were two consuls who served at the same time, and they only had terms of a single year. This prevented them from amassing too much power. Consuls had powers such as the ability to declare war and to collect taxes. The republic also had a Senate. Senators served life terms and were advisors to the consuls. The Plebian Council enabled common people, called plebians, to elect leaders, to pass laws, and to perform other roles of the government.

There were many other government officials in the republic. Each had his own responsibilities and was required to obey the law. As a general rule, this method of rule worked well for Rome despite its flaws. For instance, there were different branches of government, and corrupt officials could be punished. The Roman Republic served as the basis for modern-day democratic governments.

However, this form of government came to an end in the first century B.C. This was a time of civil war and dictatorships. The internal conflicts stopped in 27 B.C., when Augustus was crowned emperor. As emperor, Augustus—and the rulers who came after him—held sole power and ruled as an autocrat.

The Senate still existed during the time of the empire. **1** However, it had much less power than it did during the republic. **2** The emperor also relied upon numerous civil servants. **3** These men wielded an enormous amount of power since the Roman Empire covered such a vast amount of land. **4**

Unlike consuls, emperors ruled for life or until they were deposed by someone such as a general. They typically chose a successor—a biological or adopted son. When the empire was strong, the son ascended the throne easily. During troubled times, there were often problems with succession.

---

civil servant n a person who works for the government
depose v to remove from a high position, such as king or emperor

1 According to paragraph 1, which of the following is NOT true of Rome?
   Ⓐ It had different types of governments.
   Ⓑ It had the most territory when it was an empire.
   Ⓒ It lasted from 753 B.C. to 476 A.D.
   Ⓓ It was a republic before it was an empire.

2 In paragraph 2, the author's description of the Roman Republic mentions which of the following?
   Ⓐ The reason it was established
   Ⓑ The length of time it lasted
   Ⓒ The year that it was founded
   Ⓓ The types of laws it passed

3 In paragraph 3, the author discusses "consul" in order to
   Ⓐ compare its power with that of the Senate
   Ⓑ claim it was not a particularly powerful position
   Ⓒ provide various details about the position
   Ⓓ note the names of some men who served as it

4 The word "amassing" in the passage is closest in meaning to
   Ⓐ gathering
   Ⓑ abusing
   Ⓒ attempting
   Ⓓ reviewing

5 The word "flaws" in the passage is closest in meaning to
   Ⓐ promises
   Ⓑ appearances
   Ⓒ instances
   Ⓓ problems

6   Which of the following can be inferred from paragraph 5 about Rome in the first century B.C.?
    Ⓐ It was mostly an empire during that time.
    Ⓑ The republic had many great leaders then.
    Ⓒ Augustus died at the end of it.
    Ⓓ There was a lot of fighting during it.

7   The word "it" in the passage refers to
    Ⓐ the Senate
    Ⓑ the time
    Ⓒ the empire
    Ⓓ much less power

8   According to paragraph 7, which of the following is true of Roman emperors?
    Ⓐ They often served as generals in the Roman army.
    Ⓑ They were able to choose who would rule after them.
    Ⓒ They almost always had an adopted son.
    Ⓓ They were willing to give up their power at times.

9   Look at the four squares [■] that indicate where the following sentence could be added to the passage.

    In fact, those who governed rich provinces could be almost as powerful as the emperor at times.

    Where would the sentence best fit?
    Click on a square [■] to add the sentence to the passage.

10 *Directions*: Complete the table below to summarize information about Rome discussed in the passage. Match the appropriate statements to the type of government with which they are associated.

ROME

Roman Republic
Select 3 • • •

Roman Empire
Select 2 • •

STATEMENTS

Statements

1. Caused Rome to get into many wars with its neighbors
2. Was destroyed due to the actions of Julius Caesar
3. Required civil servants because of its great size
4. Was a time when corrupt individuals were punished
5. Had the Senate and the Plebian Council
6. Was ruled by two people who served one-year terms
7. Had one person who had sole power

Actual Test 2

Jane Austen

Jane Austen is well known as the author of the novel *Pride and Prejudice*. She was much more than just a novelist though. In several ways, she was a trailblazer in the field of literature. She had a great influence on literature for several reasons.

Austen lived from 1775 to 1817. At that time, female writers were extremely rare. Writing was simply not considered something acceptable for women to do. In fact, Austen's name did not appear as the author of the four books she wrote that were published during her lifetime. Instead, those books were published anonymously. It was only after she died that the works she wrote were identified as her own. Austen's novels were not immediate bestsellers. However, they gained popularity over time. In fact, the books have almost always been in print for more than 200 years. Thanks to Austen, it became more acceptable for women to be authors.

Austen's style was also influential. While she did not develop the technique, she helped popularize free indirect speech. This writing method enables the narrator of the story to let readers know what various characters are thinking. However, "he thought" and "she thought" do not appear in the text. This technique lets the author provide additional insight by showing characters' thoughts. Austen made considerable use of this method. Today, it is commonly used by writers.

Austen's novels frequently focus on ordinary people. **1** This is true of *Sense and Sensibility*, *Pride and Prejudice*, *Mansfield Park*, and *Emma*. **2** In that regard, she helped create the modern novel, which frequently focuses on the actions of everyday individual. **3** Rather than covering the actions of kings or great heroes, Austen's novels told stories about members of the middle class in nineteenth-century England. **4** This subject matter helped increase the popularity of her works. It essentially made them timeless classics that are not only read in literature classes but are also enjoyed by readers who desire a good story.

---

anonymously **adv** having no name   classic **n** a great work of literature

1. The word "trailblazer" in the passage is closest in meaning to
   - A pioneer
   - B engineer
   - C reporter
   - D author

2. Which of the following best expresses the essential information in the highlighted sentence? *Incorrect* answer choices change the meaning in important ways or leave out essential information.
   - A Austen was named as the author of four of her works only after she passed away.
   - B The four books that came out during Austen's life were published anonymously.
   - C Austen managed to write four anonymous books by the time that she died.
   - D Only four of the books that Austen wrote were published while she was alive.

3. According to paragraph 2, which of the following is true of Jane Austen?
   - A She became wealthy due to sales of her novels.
   - B She lived her entire life in the nineteenth century.
   - C She became popular as a writer after she died.
   - D She was encouraged to become a writer by her family.

4. In paragraph 2, the author implies that Jane Austen's novels
   - A have sold a large number of copies
   - B are hard to find in some places
   - C use language that is uncommon today
   - D appeal more to women than to men

5. In paragraph 3, the author uses "free indirect speech" as an example of
   - A a writing technique that Jane Austen created
   - B the most important writing method for novels
   - C a writing method that Jane Austen made popular
   - D a writing technique developed during the nineteenth century

6. The word "enables" in the passage is closest in meaning to

   Ⓐ encourages
   Ⓑ permits
   Ⓒ prepares
   Ⓓ assumes

7. The word "It" in the passage refers to

   Ⓐ The middle class
   Ⓑ Nineteenth-century England
   Ⓒ This subject matter
   Ⓓ The popularity of her works

8. In paragraph 4, the author's description of Jane Austen mentions all of the following EXCEPT:

   Ⓐ The number of copies her books have sold
   Ⓑ The subject matter of her books
   Ⓒ Her influence on the modern novel
   Ⓓ The titles of some of her novels

9. Look at the four squares [■] that indicate where the following sentence could be added to the passage.

   These were the titles of the novels that were published while she was still alive.

   Where would the sentence best fit?
   Click on a square [■] to add the sentence to the passage.

10 Directions: An introductory sentence for a brief summary of the passage is provided below. Complete the summary by selecting the THREE answer choices that express the most important ideas in the passage.

Jane Austen was an important novelist in the nineteenth century for several reasons.

-
-
-

Answer Choices

1. The method called free indirect speech was popularized by Jane Austen.
2. Only four of the six books that Jane Austen wrote were published while she was alive.
3. Jane Austen's books were not immediately popular, but they are read by people today.
4. Thanks to Jane Austen, it became more acceptable for women to write novels.
5. Many of Jane Austen's books are studied by students in English literature classes.
6. Jane Austen contributed to the making of the modern novel by writing about regular people.

Actual Test 3

The Hubble Space Telescope

No matter how large and powerful a telescope is, the images it captures are still distorted. The reason is that the Earth's atmosphere affects how starlight appears. For this reason, in 1990, a space telescope was launched. It would be the first major telescope to be sent into space. Called the Hubble Space Telescope, it has had a tremendous effect on the field of astronomy. It has taken pictures of galaxies incredibly distant from the Earth and has helped improve people's knowledge of the universe.

The Hubble is roughly the size of a school bus. It had to be lifted into orbit by a space shuttle in 1990. It was placed in orbit around the Earth roughly 600 kilometers above the planet. However, when the Hubble was activated, astronomers were disappointed. The images were not nearly as clear as they had been expecting. A close examination of the Hubble revealed that the mirror in the telescope was curved improperly. The mistake was miniscule, but it had a great effect on the quality of pictures, causing them to look blurry.

In 1993, astronauts on board another space shuttle managed to fix the Hubble over the course of five days. These repairs finally enabled the Hubble to produce the high-quality images expected of it. The Hubble was originally scheduled to have a lifetime of around fifteen years. However, as of 2023, the telescope was still active. The primary reason is that five separate missions were taken to service the telescope. These missions greatly prolonged the lifetime of the Hubble.

One of the Hubble's primary accomplishments was determining the age of the universe at around 13.7 billion years. It has taken numerous photographs of distant galaxies it discovered. **1** It also photographed the first planet outside the solar system. **2** Today, other space telescopes, such as CHEOPS and the James Webb Space Telescope, take pictures and make discoveries of their own. **3** Yet the Hubble is still contributing to the advancement of human knowledge. **4**

---

galaxy [n] a very large group of stars   **miniscule** [adj] tiny; very small

1. The word "distorted" in the passage is closest in meaning to
   - Ⓐ precise
   - Ⓑ enlarged
   - Ⓒ appreciated
   - Ⓓ inaccurate

2. Which of the following can be inferred from paragraph 1 about the Hubble?
   - Ⓐ It cost more than any other telescope in history.
   - Ⓑ It took more than ten years to be constructed.
   - Ⓒ Other telescopes were sent into space before it.
   - Ⓓ Multiple space shuttles carried it into space.

3. In paragraph 2, why does the author mention "a school bus"?
   - Ⓐ To point out a problem
   - Ⓑ To make a comparison
   - Ⓒ To discuss a solution
   - Ⓓ To consider a theory

4. The word "they" in the passage refers to
   - Ⓐ 600 kilometers above the planet
   - Ⓑ astronomers
   - Ⓒ the images
   - Ⓓ the quality of pictures

5. According to paragraph 2, there was a problem with the Hubble because
   - Ⓐ its mirror was cracked
   - Ⓑ its camera broke down
   - Ⓒ its mirror did not curve properly
   - Ⓓ its power supply was used up

6 The word "prolonged" in the passage is closest in meaning to

- Ⓐ approved
- Ⓑ extended
- Ⓒ improved
- Ⓓ revealed

7 According to paragraph 3, which of the following is NOT true of the Hubble?

- Ⓐ Several missions helped it continue working.
- Ⓑ It needed to be repaired in 1993.
- Ⓒ It had a lifetime of only fifteen years.
- Ⓓ Repairs let it produce good images.

8 According to paragraph 4, which of the following is true of the Hubble?

- Ⓐ It is less popular than the James Webb Space Telescope.
- Ⓑ Its mission is being performed by CHEOPS now.
- Ⓒ It is scheduled to be shut down soon.
- Ⓓ It learned how old the universe is.

9 Look at the four squares [■] that indicate where the following sentence could be added to the passage.

Others have been launched yet discontinued during the time that the Hubble has been active.

Where would the sentence best fit?

Click on a square [■] to add the sentence to the passage.

10 Directions: An introductory sentence for a brief summary of the passage is provided below. Complete the summary by selecting the THREE answer choices that express the most important ideas in the passage.

Since its launch in 1990, the Hubble Space Telescope has contributed greatly to the knowledge of astronomers.

-
-
-

Answer Choices

1. The Hubble is not the only space telescope looking at distant galaxies anymore.
2. The Hubble has managed to send pictures clearer than those taken on the Earth.
3. Astronomers have used the Hubble for many years thanks to the multiple missions sent to it.
4. The Hubble has taken pictures of many distant galaxies and other places.
5. Astronomers expect that the Hubble will be able to continue working for a few more years.
6. Because the Hubble had a problem, the images it sent back were poor at first.

High Score iBT TOEFL READING For Junior High Intermediate

Publisher Kyudo Chung
Editors Woonhee Park, Sangik Cho
Author Michael A. Putlack
Designers Minji Kim, Yeji Kim

First published in April 2008 by Happy House
Second edition first published in August 2023 by Darakwon, Inc.
Darakwon Bldg., 211, Munbal-ro, Paju-si, Gyeonggi-do 10881
Republic of Korea
Tel: 82-2-736-2031 (Ext. 250)
Fax: 82-2-732-2037

Copyright © 2008 Happy House, 2023 Darakwon

All rights reserved. No part of this publication may be reproduced, stored in a retrieval system, or transmitted in any form or by any means, electronic, mechanical, photocopying or otherwise, without the prior consent of the copyright owner. Refund after purchase is possible only according to the company regulations. Contact the above telephone number for any inquiries. Consumer damages caused by loss, damage, etc. can be compensated according to the consumer dispute resolution standards announced by the Korea Fair Trade Commission. An incorrectly collated book will be exchanged.

ISBN 978-89-277-8061-8 14740
978-89-277-8056-4 14740 (set)

www.darakwon.co.kr

Photo Credits
Shutterstock.com

Components Main Book / Answer Key
9 8 7 6 5 4 3   25 26 27 28 29

High Score
iBT TOEFL READING
For Junior

2nd Edition

High Intermediate

Answer Key

High Score iBT TOEFL READING For Junior

High Intermediate

Answer Key

CHAPTER 1 # Literature

Understanding TOEFL Question Types & Reading Skills
p.14

1 Question Types ▶ Sample Question

Ⓒ

해석　　　　　문학의 시대

동시대 사람들의 글은 종종 일정한 특징과 스타일을 공유한다. 이러한 유사성 때문에 사람들은 특정 시기를 하나의 문학의 시대로 분류한다. 문학의 3대 시대로는 르네상스 시대, 신고전주의 시대, 낭만주의 시대가 있다.

르네상스 시대는 1500년에서 1660년 사이에 있었다. 르네상스 시대의 작가로는 셰익스피어, 보카치오, 단테 등이 있었다. 르네상스 시대 동안에는 산문체 소설과 단편 소설이 유행했다.

신고전주의 시대는 1660년부터 1785년까지 지속되었다. 그 시대의 작가들은 고대 그리스와 로마로 회귀하여 그 영향을 받은 경우가 많았다. 알렉산더 포프와 존 드라이든이 두 명의 위대한 신고전주의 작가이다.

낭만주의 시대는 1785년부터 1830년까지 계속되었다. 이 시대의 작가들은 감정을 중시했으며 종종 합리주의에 반대했다. 존 키츠와 퍼시 비쉬 셸리가 이 시대의 두 유명한 작가들이다.

2 Reading Skills ▶ Check-Up

1 Renaissance
2 1785, 1830

• Exercise 1 •
p.16

정답　Q1 Ⓓ　Q2 Ⓑ　Q3 Ⓑ

해석　　　　　빅토리아 시대의 문학

영국의 빅토리아 여왕은 1837년부터 1901년까지 통치했다. 사람들은 이 시대를 빅토리아 시대라고 불렀다. 이 시기 동안 많은 위대한 작가들이 살았기 때문에 그 시기에는 특히 소설을 비롯하여 정말로 훌륭한 문학이 많이 쓰여졌다.

대부분의 빅토리아풍 소설들은 고난과 역경의 삶을 사는 사람들을 묘사했다. 많은 이야기들이 절망적이었지만, 책 속의 주인공들은 보통 역경을 극복하기 위해 부단히 노력했다. 결말에서는 보통 착한 사람들이 악인들을 물리쳤다. 죄인들은 그들의 악행으로 인해 종종 벌을 받았다.

빅토리아 시대의 잘 알려진 소설가 중에는 에밀리 브론테, 토머스 하디, 오스카 와일드가 있었다. 또 다른 빅토리아 시대 작가인 조지 엘리엇은 1861년에 소설 *사일러스 매너*를 썼다. 그러나 찰스 디킨스가 아마도 모든 빅토리아 시대의 소설가들 중 가장 위대한 인물이었을 것이다. 그는 수많은 인기 소설들을 썼다. 1859년에 출간된 *두 도시 이야기*와 1861년에 출간된 *위대한 유산*은 그가 쓴 최고의 두 작품이었다. 오늘날에도 사람들은 여전히 그의 작품들을 읽는다.

Reading Skills

4, 2, 1, 3

• Exercise 2 •
p.18

정답　Q1 Ⓒ　Q2 Ⓓ　Q3 Ⓐ

해석　　　　　윌리엄 셰익스피어

1564년에 태어나 1616년에 세상을 떠난 윌리엄 셰익스피어는 문학계에 막대한 영향을 끼쳤다. 실제로, 그가 죽은 지 거의 400년이 지났음에도 불구하고 그는 오늘날에도 여전히 문학에 영향을 끼치고 있다.

희곡과 시를 포함하여, 셰익스피어의 많은 작품들은 여전히 유명할 뿐만 아니라 유의미하다. 그의 희곡 중에서, 1595년 작품인 *로미오와 줄리엣*은 지금껏 가장 위대한 사랑 이야기로 많은 이들이 여기고 있다. 1600년경, 셰익스피어는 *햄릿*을 썼다. 비평가들은 종종 *햄릿*을 그가 쓴 최고의 희곡 작품으로 언급한다. 셰익스피어는 일생 동안 총 37편의 희곡을 썼다.

1593년이 시작되면서, 그는 또한 수많은 소네트를 비롯하여 여러 편의 시를 창작했다. 소네트는 14행으로 된 시이다. 사람들은 여전히 셰익스피어의 시에서 여러 시구(詩句)들을 인용하고 있다.

흥미롭게도 셰익스피어는 영어에도 지대한 공헌을 하였다. 그가 살았던 시대에는 영어가 여전히 발전 단계의 언어였다. 어떤 전문가들은 셰익스피어가 1,700개 이상의 단어를 영어로 들여왔다고 생각한다. 어떤 경우든 간에, 영어와 문학에 미친 그의 영향은 놀라웠다.

Reading Skills

1　1593
2　Romeo and Juliet

• Exercise 3 •
p.20

정답　Q1 Ⓒ　Q2 Ⓐ　Q3 Ⓒ

해석　　　　　그림 동화

오늘날, 부모들은 잠들기 전에 종종 자녀에게 동화를 읽어준다. 그래서 아이들은 *신데렐라*, *라푼젤*, *백설공주*와 같은 이야기들을 잘 알고 있다. 사실, 이러한 이야기들과 그와 비슷한 다른 이야기들은 아주 오래된 것이다. 그러나 누구도 19세기가 되기까지 이런 이야기들을 기록하지 않았다.

독일의 야코프 그림과 빌헬름 그림, 두 형제는 1803년에 동화에 관심을 갖게 되었다. 이러한 이야기들은 세대에 걸쳐 구전되고 있었지만, 그 누구도 그 이야기들을 어느 곳에도 기록하지 않았다. 그림 형제가 그것을 바꾸었다.

1812년, 그들은 동화를 엮어 첫 번째 책을 출판했는데, 그 책에는 86편의 이야기가 실렸다. 그들은 1814년에 두 번째 책을, 1822년에 세 번째 책을 출간하였다. 그들의 책에는 모두 합쳐 약 170여 편의 이야기가 실렸다.

그림 형제의 동화는 종종 아주 잔혹하다. 그 이야기들에는 죽음은 물론 과도하게 잔인한 장면들이 많이 포함되어 있다. 그 이야기들은 요즘 사람들이 들려주는 비폭력적인 동화와는 많이 달랐다. 이런 차이에도 불구하고, 그림 형제는 사람들이 즐길 수 있는 정말 많은 이야기들을 기록함으로써 매우 귀중한 공헌을 했다.

Reading Skills

1, 3, 2, 4

• Exercise 4 • ─────────────── p.22

정답 Q1 Ⓑ   Q2 Ⓐ   Q3 Ⓒ

해석   중세 영문학

중세 시대는 476년부터 대략 1500년까지 지속되었다. 그 기간 동안 영어로 쓰여진 인상적인 문학 작품들이 많이 있었다. 이들 중 대부분은 시였다.

영어로 쓰인 최초의 위대한 작품은 서사시인 *베오울프*였다. 대부분의 학자들은 이것이 8세기에 쓰여졌다고 생각한다. 이 시는 베오울프라는 이름의 위대한 스칸디나비아 전사에 관한 이야기를 들려준다. 그는 용을 포함한 괴물들을 물리치고 왕이 된다.

10세기 말에는 *몰든의 전투*라는 시가 쓰여졌다. 1370년 무렵 어느 시기에는 윌리엄 랭글런드가 *농부 피어스의 꿈*을 썼다. 14세기 말에는 익명의 시인에 의해 *진주라*는 또 다른 시가 쓰여졌다. 중세 시대의 가장 위대한 시 중 하나는 1392년경에 쓰여졌다. 바로 제프리 초서가 쓴 *캔터베리 이야기*였다. 이는 영국의 캔터베리로 순례를 떠난 한 무리의 사람들에 대한 이야기 모음집이다.

Reading Skills

1 Beowulf
2 The Canterbury Tales

• Exercise 5 • ─────────────── p.24

정답 Q1 Ⓑ   Q2 Ⓒ   Q3 Ⓐ   Q4 Ⓒ

해석   공상 과학 소설

오늘날 많은 이들이 공상 과학 소설 작품들은 단순하고 문학적 가치가 부족하다고 생각하기 때문에 진정한 문학이 아니라고 여긴다. 어떤 공상 과학 소설의 경우 이것이 사실이기는 하나, 대부분의 경우 그렇지 않으며, 공상 과학 소설의 초창기 시절에는 특히 그렇다.

19세기에 많은 유명한 공상 과학 소설 작가들이 탄생하였다. 메리 셸리가 그중 한 명이었다. 그녀의 1818년 걸작인 *프랑켄슈타인*은 프랑켄슈타인 박사가 만든 괴물의 탄생을 묘사하였으며, 사람들이 어떻게 과학을 남용할 수 있는지에 대해 고찰했다.

게다가 그 당시 또 다른 위대한 공상 과학 소설 작가로는 쥘 베른이 있었다. 그의 작품은 종종 그때까지 아무도 발명하지 않았던 장치들에 대해 묘사했다. 그는 1865년에는 *지구에서 달까지*를, 그리고 1869년에는 *해저 2만리*를 썼다. 두 책 모두 그의 다른 작품들과 마찬가지로 미래의 과학과 그것이 지닌 가능성에 대해 조명했다.

H.G. 웰스는 수많은 공상 과학 소설 작품들을 썼다. 1895년에 한 남자가 지구의 미래를 여행하는 내용의 책인, *타임머신*이 출간되었다. 그는 또한 1898년작인 *우주 전쟁*에서 화성인의 지구 침공에 대해 묘사했다.

20세기에는 로버트 하인라인과 같은 많은 공상 과학 소설 작가들이 명성을 얻었다. 그렇지만 19세기에도 그 시대만의 뛰어나고 유명한 작가들이 많이 있었다.

Reading Skills

2, 4, 1, 3

• Exercise 6 • ─────────────── p.26

정답 Q1 Ⓓ   Q2 Ⓒ   Q3 Ⓒ   Q4 Ⓐ

해석   아서왕의 전설

수백 년 동안, 사람들은 아서왕과 원탁의 기사에 대한 이야기들을 읽어 왔다. 아서왕이 실존 인물이었는지는 아무도 확신하지 못한다. 어떤 이들은 그가 4세기 내지 5세기에 영국에 살았다고 믿는다. 그렇지만 그의 모험담을 담은 수없이 많은 이야기들이 존재해 왔다.

중세 시대에, 아서왕에 대한 많은 위대한 전설들이 있었다. 12세기 초에 글을 쓰던 몬머스의 제프리라는 사람이 *브리타니아 열왕사*에서 아서왕에 대해 썼다. 12세기 후기에는 프랑스인인 트루아의 크레티앵이 아서왕의 기사들의 공적에 대한 여러 편의 시를 썼다. 토머스 맬러리는 중세 시대의 가장 위대한 작품 중 하나인 *아서왕의 죽음*을 썼다.

중세 시대에 아서왕에 대한 이야기가 많이 있었지만, 이후의 작가들도 그 전설에 대해 간과하지 않았다. 예를 들어 1885년, 앨프리드 테니슨 경은 그의 작품 *국왕목가*를 완간했다. 그리고 마크 트웨인은 1889년에 *아서왕을 만난 사나이*에서 아서왕의 전설을 해학적으로 개작했다.

오늘날까지도, 많은 작가들이 아서왕에 주목하고 있다. 그 전설은 너무나도 유명하고 사람들의 많은 사랑을 받기 때문에, 작가들은 앞으로도 계속해서 이 전설에 주목할 것이 분명하다.

Reading Skills

1 Geoffrey of Monmouth
2 Mark Twain

• Exercise 7 • ─────────────── p.28

정답 Q1 Ⓑ   Q2 Ⓓ   Q3 Ⓑ   Q4 Ⓒ

해석   버질(베르길리우스)

로마는 세계에서 가장 크고도 오래 지속된 제국 중 하나를 이루었다. 로마는 빛나는 문명은 물론 키케로, 수에토니우스, 리비우스를 비롯하여 많은 뛰어난 작가들을 배출해냈다. 그러나 모든 로마 작가들을 통틀어 가장 위대한 사람은 버질이라 불린, 푸블리우스 베르길리우스 마로였다.

기원전 70년에 태어난 버질은 수많은 다양한 작품들을 썼다. 그러나 사람들은 대부분 그를 세 편의 서사시로 알고 있다. 그 첫 번째는 *전원시*인데 버질이 기원전 44년부터 38년까지 쓴 것이다. 이 작품은 주로 전원을 배경으로 하는 시들이기는 하나, 또한 정치에도 초점을 맞추고 있었다. *전원시*를 완성한 다음 버질은 뒤이어 *농경시*를 쓰기 시작했다. 이 시들의 주제는 전원 생활과 농사였고 이 시들은 기원전 29년에 편찬되었다.

그러나 버질의 가장 뛰어나고 유명한 작품은 *아이네이스*였다. 버질은 이 작품을 기원전 29년부터 기원전 19년, 그가 사망하기까지 썼으나, 결국 그 시를 완성하지 못했다. *아이네이스*는 로마의 건립에 대한 이야기를 담았다. 그 시는 트로이의 멸망에서 시작하여, 마침내 이탈리아에 정착한 영웅 아이네이아스의 유랑을 따라갔다. 버질은 죽을 때 그 시를 없애려고 하였으나 황제가 그것을 보존하였다. 그리하여 세상은 이 전무후무한 문학 작품을 가까스로 얻게 되었다.

Reading Skills

1, 3, 4, 2

• Exercise 8 • p.30

정답 Q1 Ⓓ Q2 Ⓒ Q3 Ⓐ Q4 Ⓒ

해석 판타지 문학 작가들

판타지 문학에는 종종 마법과 이상한 나라, 그리고 신비한 짐승들이 등장한다. 많은 고대 문학 작품들이 판타지 작품이었다. 그러나 19세기 무렵이 되어서야 현대의 판타지 소설들이 시작되었다. 그때 이후로 3명의 작가가 판타지 장르에 큰 영향을 미치고 있다. 그들은 조지 맥도널드, C.S. 루이스, 그리고 J.R.R. 톨킨이다.

조지 맥도널드는 1824년에서 1905년까지 살았다. 스코틀랜드의 목사였던 그는 소설과 동화책을 썼다. 그는 또한 판타지 장르의 부활에 공헌했다. 그의 판타지 작품 중 하나는 *판테스티스*로, 요정 나라의 세계에서 한 남자가 겪는 모험을 담은 1858년 소설이었다. 그가 쓴 또 다른 판타지 소설은 1895년에 쓰여진 *릴리스*였다.

*판테스티스*는 20세기의 가장 유명한 작가 중 한 사람인 C.S. 루이스에게 커다란 영향을 끼쳤다. 루이스는 많은 기독교적 작품들을 썼으나, 7권의 시리즈인 *나니아 연대기*로 가장 유명하다. 1949년에서 1954년 사이에 걸쳐 쓰여진, 그 시리즈는 어떤 아이들이 나니아 왕국에서 겪는 모험을 묘사하고 있다. 1권인 *사자, 마녀, 그리고 옷장*은 어린이와 어른 팬들을 모두 보유하고 있다.

마지막으로 J.R.R. 톨킨은 루이스와 동시대 작가로, *반지의 제왕* 시리즈를 1954년과 1955년에 출간했다. 고대 서사시와 유사점을 가진 판타지 작품으로, 톨킨의 작품들은 수많은 현대 작가들에게 영향을 끼치고 있다.

Reading Skills

1 Lilith
2 J.R.R. Tolkien

Grammar Point p.32

✓ Grammar Check-Up

A 1 Because
   2 even though
   3 since
   4 Although
   5 When

B 1 ⓓ 2 ⓐ 3 ⓑ 4 ⓓ

C 1 ⓒ 2 ⓑ

Vocabulary Review p.34

A 1 consider
   2 emperor
   3 beasts
   4 fiction
   5 anonymous

B 1 Ⓑ 2 Ⓑ 3 Ⓓ 4 Ⓑ 5 Ⓐ

C 1 Ⓑ 2 Ⓐ 3 Ⓒ 4 Ⓒ 5 Ⓐ

D 1 fairy tales
   2 masterpiece
   3 medieval
   4 warrior
   5 lasted

Practice Test p.36

1 Ⓑ 2 Ⓑ 3 Ⓐ 4 Ⓑ 5 Ⓒ 6 Ⓐ
7 Ⓓ 8 Ⓒ 9 Ⓒ 10 ③, ⑤, ⑥

해석 존 밀턴과 실낙원

고대 그리스, 고대 로마, 메소포타미아와 같은 인근 동양 문화에 수많은 서사시들이 존재하고 있다. *일리아스*, *오디세이아*, *아이네이스*, *길가메시* 등이 이에 포함된다. 그러나 *베오울프*를 제외하고 영어로 쓰여진 위대한 서사시는 거의 없었다. 이것은 존 밀턴이 *실낙원*을 쓰면서 바뀌었다.

밀턴은 1608년에 태어나 격동의 시대를 살았다. 17세기에는 잉글랜드 내전이 있었다. 밀턴은 정치에 깊이 관여하였으나 다른 이들과는 달리 정치적 숙적들에 의해 처형되지 않았다. 어려운 시대에 살았지만, 밀턴은 많은 작품을 쓴 다작가였다. 그의 가장 위대한 작품은 *실낙원*이었다.

그 작품에서 밀턴은 성경 속 이야기들을 탐험한다. 그는 아담과 이브가 신의 은총을 잃고 에덴동산에서 추방된 것에 초점을 맞추고 있다. 밀턴은 아담과 이브는 물론 사탄에 대해서도 썼다. 실제로는, 사탄이 악마이지만, 주인공이다. 밀턴은 그가 악이라는 사실에도 불구하고 그를 서사시의 주인공으로 그려낸다. 밀턴은 *실낙원* 전반에 걸쳐 천국에서 추방되어 지옥으로 쫓겨난 사탄의 여정을 따라간다.

*실낙원*은 출간 즉시 돌풍을 일으켰다. 흥미로운 점은 밀턴이 실명한 후 그 작품을 썼다는 것이다. 이로써 그가 작품을 완성하는 데는 오랜 시간이 걸렸는데, 왜냐하면 그는 밤에 머릿속으로 시구를 지어 두었다가 아침에 조수에게 그것들을 반복해 들려주곤 했기 때문이다. 그러면 그 조수는 밀턴의 말을 종이에 기록했다. 밀턴의 작품은 엄청난 양의 출처 불명인 참조 자료들 또한 특징이다. 이것은 밀턴의 백과사전적 지식과 비상한 기억력에 기인한다. 오늘날에도 대부분의 독자들은 그 작품을 이해하기 위해서 각주들에 의지한다.

CHAPTER 2 Astronomy

Understanding TOEFL Question Types & Reading Skills p.40

 **Question Types** ▸ Sample Question

Ⓑ

해석 별의 종류

사람들이 밤하늘을 바라볼 때면 무수히 많은 별들을 보게 된다. 이 별들은 모두 외형이 똑같아 보일지 모르지만, 사실 저마다 다양한 특징들을 가지고 있다. 실제로 별에는 몇 가지 다른 등급이 존재하며 이 중 두 가지로는 청색별과 적색별이 있다.

청색별은 우주에서 가장 뜨겁고 굉장히 밝다. 지구에서 볼 때 사람들은 그 별들을 옅은 파란색으로 인식한다. 이들은 그 거대한 크기에도 불구하고 실제로는 아주 드문데, 고열 때문에 엄청나게 순식간에 타 버리기 때문이다.

반면 적색별은 지구에서 보면 붉은 주황색으로 보이며 크기가 가장 작은 별이다. 이 별들은 또한 확실히 은하계에서 가장 흔한 별들이기도 하다. 이들은 또한 에너지의 대부분이 이미 다 타버렸기 때문에 가장 차갑기도 하다.

2 Reading Skills ▶ Check-Up
ⓓ

• Exercise 1 • ——— p.42

정답 Q1 ⓒ   Q2 ⓐ   Q3 ⓑ

해석   화성과 금성

화성과 금성은 지구와 가장 가까운 두 행성이다. 이들은 비슷한 점이 몇 가지 있지만 실은 서로 다른 점도 어느 정도 있다.

두 행성 모두 지구형 행성으로 분류되며 이는 이들이 비교적 작다는 것을 의미한다. 화성은 사실 매우 작지만, 금성과 지구는 크기가 거의 같다. 사람들은 심지어 두 행성의 크기가 너무나 비슷해서 금성을 지구의 "자매 행성"이라고 부르기도 한다. 그러나 지구는 화성 크기의 거의 두 배이다. 화성과 금성은 또한 생명체가 존재할 가능성이 있을 만큼 충분히 태양과 가깝다. 과학자들이 어느 쪽 행성에서도 생명체를 찾아내지는 못했지만 두 행성 모두 생명체가 있거나 한때 살았을 가능성이 있다.

그러나 이들은 다른 점도 많다. 예를 들어, 화성에는 사실상 대기가 없으나 금성의 대기는 그곳에서 일어나는 온실 효과 때문에 생긴 두꺼운 이산화탄소층이 있다. 그리고 금성의 표면은 화성의 표면보다 훨씬 더 뜨겁다. 마지막으로, 화성에는 얼음이 있으나 금성의 모든 물은 열로 인해 오래 전에 증발되어 버렸다.

Reading Skills

D, S, S, D

• Exercise 2 • ——— p.44

정답 Q1 ⓓ   Q2 ⓑ   Q3 ⓓ

해석   유로파와 이오

1600년대에 천문학자인 갈릴레오 갈릴레이는 망원경을 이용하여 목성 행성을 관찰했다. 그는 그 행성을 돌고 있는 네 개의 천체에 주목했다. 이들은 목성의 위성 중 네 개에 해당하는 것으로 갈릴레이의 이름을 따서 갈릴레이 위성이라고 불렸다. 그중 두 개가 유로파와 이오이다.

유로파는 태양계에서 가장 밝은 위성이지만, 이러한 점 때문에 천문학자들이 유로파에 관심을 갖는 것은 아니다. 유로파는 엄청나게 차가워서 표면 온도가 높은 곳은 약 섭씨 영하 160도에 이른다. 그 결과 그곳의 표면은 얼음으로 꽁꽁 얼어 있다. 그럼에도 불구하고 천문학자들은 이러한 얼음층 아래에 액체 상태의 바다가 존재한다고 생각한다. 어떤 이들은 그곳에 생명체가 존재할 수도 있다고 추정한다.

이오에 대해 말하자면, 천문학자들은 이오의 화산에 관심을 가지고 있다. 이 위성에는 400개 이상의 활화산이 있는데, 이로써 이오는 태양계에서 화산 활동이 가장 활발한 곳이다. 분출이 끊임없이 이루어지고 있다는 점은, 이오가 차갑다는 사실에도 불구하고, 그곳 표면이 대부분 액체라는 점을 의미한다. 화산에서 흘러내리는 용암과 용융 암석이 이 위성의 표면 형태를 계속 바꾸어 놓는다.

Reading Skills

ⓐ

• Exercise 3 • ——— p.46

정답 Q1 ⓒ   Q2 ⓓ   Q3 ⓓ

해석   무인 및 유인 우주 비행

세계의 몇몇 국가들은 우주 프로그램을 가지고 있어서, 종종 우주로 탐험을 떠난다. 이것은 두 가지 방법으로 이루어지는데, 바로 무인 우주 비행과 유인 우주 비행이다.

무인 우주 비행이 분명히 가장 일반적이다. 무인 우주 비행은 소비에트 연방이 1957년에 *스푸트니크* 인공위성을 쏘아 올렸을 때부터 시작되었다. 그 이후로 몇몇 나라의 항공우주국들은 무수히 많은 무인 우주선을 발사해 왔다. 대부분은 지구 궤도를 도는 인공위성이지만, 몇몇 무인 우주 비행선들은 달 그리고 심지어는 태양계의 다른 행성들에도 무인 탐사선을 보내고 있다.

유인 우주 비행은 결코 아주 흔하지는 않은데, 특히 무인 우주 비행보다 엄청나게 많은 비용이 들고 위험하기 때문이다. 최초의 유인 우주 비행은 1961년에 소련인인 유리 가가린에 의해 이루어졌다. 그 이후 몇몇 미국인들이 달에 착륙하였다. 현재 미국과 러시아는 국제 우주 정거장으로 가끔씩 유인 우주 비행을 수행하고 있다. 그러나 오늘날에는 과거에 한때 그랬던 것처럼 그렇게 많은 유인 우주 비행은 하지 않는다.

Reading Skills

S, D, D, D

• Exercise 4 • ——— p.48

정답 Q1 ⓐ   Q2 ⓒ   Q3 ⓓ

해석   태양계의 행성들

태양계에는 8개의 행성이 있다: 수성, 금성, 지구, 화성, 목성, 토성, 천왕성, 해왕성이 그것이다. 이 행성들이 모두 공유하는 몇 가지 특징들이 있지만, 이들 사이에는 많은 차이점들이 존재한다. 실제로 천문학자들은 이 행성들을 두 종류로 나눈다: 지구형 행성과 거대 가스 행성이 그것이다.

수성, 금성, 지구, 화성은 지구형 행성이다. 이들은 암석과 금속으로 이루어져 있다. 또한 이들은 천천히 회전하고, 꽤 작은 편이며, 각 행성에는 위성이 없거나 한두 개만 있다. 이 행성들은 또한 태양과 가깝다.

거대 가스 행성은 목성, 토성, 천왕성, 해왕성이다. 이들은 지구형 행성보다 훨씬 더 크다. 수소와 헬륨이 이 행성들의 대부분을 구성하고 있다. 이 행성들은 아주 빠르게 회전하며 많은 수의 위성을 가지고 있다. 실제로 목성은 최소 95개의 위성을 가지고 있다. 거대 가스 행성들은 또한 태양에서 다소 멀리 떨어져 있어서 태양 주위를 도는 데 지구형 행성보다 훨씬 더 많은 시간이 걸린다.

Reading Skills

ⓐ

• Exercise 5 • — p.50

정답 Q1 ⓒ   Q2 ⓑ   Q3 ⓑ   Q4 ⓐ

해석   소행성과 혜성

행성과 위성 말고도 태양 주위를 돌고 있는 천체들이 셀 수 없이 많이 있다. 사실 우주는 사람들이 생각하는 것처럼 그렇게 텅 비어 있지 않다. 태양계에서 매우 흔한 두 천체는 소행성과 혜성이다. 이들은 약간의 공통점을 가지고 있지만 대부분은 다르다.

소행성은 태양계가 생성된 46억년 전 무렵에 형성되었다. 지금까지 천문학자들은 화성과 목성 사이에 위치한 소행성 벨트에 9만 개 이상의 소행성이 있음을 확인하였다. 소행성은 단순하게는 큰 바위 덩어리지만, 그 크기가 모두 다르다. 어떤 것들은 길이가 겨우 몇 피트 정도이지만, 다른 어떤 것들은 몇 마일에 이른다. 가장 큰 것으로 알려진 소행성인 세레스는 직경이 590마일에 이른다.

소행성과 마찬가지로 혜성 또한 태양계 생성 시기에 형성되었다. 그러나 그 구성 성분은 소행성과 다르다. 혜성은 암석과 얼음으로 이루어진 커다란 구이다. 이들이 태양 가까이에 다가가면 얼음이 녹아 백만 마일에 이르는 꼬리를 형성한다. 천문학자들은 태양계에 수조 개의 혜성이 있을 것이라고 생각한다. 그러나 대부분의 혜성은 명왕성 너머에 위치해 있다. 소행성과는 다르게 혜성은 모두 각기 다양한 궤도를 따른다. 어떤 것은 태양계를 통과하기도 하고 어떤 것은 항상 태양계 바깥에 머물기도 하므로, 어떤 혜성의 궤도는 수천 년 동안 지속될 수도 있다.

Reading Skills

D, S, D, S

• Exercise 6 • — p.52

정답 Q1 ⓐ   Q2 ⓓ   Q3 ⓑ   Q4 ⓑ

해석   망원경

갈릴레오 시대 이후, 사람들은 망원경을 사용해 우주를 관찰해 왔다. 사람들은 망원경으로 우주에 있는 별과 행성, 그리고 다른 천체들을 가까이 볼 수 있게 되었다. 망원경에는 몇 가지 종류가 있는데, 가장 일반적인 두 가지는 반사 망원경과 굴절 망원경이다.

반사 망원경은 관찰하고 있는 천체의 크기를 커 보이게 하는 거울을 사용한다. 첫 번째 거울은 구(球)의 형태이며 빛을 모은다. 그런 다음 두 번째 거울 위에 그 빛을 집중시킨다. 이 두 번째 거울이 접안 렌즈에 빛을 모아주고 그 결과 관찰자는 그때 접안 렌즈를 통해 볼 수 있게 된다. 반사 망원경은 멀리 있는 천체를 관찰하는 데 좋으며 가격 또한 다소 저렴하다. 안타깝게도, 그것은 지구에서 항상 잘 작동하는 것은 아니고 어떤 경우 잘못된 이미지를 제공할 수도 있다.

굴절 망원경은 다양한 천체를 관찰하는 렌즈들을 이용한다. 전면에는 주로 두 개의 렌즈가 있는데, 이것들이 이미지를 포착한 다음 접안 렌즈 쪽으로 빛을 굴절시킨다. 굴절 망원경은 사용이 쉽고 달과 행성, 쌍성을 보는 데 탁월하다. 그러나 가격이 비쌀 수 있으며 멀리 있는 천체를 관찰하는 데에는 효과적이지 않다.

Reading Skills

D

• Exercise 7 • — p.54

정답 Q1 ⓒ   Q2 ⓐ   Q3 ⓐ   Q4 ⓓ

해석   우주 식민지

결국에는 유인 우주 비행이 더욱 일반화되어, 인류는 태양계, 그리고 아마도 심지어는 은하계 어딘가에 정착하기 시작할 것이다. 현재로서는 달과 화성이 인류가 식민지를 건설할 수 있는 장소가 될 가능성이 있다. 어떤 사람들은 다른 행성을 식민지로 삼는 것에 아주 많이 찬성하지만, 또 다른 사람들은 그것에 강하게 반대한다.

우주 식민지를 찬성하는 사람들은, 인류가 종으로서의 생존을 보장받기 위해서는 지구를 떠나야 한다고 생각한다. 그들은 핵전쟁이나 치명적인 질병이 지구상의 모든 인류를 멸종시킬지 모른다고 염려한다. 지구의 인구가 증가하고 있다는 이유로, 이들은 넘치는 사람들을 다른 행성에 있는 식민지로 보내기를 원한다. 이들은 또한 이러한 외계 식민지가 지구에 사는 사람들에게 유용할 수 있다고 믿는다. 예를 들어 지구의 자원이 줄어들고 있기 때문에 다른 행성의 천연 자원을 이용할 수 있다는 것이다. 이 천연 자원이 인류를 결국 다른 별에 도달하게 해줄 수도 있을 것이다.

놀라울 만큼 많은 사람들이 우주 식민지가 좋지 않은 생각이라고 믿는다. 그들은 인류가 그것을 이룰 만한 기술을 가지고 있지 않다고 생각한다. 행성들이 지구와 비슷하게 되려면 인간이 그 행성들을 지구처럼 만들어야 한다는 것을 모두가 알고 있다. 이렇게 하는 데는 막대한 비용이 들 것이다. 그들은 또한 그 일이 너무나 위험해서 많은 사람들이 죽을 수도 있다고 생각한다.

Reading Skills

D, D, S, D

• Exercise 8 • — p.56

정답 Q1 ⓐ   Q2 ⓓ   Q3 ⓐ   Q4 ⓓ

해석   태양계에 대한 이론들

고대 사회에서는 종종 태양계 연구에 집중했다. 그들은 여러 행성들을 발견했고, 태양과 별에 대해 많은 것을 알아냈다. 그러나 지구와 태양계의 관계에 대한 그들의 생각은 오늘날 사람들이 믿고 있는 것과는 매우 달랐다.

고대 그리스인들은 주기적으로 천문학을 연구했고, 우주에 대한 많은 가설들을 정확하게 세웠다. 그러나 그들은 지구가 우주의 중심이라고 확신했다. 사람들은 이것을 천동설(지구 중심설)이라고 부른다. 그리스인들은 지구가 둥글며 편평하지 않다는 것을 깨달았다. 그럼에도 불구하고 그들은 달, 행성, 별, 그리고 심지어는 태양조차 지구를 중심으로 돌고 있다고 생각했다. 그들의 의견에 따르면 지구는 움직이지 않고 고정되어 있으며 반면에 다른 모든 것이 지구 주위를 돌았다.

17세기에 이러한 사고 방식은 바뀌기 시작했다. 갈릴레오 갈릴레이와 요하네스 케플러와 같은 천문학자들이 지동설(태양 중심설)에 믿음을 둔 새로운 이론들을 제시했다. 즉, 그들은 행성 모두가 태양을 중심으로 돌며, 그로 인해 각각의 행성들이 얼마나 빨리 도는지가 결정된다고 생각했다. 그들은 행성들의 궤도가 완벽한 원이 아니라는 것을 인지했다. 그들은 망원경의 도움으로 이것을 파악할 수 있었다. 이제 사람들은 갈릴레오와 케플러의 생각이 완벽하지는 않으나 고대 그리스인들의 생각보다는 훨씬 더 사실에 가까웠다는 것을 알고 있다.

Reading Skills

S, S, D, D

Grammar Point p.58

✓ Grammar Check-Up

A
1 and
2 so
3 yet
4 but
5 or

B 1 ⓑ   2 ⓒ   3 ⓐ   4 ⓑ

C 1 ⓒ   2 ⓐ

Vocabulary Review p.60

A
1 Reflecting
2 volcanoes
3 terraform
4 unmanned
5 rotates

B 1 ⓒ   2 ⓓ   3 ⓑ   4 ⓑ   5 ⓓ

C 1 ⓒ   2 ⓐ   3 ⓑ   4 ⓐ   5 ⓓ

D
1 heliocentric
2 orbit
3 terrestrial
4 comprised
5 evaporate

Practice Test p.62

1 ⓑ   2 ⓒ   3 ⓐ   4 ⓐ   5 ⓓ   6 ⓓ
7 ⓒ   8 ⓒ   9 ⓐ   10 ②, ④, ⑤

해석 성간 여행의 문제점

미국, 구소련, 그리고 다른 국가들이 특히 금성과 화성과 같은 몇몇 행성들에 탐사선을 보내고 있다. 게다가 미국의 우주비행사들은 여러 차례 달을 방문하기도 했다. 하지만 다른 항성계로 가는 것은 현재로서 불가능하다.

주된 이유는 그와 관련된 거리가 엄청나기 때문이다. 태양에서 지구까지의 거리는 대략 9천3백만 마일로, 1천문단위(AU)에 해당한다. *아폴로 11*호의 달 탐사는 도착하는 데 4일이 걸렸다. 동일한 속도로 우주선이 태양까지 가는 데는 2년 이상이 걸릴 것이다. 지구에서 가장 멀리 떨어져 있는 해왕성은 약 29AU의 거리에 있다. *아폴로*와 비슷한 속도로 이동을 한다면 수십 년이 걸릴 것이다.

항성에 대해 말하자면, 가장 가까이에 있는 항성은 프록시마 켄타우리로, 이는 4.2광년 거리에 있다. *아폴로*와 비슷한 속도로 그곳까지 가려면 수천 년이 걸릴 것이다. 간단히 말해서, 광속과 비슷한 속도로 비행할 수 있는 우주선이 나오기 전까지는 또 다른 항성계로 가는 데 너무 많은 시간이 걸릴 것이다.

게다가 광속으로 이동하는 우주선이 프록시마 켄타우리에 도착한다 해도 4.2년이 걸릴 것이다. 우주비행사들은 충분한 식량을 가져가거나 식량을 재배할 수 있는 장소를 갖춰야 할 것이다. 또한 충분한 양의 산소와 물도 있어야 한다. 대부분의 사람들은 여러 해 동안 작은 공간에 갇혀 있는 일을 감당해내지 못할 것이다. 우주비행사들을 동면 상태에 들어가게 하자고 주장하는 사람들도 있지만, 이러한 기술은 현재 존재하지 않는다.

관련된 거리 문제는 성간 여행에 너무 많은 어려움을 안겨주고 있다. 인류의 기술 수준이 엄청나게 향상되기 전까지 인류는 태양계에 남아 있을 것이다.

CHAPTER 3 Zoology

Understanding TOEFL Question Types & Reading Skills p.66

1 Question Types ▶ Sample Question
ⓑ

해석 파충류와 양서류

호수에 가면 보통 개구리, 두꺼비, 거북이, 도마뱀, 심지어는 뱀도 볼 수 있다. 그러나 생물학자들은 이들을 따로 분류하기 때문에 이 동물들이 같은 종류는 아니다. 어떤 것은 파충류인 반면 어떤 것은 양서류이다.

파충류와 양서류는 둘 다 냉혈 동물이고, 땅 위나 물속 어디에서나 살 수 있다. 그럼에도 불구하고 뱀, 도마뱀, 거북이 등의 파충류는 개구리와 두꺼비 등의 양서류와는 별개의 종으로 분류된다.

파충류와 양서류는 알에서 태어난다. 그러나 파충류의 알은 땅 위에서 부화하고, 양서류의 알은 물속에서 부화한다. 새끼 양서류들은 심지어 물속에서 호흡할 수 있도록 한시적으로 아가미를 가지고 있다. 또한 파충류의 메마르고 비늘이 있는 피부와는 다르게 양서류는 부드럽고 축축한 피부를 지니고 있다. 또한 양서류는 물을 마실 수 있고 피부를 통해 숨을 쉴 수 있다.

2 Reading Skills ▶ Check-Up
ⓓ

• Exercise 1 • p.68

정답 Q1 ⓒ   Q2 ⓐ   Q3 ⓐ

해석 동물학의 분야

동물에 대한 학문을 동물학이라고 한다. 하지만 동물학자들이 연구를 하면서는 동물 연구에 여러 다른 접근법을 취한다. 그 결과, 동물학에는 몇 가지 다른 분야가 존재한다. 그중 두 가지는 비교 해부학과 동물 행동학이다.

비교 해부학에서 동물학자들은 다양한 동물의 신체를 연구한다. 그들은 다양한 방식으로 이를 수행할 수 있다. 그들은 각 동물의 개별적인 특성을 분류한다. 동물학자들은 그 동물이 동일한, 혹은 관련 있는 속의 다른 동물들과 어떻게 다른지 알아보기 위해 동물들을 검사한다. 그들은 또한 동물들 간의 유사성에도 주목한다.

동물 행동학은 비교적 새로운 분야의 동물학이다. 그것은 동물의 행동을 조사한다. 동물 행동학자들은 동물이 서로, 그리고 인간과 어떻게 상호작용하는지에 관심을 갖는다. 그들은 동물의 문화를 조사하고 동물들이 서로 어떻게 어울

려 지내는지 연구한다. 동물의 감정과 그들이 다른 상황에서는 어떻게 반응하는지를 관찰하기도 한다.

동물학에는 다른 많은 분야들이 있다. 그러나 이 두 분야가 오늘날 비교적 인기 있는 분야이다.

Reading Skills
Ⓑ

• Exercise 2 • ──────────────────── p.70

정답 Q1 Ⓓ   Q2 Ⓒ   Q3 Ⓒ

해석   패류

많은 동물 종들이 물속 가장 밑바닥에서 서식한다. 과학자들은 이들 대부분을 패류로 분류한다. 패류에는 두 가지 다른 종류가 있다: 연체 동물과 갑각류가 그것이다.

모든 패류와 같이, 연체 동물은 등뼈와 지느러미가 없고, 몸통을 껍데기 속에 넣어 산다. 보통 연체 동물은 몸통을 껍데기 안에 완전히 넣어 산다. 그러나 어떤 연체 동물은 부분적으로만 껍데기 안에 넣어 산다. 대부분의 연체 동물들은 얕은 물속에서 살지만 아주 극소수가 깊은 심해에 살 수도 있다. 조개, 가리비, 굴은 연체 동물의 세 종류이다. 문어와 오징어 또한 연체 동물로 여겨진다. 인간에게 알려진 연체 동물만 해도 다 합쳐 25만 종이 넘는다.

갑각류는 연체 동물과 동족이기는 하나 몇 가지 차이점이 있다. 갑각류의 몸통은 대체로 가늘고 길며 마디로 분절되어 있다. 이 점은 가장 잘 알려진 두 갑각류인 게와 랍스터 같은 동물에게서 분명히 볼 수 있다. 또한 갑각류의 눈은 몸통이 아닌 머리에 있는 자루 위에 있다. 또한 몸통이 항상 대칭형은 아니며 따라서 때로는 모양이 독특한 경우도 있다.

Reading Skills
Ⓒ

• Exercise 3 • ──────────────────── p.72

정답 Q1 Ⓓ   Q2 Ⓒ   Q3 Ⓐ

해석   영장류

영장류는 인간, 원숭이, 긴팔원숭이, 침팬지, 안경원숭이 등의 포유류 집단이다. 이들은 잡식성인 경향을 띠기 때문에 육류와 채소를 모두 먹는다. 300종 이상의 영장류가 존재한다. 그중에서 유명한 두 종으로는 원숭이와 긴팔원숭이가 있다.

많은 사람들이 원숭이와 긴팔원숭이를 같은 종으로 생각하지만, 그렇지 않다. 이들은 많은 차이점을 가지고 있다. 예를 들어 대부분의 원숭이는 꼬리를 가지고 있는 반면, 긴팔원숭이는 전혀 그렇지 않다. 마찬가지로, 긴팔원숭이는 원숭이보다 몸집이 더 큰 편이다. 이들의 흉부 또한 원숭이보다 더 넓다. 이 덕분에 긴팔원숭이들은 덩굴에 매달려 나무 사이를 다닌다. 일반적으로 원숭이들은 매달려 다니지 못한다. 대신 원숭이들은 나뭇가지에서 나뭇가지로 달리거나 점프해서 나무 사이를 다닌다.

또 다른 차이점은 지능에 있다. 일반적으로 긴팔원숭이들이 원숭이보다 더 똑똑하다. 포획된 긴팔원숭이 중에는 수화를 이용해 인간과 의사소통하는 법을 배우기도 했다. 또한 많은 긴팔원숭이 종들이 도구를 사용한다.

Reading Skills
Ⓒ

• Exercise 4 • ──────────────────── p.74

정답 Q1 Ⓒ   Q2 Ⓑ   Q3 Ⓒ

해석   척추동물과 무척추동물

모든 동물을 두 개의 범주로 나눈다는 것은 사실상 불가능하다. 그러나 척추동물과 무척추동물로 나누는 경우에는 가능하다. 이들은 등뼈가 있는 동물과 그렇지 않은 동물들을 말한다.

동물계에는 5개의 척추동물 군이 있다: 바로 포유류, 파충류, 양서류, 조류, 어류이다. 이 범주에 속하는 모든 동물들은 척추를 가지고 있다. 척추는 동물 몸 속의 신경색을 보호하는 역할을 한다. 척추동물들은 또한 몇 가지 다른 특징들도 공유하고 있다. 이들의 뇌는 상당히 발달되어 있으며 대체로 복잡한 구조의 눈 또한 가지고 있다.

반면 무척추동물은 등뼈가 없는 동물이다. 환형 동물, 연체 동물, 절지 동물, 그리고 극피 동물이 모두 척추가 없는 동물 군에 속한다. 이 동물들은 보통 아주 부드러운 몸을 가지고 있다. 그들의 몸은 또한 마디마다 분절될 수 있다. 흥미롭게도 지구에 사는 동물의 90퍼센트 이상이 무척추동물이다. 이 동물들은 주로 진화론적으로 낮은 단계에 속하며 척추동물에 비해 훨씬 덜 복잡하다.

Reading Skills
Ⓐ

• Exercise 5 • ──────────────────── p.76

정답 Q1 Ⓒ   Q2 Ⓐ   Q3 Ⓐ   Q4 Ⓓ

해석   토착종과 외래종

이 세상에는 셀 수 없이 많은 생태계라고 하는 특정한 영역이 있으며, 그곳에서 동물들과 식물들이 살아간다. 어떤 생태계 안에 사는 동물들을 토착종이라고 부른다. 그러나 이따금 한 생태계의 동물들이 다른 생태계로 옮겨가는 경우가 있다. 이들을 침략종, 혹은 외래종이라고 한다.

토착종은 하나의 특정한 생태계에 속하는 동물들이다. 이들은 일반적으로 그 지역에 사는 다른 동물들과 조화를 이루는 상태에 이른다. 그러므로 이 동물들의 수는 너무 많지도, 적지도 않다. 완벽한 조화를 이룰 만큼 딱 적정한 수가 존재한다. 예를 들어 숲속 생태계에서는 보통 토끼, 다람쥐, 사슴, 곰, 그리고 다른 숲속에 사는 동물들이 비교적 조화를 이루며 함께 산다.

안타깝게도 주로 외래종이 한 생태계의 균형을 깨뜨린다. 사람들이 뜻하지 않게 이러한 동물들을 들여오거나, 혹은 동물들이 스스로 새로운 지역으로 이동할 수 있다. 외래종은 보통 새로운 지역에 해를 입힌다. 이들은 그 지역의 먹이를 몽땅 먹어치우거나 심지어는 한 동물 종 전체를 멸종시킬 수도 있다. 한 예로, 예전에는 늑대가 단 한 마리도 없었던 숲에 늑대들이 들어간다고 해보자. 그렇게 되면 그 늑대들은 사슴, 다람쥐, 토끼와 같은 많은 수의 동물들을 잡아먹을 것이다. 그 결과로 그 생태계의 균형이 깨지게 될 것이다.

Reading Skills
Ⓒ

• **Exercise 6** • ──────────── p.78

정답 Q1 ⓒ   Q2 ⓑ   Q3 ⓑ   Q4 ⓒ

해석   **포식 동물과 먹이 동물**

지구에는 많은 다른 종류의 동물들이 있지만, 그들은 모두 포식 동물과 먹이 동물이라는 두 가지 큰 범주로 분류될 수 있다. 포식 동물은 먹잇감으로 다른 동물들을 사냥하는 동물들이고, 먹이 동물은 사냥을 당하는 동물들이다. 흥미롭게도 이러한 동물들에는 많은 차이점이 있다.

먹이를 잡기 위해, 포식 동물들은 본성이 공격적이어야 한다. 동물은 살육 본능이 없는, 성공적인 사냥꾼이 될 수 없다. 포식 동물은 또한 머리의 전면에 눈이 있는 편이다. 이 때문에 목표물을 더 잘 집중해서 볼 수 있다. 자연히 포식 동물은 다른 동물들의 고기를 먹는 육식 동물이다. 잘 알려진 포식 동물로는 북극곰, 사자, 호랑이, 그리고 그중에서도 가장 무서운 인간이 있다.

먹이 동물은 포식 동물로부터 달아나거나 피할 수 있도록 일정한 특징들을 발달시켜 왔다. 그래서 이들은 위장술은 물론 색을 바꾸는 능력과 같은 방어 기제를 갖고 있는 경우가 많다. 가젤과 같은 어떤 동물들은 포식 동물을 피해 아주 빠르게 달릴 수 있다. 먹이 동물들은 주로 눈이 머리의 양 옆에 있다. 이 때문에 이들은 공격하는 포식 동물들을 훨씬 더 잘 경계할 수 있다. 먹이 동물은 보통은 그저 초식성이지만, 항상 그런 것은 아니다. 사슴과 다람쥐, 토끼가 북아메리카의 흔한 먹이 동물들이다.

Reading Skills

ⓑ

• **Exercise 7** • ──────────── p.80

정답 Q1 ⓒ   Q2 ⓒ   Q3 ⓑ   Q4 ⓓ

해석   **고래류**

엄청나게 많은 수의 큰 동물들. 즉, 고래과에 속하는 많은 수의 동물들이 대양의 바닷속 세계에서 서식한다. 고래류에는 고래, 만새기, 돌고래인 세 가지 종류가 있다.

일부 대왕고래는 그 길이가 110피트 이상에 달하는 등 고래는 엄청난 크기로 자란다. 이들은 또한 포유류라서 숨을 쉬기 위해서는 물이 아닌 공기가 필요하다. 과학자들은 이들을 수염 고래류와 이빨 고래류로 세분화하여 나누고 있다. 수염 고래류는 새우와 해조류인 켈프와 같이 아주 작은 동물들을 입으로 빨아들여 먹이로 섭취한다. 이빨 고래류는 먹이를 사냥하여 그것을 통째로 삼킨다. 대부분의 고래들은 수염 고래류이며 반면에 이빨 고래류의 수는 적다.

반면, 만새기는 고래보다는 그 크기가 훨씬 더 작게 자라, 보통 길이가 6피트에서 15피트 사이이다. 사람들은 그들의 작은 크기로 만새기와 고래를 구별한다. 게다가 모든 만새기는 이빨 고래류이기 때문에 이들은 먹이를 통째로 먹는다. 만새기는 인간과 함께 종종 수영을 하기도 하고 때로는 심지어 상어의 공격에서 사람들을 구해주는 등 그 쾌활한 성격으로도 잘 알려져 있다.

돌고래는 외양이 만새기와 거의 비슷해 보이며 몇 가지 특징들을 공유하고 있다. 이들 또한 이빨 고래류이며 다소 쾌활하다. 그러나 이들은 해안 가까이에 사는 경우가 많다. 또한 돌고래는 편평한 이빨을 가지고 있으며, 반면에 만새기의 이빨은 원뿔 모양이다.

Reading Skills

ⓓ

• **Exercise 8** • ──────────── p.82

정답 Q1 ⓓ   Q2 ⓓ   Q3 ⓒ   Q4 ⓐ

해석   **동물의 진화**

동물계의 생물들은 끊임없이 다양한 변화를 겪는다. 이러한 변화의 대부분은 자연 선택이라고 하는 과정 속에서 오랜 시간에 걸쳐 일어난다. 그러나 인위 선택이라고 하는 또 다른 종류의 변화도 있다. 여기서는 인간이 동물을 진화하게 만드는 역할을 담당한다.

자연 선택하에서는 종에 바람직한 형질을 가진 동물들이 이런 형질을 가지지 못한 동물들보다 더 빠르고 더 성공적으로 번식한다. 이로 인해 더 우수한 동물들이 그 종을 지배하게 된다. 자연에서 이러한 형질들은 주로 대부분이 유전적 변화이다. 그 변화들은 또한 동물들에게 항상 어떤 방식으로든 도움이 된다. 이러한 변형은 주요하거나 사소할 수 있다. 또한 단 한 세대에 걸쳐 빠르게 발생할 수도 있고 혹은 몇 세대에 걸쳐 발생할 수도 있다.

반면에 인위 선택은 인간이 발생시키는 것이다. 인간은 어떤 특성을 얻기 위해 동물을 사육하기도 한다. 인간은 수백 년 동안 말과 개를 이런 식으로 사육해 왔다. 또 다른 방법은 근친교배로, 아주 가까운 동족류의 동물들끼리 서로 교배하는 것이다. 그러나 이 결과가 항상 바람직한 것은 아니다. 오늘날 과학자들은 동물의 유전적인 구조를 바꾸기 위해 심지어 유전자 요법을 사용하기도 한다.

자연 선택이든 인위 선택이든 모두의 결과로 동물은 변화하거나 진화한다. 이러한 변화는 자연적으로 혹은 의도적으로 일어날 수 있다.

Reading Skills

ⓑ

Grammar Point   p.84

Grammar Check-Up

A 1 ✓ Some animals have one cell; others have many.
 2 ✓ There are more than twenty-two dolphins living in the aquarium.
 3 ☐ There are three kinds of cetaceans: dolphins—whales—and porpoises.
 4 ☐ In addition; most predators are very aggressive animals.
 5 ✓ Natural selection—which Darwin discussed—happens in many species.
 6 ☐ Ethology is a field of zoology. and so is comparative biology.

B , / : / ; / — / .

C 1 ⓒ   2 ⓐ   3 ⓓ   4 ⓑ   5 ⓒ

Vocabulary Review   p.86

A 1 harmoniously
 2 omnivorous
 3 Carnivorous
 4 moist
 5 artificial

B 1 Ⓑ 2 Ⓒ 3 Ⓒ 4 Ⓐ 5 Ⓒ

C 1 Ⓓ 2 Ⓑ 3 Ⓑ 4 Ⓐ 5 Ⓓ

D
1 ecosystem
2 hatches
3 transformations
4 swing
5 breathe

Practice Test   p.88

1 Ⓒ 2 Ⓓ 3 Ⓐ 4 Ⓑ 5 Ⓒ 6 Ⓑ
7 Ⓐ 8 Ⓒ 9 ① 10 ①, ③, ④

해석 물새

전 세계의 강, 호수, 시내, 그리고 바다에서, 혹은 그 근처에서 서식 중인 물새를 찾아볼 수 있다. 물새는 오리와 거위, 백조와 같은 조류이다. 많은 물새들이 유사한 특성을 가지고 있다. 예를 들어 이들은 물갈퀴와 방수 기능이 있는 깃털을 가지고 있다. 이러한 깃털은 새들이 물속으로 잠수할 때조차 물에 젖지 않게 도와준다.

오리, 거위, 백조 중에서는 오리가 가장 색이 다양하다. 수컷들은 색이 다양할 수 있다. 동아시아가 원산지인 원앙새는 파란색, 초록색, 빨간색, 주황색, 그리고 자주색을 띨 수 있다. 다른 종들의 수컷들은 그보다 색이 다소 덜 다양한 편이다. 암컷들은 갈색이나 흰색을 띠는 경향이 있다. 거위와 백조의 수컷과 암컷은 보통 하얀색이나 회색을 띤다.

물새는 보통 잡식성이기 때문에 다양한 먹이를 먹는다. 한 가지 예외는 캐나다 구스인데, 이들은 초식성으로 수중 식물과 같은 식물성 물질만을 먹는다. 다른 종류의 거위들도 식물을 먹지만, 벌레, 조개, 작은 물고기까지 잡아먹기도 한다. 백조와 대부분의 오리 종들도 마찬가지이다.

물새의 또 다른 특징은 자주 이동을 한다는 점이다. (이들이 이렇게 이동하는 이유는 먹이를 찾고 짝짓기 장소에 도달하기 위해서이다.) 북아메리카에서 가을에 흔히 볼 수 있는 장면은 거위 무리가 V자 형태로 비행을 하면서 남쪽으로 이동하는 모습이다. 일부 물새들은 엄청난 속도로, 심지어는 시속 100킬로미터를 넘는 속도로 비행을 할 수 있다. 이로써 이 새들은 불과 몇 시간 만에 수백 킬로미터를 날아갈 수 있다. 예컨대 오리의 일종인 청둥오리는 반나절 만에 800킬로미터 이상을 날아갈 수 있다.

CHAPTER 4 Art

Understanding TOEFL Question Types & Reading Skills   p.92

1 Question Types ▶ Sample Question
Ⓐ

해석 채식 필사본

중세 시대의 가장 아름다운 미술 작품 중에는 회화의 결과가 아니라 오히려 책에서 발견되는 경우가 있다. 이 시기의 채식 필사본 속에는 그림이 담겨 있었다.

몇 세기 전에는, 책이 엄청나게 비쌌고 그래서 부유한 사람들만이 책을 샀다. 이들은 보통 특별하게 제작된 책들을 주문했다. 그 책들이 평범했다면 이들이 좋아하지 않았을 것이다. 그래서 책 제조업자들은 흔히 글에 삽화를 그려 넣었다.

성경은 중세 시대에 가장 흔한 책이었고 그래서 많은 채식 필사본들이 성경의 장면들을 묘사했다. 또한 주로 종교적인 글이 담긴 다른 책들에도 삽화를 그려 넣었다. 이러한 책들에 있는 그림들은 오늘날에도 여전히 훌륭하다. 그 이유는 화가들이 사용한 물감 때문인데, 그 물감에는 다양한 허브가 함유되어 있었고 어떤 물감에는 심지어 진짜 금과 은이 함유되어 있었다.

2 Reading Skills ▶ Check-Up
C, E

• Exercise 1 •   p.94

정답 Q1 Ⓓ Q2 Ⓑ Q3 Ⓒ

해석 아르 데코

1920년대에 세계는 제1차 세계 대전으로 인한 피해에서 회복되고 있었다. 사람들은 당시의 번영과 화려함을 나타낼 수 있는 새로운 스타일을 원했다. 그 결과 아르 데코가 등장했다. 그것은 매우 장식적인 예술 양식이었다.

아르 데코는 많은 영향을 받았다. 여기에는 입체주의와 미래주의가 포함되었다. 고대 이집트, 그리스, 그리고 로마 양식 또한 아르 데코 예술가들에게 영향을 끼쳤다. 아르 데코는 기하학적인 형태뿐만 아니라 양식화된 자연적인 형태를 만들어내는 일에 초점을 맞추었다. 아르 데코는 호화로운 장식을 강조했다. 하지만 이것이 하나의 예술 운동에 그친 것은 아니었다. 이것은 건축가, 인테리어 디자이너, 그리고 패션 디자이너들에게도 영향을 끼쳤다.

미국의 건축가들은 아르 데코에 매료되었다. 그래서 이들은 종종 이러한 양식으로 건물을 설계했다. 뉴욕에서는 크라이슬러 빌딩이 아르 데코 양식으로 지어졌다. 엠파이어 스테이트 빌딩도 마찬가지였다. 아르 데코는 플로리다의 마이애미에서 유행했다. 오늘날 그 도시에는 아르 데코 양식의 건물들이 세계에서 가장 많이 있다.

Reading Skills

1 E, C   2 C, E

• Exercise 2 •   p.96

정답 Q1 Ⓑ Q2 Ⓓ Q3 Ⓓ

해석 레오나르도 다 빈치

레오나르도 다 빈치는 이상적인 르네상스적 인물이었다. 그는 미술, 공학, 과학, 자연주의 등 수많은 분야에 능통한 사람이었다. 이런 재능으로 그는 일생 동안 놀라운 업적들을 이룰 수 있었다. 사람들은 레오나르도를 여러 가지 방면에서 알고 있지만 그에게 최고의 명성을 가져다 준 것은 화가로서의 그의 재능이었다.

인생 전반기에 레오나르도는 밀란에서 작업하면서 상당한 시간을 보냈다. 그곳에서, 그는 자신의 가장 유명한 작품들 중 일부를 완성하였다. 이 중 하나가 예수 그리스도와 그의 제자들의 마지막 저녁식사 장면을 묘사한 벽화인 최후의 만찬이었다. 레오나르도는 이 작품을 의뢰한 후원자인 루도비코 스포르차 공작을 위해 이 그림을 그렸다.

그 후 레오나르도는 플로렌스로 갔다. 그곳에서, 한 부유한 상인이 자신의 아내를 그린 그림을 원했고 레오나르도에게 그림을 그리는 데 대한 값을 지불하였다. 레오나르도가 그 그림을 그리는 데는 몇 년의 시간이 걸렸는데, 마침내 인생 말년이 되어서야 모나리자를 완성했다. 이것은 거의 틀림없이 세계에서 가장 유명한 그림이다. 확실히 가장 잘 알려진 그림 중 하나이다.

Reading Skills

1 C, E 2 E, C

• Exercise 3 • ——————————————— p.98

정답 Q1 Ⓐ Q2 Ⓒ Q3 Ⓓ

해석 인상주의

때때로 많은 화가들이 비슷한 양식으로 그림을 그리기 시작한다. 그 결과 새로운 예술 운동이 탄생한다. 역사적으로 다양한 예술 운동이 많이 있어 왔지만, 아마도 가장 유명한 것은 인상주의 운동일 것이다.

인상주의는 1860년대에 시작되었고, 그 이름은 클로드 모네가 그린 인상, 해돋이라는 그림에서 가져왔다. 인상주의는 그 당시 미술계의 유행에 대한 반작용으로 시작되었다. 19세기에는 종교적인 이미지와 역사적인 주제가 매우 인기였다. 그러나 인상파 화가들은 이러한 주제에 특별히 관심이 없었다. 그래서 그들은 주로 사람이나 심지어는 그냥 과일 접시같은 일상적인 대상들을 그렸다.

마찬가지로, 인상파 이전의 화가들은 주로 어두운 색을 사용하였다. 그러나 인상파 화가들은 그리는 대상에 미치는 햇빛의 효과에 대해 관심이 있었고, 그에 따라 그림에 밝은 색을 사용했다.

세계적으로 가장 유명한 인상파 화가들로는 폴 세잔, 피에르 오귀스트 르누아르, 에두아르 마네 등이 있다. 오늘날 그들의 그림은 종종 수백만 달러에 팔린다.

Reading Skills

1 C, E 2 E, C

• Exercise 4 • ——————————————— p.100

정답 Q1 Ⓒ Q2 Ⓑ Q3 Ⓑ

해석 네덜란드 황금 시대

17세기에 네덜란드는 유럽의 선도적인 국가였다. 네덜란드는 국제 무역에 활발히 개입하고 있었고, 네덜란드의 과학자들은 위대한 발견과 발명을 이루었다. 막대한 부(富) 덕분에, 네덜란드의 시민들은 미술 작품을 만드는 데 상당한 시간을 할애했다. 그 결과가 바로 약 1세기 가까이 지속되었던 네덜란드 황금 시대였다.

흥미롭게도 네덜란드의 화가들이 모두 동일한 화풍을 가지고 있지는 않았다. 오히려 그들은 풍경화, 역사화, 초상화 등 온갖 종류의 그림을 그렸다. 이것이 네덜란드 황금 시대를 아주 다양한 예술의 시기로 만들었다.

렘브란트와 페테르 파울 루벤스가 이 시대의 가장 유명한 두 명의 네덜란드 화가들이었다. 그렇지만 이 둘은 아주 다른 화풍을 가지고 있었다. 렘브란트는 자화상과 성서화를 주로 그렸다. 그는 또한 많은 네덜란드 화가들을 가르쳤고, 그 때문에 사후에도 더 많은 지속적인 영향을 끼쳤다. 반면 루벤스는 작품에서 움직임과 색을 강조했다. 그들의 작품 모두 이 시대가 미술 작품에 있어서 얼마나 찬란했는지를 보여준다.

Reading Skills

1 C, E 2 E, C

• Exercise 5 • ——————————————— p.102

정답 Q1 Ⓐ Q2 Ⓒ Q3 Ⓑ Q4 Ⓓ

해석 미켈란젤로

르네상스 시대는 유럽에서 많은 뛰어난 사람들 덕분에 지식이 재탄생했던 시기였다. 그중 가장 위대한 인물 중 한 명이 미켈란젤로였다. 1475년에 이탈리아의 카프레세에서 태어난 조각가였던 그는 모든 시대를 통틀어 가장 위대한 예술가 중 한 사람이 될 예정이었다.

미켈란젤로는 12살 때 한 화가의 도제가 되었다. 그러나 그는 조각을 배우는 것을 더 좋아했고 그래서 그 대신에 조각을 공부하기 시작했다. 10대 초반에, 플로렌스의 메디치 통치 가문의 한 사람이 미켈란젤로를 알아보고 그의 후원자가 되었다. 미켈란젤로가 메디치 통치 가문을 만나지 못했다면 그의 인생은 아주 달라졌을 것이다.

청년이 되면서, 미켈란젤로는 위대한 작품들을 빠른 속도로 만들어 내기 시작했다. 그는 겨우 23살에 피에타를 완성했다. 2년 후 그는 다비드를 조각하기 시작했다. 그는 다비드를 다른 조각가들의 다비드와 다른 모습으로 보여주고 싶었다. 그래서 그는 다비드를 노인이 아닌 젊은 청년으로 조각했다.

그러나 미켈란젤로의 가장 위대한 작품은 바티칸에 있는 시스티나 성당의 천장화였다. 그는 스스로를 화가가 아니라 조각가로 여겼기 때문에 처음에는 그 프로젝트에 관심이 없었다. 그러나 교황이 그를 설득해 그 작품을 시작하고 완성하게 되었다. 그 결과 미켈란젤로는 1508년부터 1512년까지 작업하여 그의 역작을 완성했다.

Reading Skills

Ⓒ

• Exercise 6 • ——————————————— p.104

정답 Q1 Ⓑ Q2 Ⓒ Q3 Ⓑ Q4 Ⓓ

해석 앤설 애덤스

사람들은 보통 예술을 생각하면 회화와 그림을 떠올리지만, 다른 많은 종류의 예술이 있다. 사진이 그중 하나이다. 그리고 지금껏 가장 위대한 사진작가 중 한 사람이 바로 앤설 애덤스였다.

애덤스는 고독한 성장기를 지냈고, 그로 인해 상당한 시간을 야외에서 보냈다. 이것은 그를 자연 예찬론자가 되게 하였고, 이 점은 그의 전 생애에 영감을 주었다. 애덤스는 캘리포니아 북부에서 성장했기 때문에 그의 자연 산책은 종종 요세미티 국립공원 방문이 포함되었다. 1916년, 그가 처음 요세미티를 방문했을 때, 그것은 그가 자신의 삶을 자연에 바치도록 그를 변화시켰다. 그는 또한 최소 1년에 한 번은 그 공원을 찾겠다고 결심했다. 1984년, 사망할 때까지 그는 이것을 지켰다.

애덤스는 1919년에 시에라 클럽에 가입했다. 이 조직은 환경 보존에 관심을 가졌다. 2~3년간 그는 시에라 클럽의 회보에 자신의 사진과 그림을 발표하기 시작했다. 사람들이 그의 작품에 주목하기 시작했고, 이는 그에게 엄청난 명성을 가져다 주었다. 그는 곧 사진 작품만으로 살아가기 시작했다. 애덤스는 일생 동안 자신이 찍는 사진의 품질을 계속해서 향상시켰다. 이로 인해 사진작가로서 그가 가진 기술적인 천재성이 인정을 받게 되었다. 그가 죽었을 때, 그는 거의 틀림없이 세계에서 가장 유명한 사진작가였다.

Reading Skills
ⓒ

• Exercise 7 • p.106

정답 Q1 ⓒ   Q2 ⓑ   Q3 ⓒ   Q4 ⓐ

해석 동굴 벽화

1879년, 마르셀리노 사우투올라와 그의 딸이 한 동굴 속에서 그림 몇 점을 발견하였다. 많은 연구 끝에 사우투올라는 그가 발견한 것을 대중에게 발표했다. 대부분의 사람들이 그 그림들이 가짜라고 생각했기 때문에 사우투올라가 발견한 것이 진짜라고 믿으려 하지 않았다. 그러나 유럽인들은 곧이어 더 많은 동굴 벽화들을 발견하기 시작하였다. 그 결과 사람들은 동굴 벽화가 정말로 존재한다고 인식하게 되었다.

동굴 벽화는 32,000년 전부터 10,000년 전에 이르기까지 어느 시기에나 존재한다. 동굴 벽화는 보통 들소, 사슴, 말과 같은 동물은 물론 사람의 손을 모사한 그림 등 다양한 대상을 단순하게 묘사한다. 사람을 그린 그림은 아주 드물다. 그림들은 매우 단순한 경우가 많다. 그러나 라스코 동굴 벽화와 같이 최근에 발견되는 동굴 벽화 중에는 더 정교한 경우들이 있다. 이로 인해 사람들이 이러한 동굴의 연구에 집중하게 되었다.

왜 고대인들이 이러한 벽화를 그렸는지는 아무도 알지 못한다. 어떤 이들은 종교적인 목적으로 그림이 그려졌다고 생각하고 또 어떤 이들은 그림으로 의사소통을 시도한 것이라고 생각한다. 그러나 단순하기는 해도 이러한 벽화가 존재하지 않는다면, 과거에 대한 인류의 지식도 달라질 것이다. 예를 들어, 인류학자들은 지금은 유럽에 살고 있지 않은 동물들을 그린 그림들을 목격해 왔다. 그 결과 이제 그들은 코뿔소와 하이에나와 같은 이러한 동물들이 한때는 유럽의 일부 지역에 실제 살았다는 사실을 깨닫게 된다.

Reading Skills
ⓑ

• Exercise 8 • p.108

정답 Q1 ⓑ   Q2 ⓓ   Q3 ⓐ   Q4 ⓐ

해석 르네상스 시대의 원근법

중세 시대에는 대부분의 화가들이 3차원적인 그림을 그리지 못했기 때문에 2차원적인 모습을 그렸다. 그러나 르네상스 시기에 화가들은 새로운 화법을 익혀 그들의 작품에 원근법을 도입하기 시작했다.

원근법이란 사물을 실제 보이는 대로 그리는 기술이다. 이것은 전경에 있는 형상은 더 크게 그려지는 반면 배경에 있는 형상은 더 작아 보인다는 것을 의미한다. 고대 그리스의 화가들은 이 방법에 대해 이해하고 있었지만, 몇 세기 동안 그 방법은 서양에서 잊혀졌다. 후에 이슬람교도들이 서양에 원근법을 다시 소개했다. 이탈리아의 화가인 조토는 원근법으로 그림 그리기를 시도한 최초의 화가 중 한 명이었다.

조토가 죽은 뒤 몇 년 후에 르네상스 시대가 시작되자, 더 많은 화가들이 원근법을 사용한 작업을 시도하였다. 그들은 원근법으로 그림을 그리기 위해 수학적인 공식을 도입하기 시작했다. 또 다른 화가들은 단순히 다양한 사물이 거울에 비치는 모습을 그리면서 연습했다. 이러한 방식으로, 그들은 여러 다른 사물의 크기를 다양하게 그리고 그림자를 이용하여 작업하는 방법에 대해 배웠다.

플로렌스의 많은 화가들은 원근법으로 실험을 하기 시작했다. 그들이 없었다면 르네상스 시대의 회화는 아주 다르게 보였을 것이다. 그들의 방식은 유럽의 나머지 지역 곳곳에 급속도로 퍼져나갔고, 이에 따라 화가들이 자신의 작품을 관찰하고 그리는 방식에 변화를 일으켰다.

Reading Skills
ⓐ

Grammar Point p.110

✓ Grammar Check-Up

A
1 Imperative
2 Indicative
3 Indicative
4 Subjunctive
5 Imperative
6 Subjunctive

B 1 ⓒ   2 ⓓ   3 ⓑ

C
1 ✓ Till someone purchases that painting, it will remain in the art gallery.
2 ☐ What kind of paint did the artist use to make that work over there?
3 ✓ If Picasso were alive today, he would still be making great art.
4 ☐ That was one of the most important periods for artwork.
5 ☐ Take a close look at the vase and then begin painting it.

Vocabulary Review p.112

A
1 engineering
2 legitimate
3 photographer
4 fascinated
5 Middle

B 1 ⓓ   2 ⓓ   3 ⓑ   4 ⓓ   5 ⓐ

C 1 ⓑ   2 ⓐ   3 ⓐ   4 ⓓ   5 ⓒ

D
1 solitary
2 bookmaker
3 sculptor
4 images
5 quality

Practice Test   p.114

1 Ⓐ	2 Ⓐ	3 Ⓓ	4 Ⓒ	5 Ⓒ	6 Ⓑ
7 Ⓐ	8 Ⓑ	9 1	10 1, 3, 4		

해석 허드슨 리버파

허드슨강은 뉴욕주를 가로지르는데 북쪽 지역부터 뉴욕시까지 남하하며 흐른다. 그 강의 일부는 애디론댁 산맥을 가로질러 흐른다. 강이 산과 언덕, 들판, 그리고 숲을 통과하기 때문에 그 강이 흐르는 지역은 경치가 매우 뛰어나. 뉴욕주 북쪽의 다른 지역들과 마찬가지로 이 지역이 바로 19세기 한 계파의 화가들에게 영감을 주었다. 그들이 시작한 운동은 허드슨 리버파라고 알려지게 되었다.

허드슨 리버파의 화가들은 낭만주의의 영향을 받았다. 이들은 주로 허드슨강에 특징적으로 자주 나타나는 풍경을 그렸다. 인근의 캐츠킬 산맥이나 화이트 산맥의 자연 풍경을 나타내는 화가들도 있었다. 이 운동을 시작한 화가는 토머스 콜이었다. 1825년, 그는 허드슨강에서 증기선을 타고 산속으로 들어가 그림을 그리기 시작했다. 또 다른 화가인 애셔 브라운 뒤랑은 콜의 친구였다. 그 역시 이 지역의 풍경을 그렸다. 화파의 인기가 높아지자 더 많은 화가들이 여기에 합류했다. 그들은 민족주의, 발견, 그리고 자연이라는 주제에 초점을 맞추었다.

운동이 확대되면서 주제가 다양해지기 시작했다. 화가들은 뉴잉글랜드와 캐나다 일부를 기반으로 한 풍경화를 그렸다. 미 서부와 남아메리카와 같이 멀리 떨어진 곳의 풍경을 그린 화가들도 있었다. (그에 따라 이러한 화가들의 그림은 광범위한 야외 풍경을 보여준다.) 프레더릭 에드윈 처치와 존 프레더릭 켄셋 등이 운동의 신진 화가들이 유명해졌다. 오늘날에도 어떤 화가들은 여전히 이러한 화풍으로 그림을 그린다. 초창기 화가들의 그림 또한 여전히 수요가 높다.

CHAPTER 5 Physiology

Understanding TOEFL Question Types & Reading Skills   p.118

1 Question Types ▶ Sample Question
Ⓑ

해석 소화기관

음식을 먹음으로써 사람들은 건강하고, 튼튼하고, 행복하게 살 수 있다. 음식이 없다면 사람들은 생존할 수 없을 것이다. 그리고 신체에 소화기관이 없다면 섭취한 어떤 음식물도 처리될 수 없을 것이다. 수많은 신체 기관들이 소화기관을 구성한다. 이들에는 입, 식도, 위, 소장과 대장, 직장과 항문이 있다. 이러한 기관들을 통하여 음식물이 체내로 들어가고 영양소로 바뀌며, 노폐물로서 체외로 배출된다.

소화기의 모든 기관들은 속이 비어 있어서 음식물이 그 기관들을 통해 이동할 수 있다. 이 기관들에는 또한 음식물을 밀어내 체내로 통과시키는 근육이 함께 있다. 많은 기관들에 점막, 즉, 음식물을 소화시키는 분비선이 있는 내막이 있다. 이러한 다양한 신체 기관들 덕분에 사람들은 음식물을 쉽게 소화시킬 수 있다.

2 Reading Skills ▶ Check-Up
Ⓑ

• Exercise 1   p.120

정답 Q1 Ⓐ Q2 Ⓒ Q3 Ⓒ

해석 심장의 방

심장은 신체에서 가장 중요한 장기 기관인데, 그 이유는 심장이 없으면 신체의 어느 곳으로도 혈액을 펌프 작용을 통해 내보낼 수 없고, 그렇게 되면 사람이 사망에 이르기 때문이다. 심장의 무게는 대략 1파운드 정도지만, 방을 4개나 가지고 있으며, 이 방들이 모두 중요한 목적에 기여한다.

심장은 4개의 방이 분리되어 나뉘어져 있다. 좌심방과 우심방, 좌심실과 우심실이 그것이다. 혈액은 심장의 오른쪽 윗부분에 위치한 우심방에서 심장으로 들어간다. 다음으로 혈액은 우심방에서, 우심방의 바로 아래쪽에 위치한 우심실로 이동한다. 우심실은 혈액을 폐로 이동시키는데, 폐에서 혈액은 산소를 받아들여 이산화탄소를 제거할 수 있다.

그런 다음 폐 속의 혈액은 좌심방을 통해 심장으로 다시 들어간다. 혈액은 마지막으로 좌심실로 한 번 더 내려가고 이곳에서 신체의 가장 큰 동맥인 대동맥이 펌프 작용을 통해 혈액을 신체 곳곳으로 내보내는 과정을 되풀이한다.

Reading Skills
Ⓐ

• Exercise 2   p.121

정답 Q1 Ⓑ Q2 Ⓐ Q3 Ⓓ

해석 암

인체에는 수백만 개의 세포가 있다. 이러한 세포들은 종종 새로운 세포를 만들어 내기 위해 분열하지만, 노화된 세포가 끊임없이 죽기 때문에 인체에 세포가 초과하는 일은 없다. 그러나 어떤 비정상적인 세포들이 있는데 이들은 절대 죽지 않고 성장을 멈추지 않으며 무시무시한 속도로 그 수를 증가시킨다: 이것이 암세포이다.

여러 다른 종류의 암이 존재한다. 그러나 모두 한 가지 공통점이 있다: 바로 있지 말아야 할 자리에서 자라는 세포라는 점이다. 암세포는 또한 돌연변이이기 때문에, 정상 세포와 비슷한 모습이 이미 아니다. 과학자들은 사실 무엇이 암을 유발하는지 확신하지 못한다.

안타깝게도 암세포는 종종 여러 장기에서 결합하여, 암세포의 거대한 덩어리인 종양을 형성한다. 어떤 종양은 양성이어서 신체의 다른 부위로 전이되지 않지만, 어떤 악성 종양은 신체 구석구석으로 퍼진다. 많은 암 때문에 결국 환자들이 사망에 이르지만, 의사들이 일부 암에 대한 치료제를 발견하기 위해 애쓰고 있다.

Reading Skills
Ⓒ

• Exercise 3   p.122

정답 Q1 Ⓑ Q2 Ⓐ Q3 Ⓒ

해석 노화

노화는 사람이 나이가 들며 겪는 과정이다. 성인이 중년의 나이에 이르고 나이가 들면서, 노화는 그들에게 많은 부정적인 영향들을 미칠 수 있다. 이는 본질적으로 신체적인 영향과 정신적인 영향 둘 다일 수 있다.

사람은 나이가 들면서 질병에 더 취약해진다. 젊은 성인들은 쉽게 회복하는 병이라도 나이가 든 사람들은 이로 인해 죽을 수도 있다. 사람의 장기 또한 많은 변화를 겪는다. 예를 들어 심장의 기능은 시간이 지남에 따라 약화된다. 노년층의 주요 사망 원인이 심장병이라는 점이 그 결과 중 하나이다. 나이가 들면서 보통 시력이 나빠진다. 소화와 관련된 문제들 또한 더 많이 겪게 된다.

정신적으로는 노화 때문에 뇌의 기능 역시 둔화된다. 다양한 자극에 대한 반응이 느려진다. 또한 노년층에게는 종종 기억력 문제가 발생한다. 알츠하이머병과 치매는 노년층의 정신에 영향을 미치는 두 가지 문제들이다. 노인들은 종종 젊었을 때처럼 명확하게 사고하는 데 어려움을 겪는다.

Reading Skills

Ⓒ

• Exercise 4 • ─────── p.123

정답 Q1 Ⓓ   Q2 Ⓓ   Q3 Ⓐ

해석   반사 신경

때때로 신체가, 개인이 의도하거나 원하지 않는 어떤 일을 본의 아니게 행하는 경우가 있을 것이다. 이것의 가장 흔한 예는 어떤 사람이 병원에 갔는데, 그때 의사가 환자의 무릎을 탁 치는 경우에 발생한다. 본의 아니게, 그 사람은 자신의 무릎을 뻗을 것이다. 의사들은 이것을 반사 신경이라고 부른다.

신체에는 여러 다른 반사 신경들이 있다. 이는 사람이 해를 입지 않도록 예방하기 위해 혹은 사람을 어느 정도 보호하려는 의도이다. 흔한 두 가지 반사 신경은 재채기와 기침이다. 사람은 비강 안에 자극적인 무언가가 걸리면 대체로 재채기를 한다. 재채기를 함으로써 사람은 그 외부 물질의 유입을 막을 수 있다. 기침도 이와 마찬가지이다. 사람의 목에 이물질이나 성가신 것이 있을 수 있다. 기침을 해야 한다는 것은 사람이 제어할 수 없는 반사적인 행동이다. 사람은 몸이 그렇게 하라고 말하기 때문에 기침을 할 뿐이다.

Reading Skills

Ⓒ

• Exercise 5 • ─────── p.124

정답 Q1 Ⓑ   Q2 Ⓒ   Q3 Ⓐ   Q4 Ⓐ

해석   피부층

피부는 사실상 신체의 노출된 모든 부위를 감싸고 있다. 겉으로는 복잡해 보이지 않지만 실제로 피부는 세 개의 다른 층으로 구성되어 있으며, 이 층은 모두 각각의 고유한 목적을 지니고 있다.

가장 바깥에 보이는 피부층은 표피인데, 표피는 피부가 손상되지 않게 보호해야 하므로 단단하다. 표피에는 사람들의 피부색을 결정하는 물질인 멜라닌이 함유되어 있다. 멜라닌이 많은 사람일수록 멜라닌이 적은 사람보다 외형이 더 어둡다. 멜라닌은 신체가 햇빛에 과다 노출되면 피부를 그을려 태양광선으로부터 몸을 보호한다.

진피는 피부의 두 번째 층이다. 진피는 표피 아래에 보이지 않게 숨어 있다. 진피에는 땀샘과 지방 분비선은 물론 말단 신경과 혈관들이 있다. 신체의 말단 신경은 사람이 사물을 느끼고 지각하게 해 주며, 혈관은 산소와 영양분을 피부에 제공하는 동시에 노폐물을 처리한다. 지방 분비선은 몸을 매끄럽게 유지해 주고, 땀샘은 땀이 신체 밖으로 배출되게 한다.

피하지방이 세 번째 층이다. 당연히도, 이 층은 대부분이 지방으로 이루어져 있다. 피하지방층은 신체를 따뜻하게 유지시켜 주고, 피부가 신체의 나머지 부위와 연결된 상태를 유지하게 해 준다.

Reading Skills

Ⓓ

• Exercise 6 • ─────── p.126

정답 Q1 Ⓒ   Q2 Ⓑ   Q3 Ⓓ   Q4 Ⓑ

해석   치아

어떤 사람이 음식을 먹을 때마다 그 사람의 치아는 음식물을 부수고 씹어야 한다. 사람은 다 합쳐 32개의 영구치를 가질 수 있고, 이 치아들은 각기 다른 5가지 종류로 나누어질 수 있다.

앞니는 전면에 있는 4개의 치아로 입의 위와 아래에 위치해 있다. 앞니는 음식물을 작은 조각으로 자르며 그래서 보통 앞니의 끝부분은 약간 날카롭다. 앞니의 바로 옆에는 송곳니가 있으며, 송곳니는 입 안의 치아 중 4개를 차지한다. 음식물을 자르는 데 이용되는 송곳니는 앞니처럼 다소 뾰족하다.

2개의 작은어금니, 즉 쌍두치는 각 송곳니 옆에 있으며 모두 합쳐 8개가 난다. 작은어금니는 비교적 커서 음식물을 으깨고 짓이기는 역할을 한다. 그 옆에는 큰어금니가 있으며, 8개가 난다. 큰어금니는 작은어금니보다 더 크고, 음식물을 수월하고 안전하게 삼킬 수 있을 정도로 작아질 때까지 완전히 분쇄함으로써 혀가 음식물을 삼키도록 도와준다.

마지막 치아는 사랑니라고 불린다. 입 안의 각 면마다 하나씩 있다. 그러나 그것은 사람의 10대 후반 시기에 발달하고, 본질적으로는 아무런 목적도 수행하지 않기 때문에 사람들은 보통 이 치아를 뽑는다. 그래서 사람의 입은 32개의 치아가 들어갈 자리를 갖추고 있지만 대부분의 사람들은 28개의 치아만을 가지고 있다.

Reading Skills

Ⓑ

• Exercise 7 • ─────── p.128

정답 Q1 Ⓒ   Q2 Ⓐ   Q3 Ⓑ   Q4 Ⓓ

해석   혈액의 구성

사람의 혈액은 한 가지 종류의 물질로 보이지만, 의사들이 원심분리기를 이용하면 분리될 수 있다. 과학자들은 혈액을 두 가지 성분으로 분류하고 있다: 혈장과 혈중유형성분이 그것이다.

일단 나누어지면, 혈액의 약 55퍼센트가 혈장으로 분리된다. 혈장은 약 90퍼센트가 물이며 나머지가 여러 가지 단백질, 무기질, 탄수화물, 지방이다. 혈액 속 혈장의 역할은 신체 구석구석에 영양분과 노폐물을 옮기는 것이다.

혈액 내의 혈중유형성분은 적혈구, 백혈구, 혈소판이다. 이 세 가지 중에는, 적혈구의 양이 훨씬 더 풍부하다. 적혈구는 주로 신체 구석구석에 산소를 나르고 약간의 이산화탄소도 옮긴다. 혈액 속에는 그보다 훨씬 더 적은 양의 백혈구가 있다. 백혈구는 주로 신체를 돌보고 건강하게 유지시켜 준다. 백혈구는 항체를 형성해 질병과 싸우고 체내의 박테리아와 세균, 그 밖의 해로운 유기체들을 공격하는 데 도움을 준다. 혈소판은 혈관이 파괴되거나 손상되어 혈액의 흐름을 막거나 천천히 흐르게 해야 할 때마다 혈액을 응고시키는 작은 세포 조각이다.

이 모두가 혈액을 신체에서 가장 강력한 물질 중 하나로 만든다.

Reading Skills

Ⓐ

• Exercise 8 • ────────────────────── p.130

정답 Q1 Ⓒ Q2 Ⓒ Q3 Ⓐ Q4 Ⓐ

해석 뼈의 기능

사람이 태어날 때, 사람의 몸에는 대략 350개의 뼈가 있다. 성인이 되는 시기에는 일부 뼈들이 서로 합쳐지기 때문에 그 수가 약 206개 정도로 줄어든다. 전체적으로 뼈는 신체의 골격계를 형성한다. 뼈는 신체가 건강하면서 적절하게 작동하기 위해 반드시 수행해야 하는 5가지 기능을 가지고 있다.

뼈의 첫 번째 기능은 심장, 간, 폐, 신장 등 신체의 내부 장기를 보호하는 것이다. 쉽게 부상 당하지 않고 더 간편히 보호하기 위해서 많은 장기들이 뼈의 바로 뒤쪽에 위치해 있다. 한 예가 심장인데, 심장은 흉곽 바로 뒤에 자리잡고 있다.

뼈의 또 다른 기능은 사람의 몸을 이리저리 움직일 수 있게 함으로써 신체를 지탱하는 것이다. 뼈는 또한 신체의 근육이 뼈에 붙어 있게 한다. 근육이 없으면, 사람들은 움직이는 데 필요한 힘이 부족할 것이다.

뼈는 또한 신체의 혈액 세포를 만든다. 이것은 골수에서 이루어지는데, 골수는 다양한 뼈의 중간 공간에서 발견된다. 마지막으로 뼈는 체내에 흡수된 무기질, 즉 철분과 칼슘을 저장한다.

뼈 덕분에 사람들의 삶은 훨씬 더 수월하고, 더 나으며, 더 편안하다.

Reading Skills

Ⓑ

Grammar Point p.132

Grammar Check-Up

Ⓐ 1 ☑ The layers of the skin are the epidermis, the dermis, and subcutaneous fat.
   2 ☐ The bones protect the organs, support the body, and are making bone marrow.
   3 ☐ Some of the teeth are premolars, bicuspids, and there are wisdom teeth.
   4 ☐ Sneezing, kicking, and to cough are some involuntary reflexes.
   5 ☑ The digestive system moves food through the body, processes it, and removes it from the body.

Ⓑ 1 the intestines
   2 goes
   3 fingers
   4 move
   5 connecting

Ⓒ 1 ⓑ 2 ⓑ 3 ⓓ 4 ⓑ 5 ⓒ

Vocabulary Review p.134

Ⓐ 1 benign
   2 centrifuge
   3 pumps
   4 enable
   5 Melanin

Ⓑ 1 Ⓑ 2 Ⓐ 3 Ⓐ 4 Ⓒ 5 Ⓓ

Ⓒ 1 Ⓑ 2 Ⓒ 3 Ⓓ 4 Ⓐ 5 Ⓐ

Ⓓ 1 organs
   2 swallow
   3 digestive
   4 cells
   5 mutated

Practice Test p.136

1 Ⓓ 2 Ⓐ 3 Ⓓ 4 Ⓒ 5 Ⓑ 6 Ⓐ
7 Ⓑ 8 Ⓑ 9 ❷ 10 ②, ③, ④

해석 유당 불내증

어떤 사람들은 우유를 마시지 못한다. 또한 치즈와 요구르트, 그리고 우유가 포함된 다른 제품들도 먹지 못한다. 이러한 유제품을 섭취하는 경우, 이들은 다양한 문제를 겪을 수 있다. 여기에는 설사, 메스꺼움, 위경련, 구토 등이 포함된다. 이러한 사람들은 유당 불내증을 겪고 있는 것이다.

유당은 우유에서 발견되는 당이다. 소장에서 효소의 일종인 락타아제가 생성된다. 이것이 유당을 소화시키는 역할을 한다. 하지만 모든 사람의 신체에서 충분한 양의 락타아제가 만들어지는 것은 아니다. 이 때문에 사람들이 유당 불내증을 겪게 된다. 충분한 양의 락타아제가 만들어지지 않으면 신체는 유당을 처리하지 못한다. 대신에 유당이 결장으로 이동을 하는데, 여기에서 박테리아와 상호 작용을 하게 된다. 이곳에서 유당 불내증의 증상들이 생성된다.

학자들은 유당 불내증이 유아와 어린이에게는 거의 나타나지 않는 문제라는 점을 밝혀냈다. 대신 이것은 보통 성년기의 사람들에게서 나타난다. 또한 유럽인들보다는 아프리카계, 아시아계, 히스패닉계 사람들, 그리고 아메리카 원주민의 혈통이 유당 불내증에 걸릴 가능성이 더 높다.

유당 불내증을 겪는 많은 사람들이 충분한 양의 칼슘을 섭취하지 못할까 봐 염려한다. (이것은 뼈와 치아에 모두 도움이 되는 무기질이다.) 다행히도 그들은 보충제를 섭취해도 된다. 또한 오늘날 많은 식품들이 유당 불내증을 겪는 사람들을 위해 만들어지고 있다. 심지어 많은 식료품점에서 유당이 없는 우유를 구입할 수도 있다. 사람들은 또한 아몬드 우유와 두유 등의 대체 식품을 섭취한다. 따라서 유당 불내증 때문에 생활 습관을 크게 바꿀 필요는 없다.

CHAPTER 6 Archaeology

Understanding TOEFL Question Types & Reading Skills
p.140

1 Question Types ▶ Sample Question
Ⓑ

해석 **아마추어 고고학자들**

전문적인 고고학자들은 이따금 어느 정도의 화려함과 명성을 얻기도 합니다. 그러나 거의 그들만큼 중요한 이들이 있는데, 바로 이름이 알려져 있지 않은 아마추어 고고학자들이다. 아마추어 고고학자들이 없다면, 많은 고고학적 발굴이 이루어지지 못할 것이다.

아마추어 고고학자들은 많은 경우 취미로 즐기는 사람들이다. 그들은 그저 고고학에 관심이 있는 사람들일 수도 있다. 아마 그들은 대학에서 고고학을 전공했거나 나중에 어느 시점에 고고학을 다시 시작했을지도 모른다. 그러나 그들이 다양한 채굴과 발굴에 값진 조력을 제공하는 경우는 빈번하다.

대부분의 고고학적 발굴을 위한 자금은 부족하다. 그에 반해 고고학은 노동 집약적이다. 따라서 많은 아마추어 고고학자들이 발굴에 자비를 부담한다. 그들은 자원봉사를 하기 때문에 보수를 받지 않고 오랜 시간 동안 작업한다. 어떤 사람들은 매우 숙련되고 지식이 풍부해지기도 하지만, 그들은 거의 늘 무명으로 남는다.

2 Reading Skills ▶ Check-Up
Ⓒ

• Exercise 1 •
p.142

정답 Q1 Ⓑ   Q2 Ⓒ   Q3 Ⓒ

해석 **모헨조다로**

4대 초기 인류 문명의 발생은 메소포타미아, 이집트, 중국, 그리고 인더스강 계곡에서 이루어졌다. 인더스강 주변의 문명은 기원전 3300년 무렵에 시작되었다. 이는 기원전 1300년경까지 유지되었다. 기원전 2500년 무렵, 이 문명에서 가장 거대한 도시가 세워졌다. 그곳은 모헨조다로라고 불렸다.

이 고대 도시에 대한 첫 번째 발굴은 1922년에 이루어졌다. 그 이후로 그곳에 관한 많은 것이 밝혀졌다. 이 도시는 정확한 격자 모양으로 설계되었다. 홍수로 불어난 인더스강의 강물로부터 도시를 보호하기 위한 장벽을 갖추고 있었다. 도시 내에는 성채가 있었다. 이곳은 다른 곳보다 더 높게 지어졌다. 이곳은 도시의 통치 기관이 있었던 곳으로 여겨진다. 그곳에서는 또한 종교적인 기능도 수행했을 가능성이 있다.

많은 주택들이 2층으로 이루어져 있었고 욕실을 구비하고 있었다. 위생을 위한 배수구와 하수구는, 로마 시대 이전에는 갖추고 있던 곳이 거의 없던 시설이었는데, 그곳에서 발굴되었다. 이는 모헨조다로의 주민들이 당시로서는 매우 진보했음을 암시한다.

Reading Skills
Ⓐ

• Exercise 2 •
p.144

정답 Q1 Ⓑ   Q2 Ⓑ   Q3 Ⓐ

해석 **스톤헨지의 축조**

과거에 고대 문화들은 몇 가지 놀라운 공학적 업적들을 이루었다. 이 중 하나가 영국 솔즈베리 근처에 위치한 스톤헨지에 오늘날까지 남아 있다. 오늘날 스톤헨지에 남아 있는 것은 원형으로 늘어선 수많은 돌 기둥들이다.

스톤헨지의 축조는 기원전 3100년경에 시작되었다. 그러나 그 기념비는 오늘날 남아 있는 거대한 돌들이 아닌 목재를 사용하여 세워졌다. 기원전 2500경에 돌을 사용하여 스톤헨지는 다시 지어졌다. 어떤 돌은 무게가 5톤이 넘을 만큼 어마어마하게 컸다. 이러한 돌들은 거의 250마일이나 떨어진 웨일즈의 한 지방에서 온 것이어서 이 점이 고고학자들을 놀라게 하고 있다.

마지막으로 기원전 2300년에 스톤헨지는 다시 한 번 개조되었다. 오늘날 볼 수 있는 유적은 세 번째 시기의 것들이다. 어떤 것은 무게가 45톤에 이르는 등 훨씬 더 큰 돌들이 사용되었다. 놀랍게도 이 돌들 중 어떤 것은 겹겹이 놓여 있다. 고대 브리튼 시대의 사람들이 어떻게 이것을 해냈는지는 아무도 확실하게 알지 못한다. 그것은 앞으로 고고학자들이 풀어야 할 수수께끼이다.

Reading Skills
Ⓑ

• Exercise 3 •
p.146

정답 Q1 Ⓑ   Q2 Ⓐ   Q3 Ⓒ

해석 **앙코르 유적지**

대부분의 고대 유적지에 대한 발견은 몇 개월 혹은 몇 년의 주의 깊은 연구 끝에 이루어진다. 그러나 때로는 단순히 사람들이 우연히 발견하기도 한다. 캄보디아의 정글 속 거대한 사원 단지인 앙코르와트가 그러한 경우였다.

19세기에 프랑스인들은 캄보디아를 식민지화했다. 그들은 이따금 정글 속 사라진 사원 혹은 건축물에 대한 소문을 들었으나 대부분은 그것에 대해 믿지 않았다. 그러나 1860년, 몇몇 프랑스 선교사들이 씨엠립시 근처에서 그곳을 발견하였다. 발견된 것은 15세기에 사라진 크메르 제국의 유적지로 믿을 수 없을 만큼 잘 보존되어 있었다.

많은 건물들이 여전히 위용을 자랑하고 있다. 그중 가장 인상적인 것은 앙코르와트로, 그 크기가 약 가로 4,900피트, 세로 4,200피트에 이르는 피라미드 모양의 거대한 건축물이다. 그것은 크메르 건축의 가장 위대한 본보기이다.

오늘날 고고학자들은 1,100평방마일 이상의 면적에 이르는 앙코르 지역을 계속 탐험하고 있다. 연구를 통해, 그들은 오래 전에 사라진 크메르 왕국과 그 건축물들에 대해 계속해서 알아내고 있다.

Reading Skills
Ⓓ

• Exercise 4 •
p.148

정답 Q1 Ⓒ   Q2 Ⓐ   Q3 Ⓑ

해석 **수중 고고학**

사람들은 고고학자라고 하면 종종 사막이나 정글에서 발굴을 수행하는 모습을 떠올린다. 물론 이런 경우가 흔하게 발생하지만, 고고학자들이 과거의 유적을 찾는 장소가 한 곳 더 있다: 바로 물속이다.

난파선은 수중 고고학을 수행하는 중요한 현장이다. 그중 가장 유명한 것은 북대서양 깊은 곳에 위치한 *타이타닉*호이다. 하지만 다른 중요한 현장들도 많이 있다. 고대 난파선을 탐험함으로써 고고학자들은 그 배가 항해하던 시대의 문화에 대해서 알 수 있다. 게다가 때로는 선박 자체가 매우 가치 있는 경우도 있다. 예를 들어 초창기 잠수함인 *헌리*호는 역사학자들에 의해 복원되고 조사되었다.

때로는 심지어 수중에 묻힌 건물들이 발견되기도 한다. 그 건물들은 지진 때문에 혹은 심지어 강줄기의 변화로 인해 물속으로 사라졌을 가능성이 있다. 실제로 이집트에 위치했던, 그 유명한 알렉산드리아 도서관은 그 유적의 일부가 지중해에서 발견되고 있다. 이 외에도 이와 같은 많은 건물들이 또한 수중 무덤 속에 있으며 발굴되길 기다리고 있다.

Reading Skills
Ⓓ

• Exercise 5 • ——————————— p.150

정답 Q1 Ⓓ   Q2 Ⓒ   Q3 Ⓑ   Q4 Ⓒ

해석 **고고학적인 방법들**

현대 영화들은 인디아나 존스와 앨런 쿼터메인과 같이, 두 시간이 채 안 되는 시간 동안 세계를 돌아다니며, 악당들과 싸우고, 보물을 찾아 발견하는 용감한 고고학자들을 보여준다. 그러나 실제 고고학자들은 이러한 것들을 찾을 때 전혀 다른 방법들을 사용한다.

첫째로, 고고학자들은 현장으로 나가기에 앞서 많은 시간을 들여 연구를 수행해야 한다. 이는 도서관과 교회 그리고 기록이 보존되어 있는 그 외 다른 장소들에서 이루어질 수 있다. 고고학자들은 보통 고대 언어를 배워야 한다. 지중해와 같은 언어 집약적인 지역에 대해 연구하려면 몇 가지 고대 언어들을 반드시 알아야 한다.

무엇을 찾을지 알게 되면, 고고학자들은 어디를 발굴해야 할지 결정해야 한다. 어떤 면에서, 그들은 고대인들처럼 생각해야 한다. 고고학자들은 그들이라면 자신들의 도시나 다른 장소들을 어디에 세웠을지 잘 생각해 볼 필요가 있다. 그러고 나면 발굴을 시작할 수 있다.

고고학자들이 발굴을 하는 동안 무언가를 발견하게 된다면 그들은 굉장히 조심해야 한다. 현장에서 작업을 하면서 발굴하고 있는 유물을 파괴하지 않도록 주의를 기울여야 한다. 연구실과 사무실로 돌아간 이후에는 발견한 유물에 대해 분석을 해야 한다. 신중한 분석을 통해야, 이 물건들의 의미가 밝혀지거나 최소한 짐작이라도 할 수 있을 것이다. 그러므로 고고학자들의 삶은 화려하지 않으며, 그들은 굉장히 바쁜 직업을 가지고 있다.

Reading Skills
Ⓐ

• Exercise 6 • ——————————— p.152

정답 Q1 Ⓒ   Q2 Ⓑ   Q3 Ⓒ   Q4 Ⓓ

해석 **하인리히 슐리만**

일반적으로 사람들은 고고학자들의 이름을 거의 알지 못한다. 그들은 열심히 일하지만 여전히 알려지지 않는 경우가 많다. 그러나 하인리히 슐리만은 고고학 분야에서 많은 사람들이 들어 본 이름이다.

정확히 말하면 전문적인 고고학자는 아니었지만, 슐리만은 현장에서 많은 성과를 이루어 냈다. 그는 사실상 보물 사냥꾼에 가까웠다. 그는 또한 *일리아스*와 *오디세이아*를 쓴 그리스의 시인 호머에 관심이 아주 많았는데, *일리아스*와 *오디세이아*는 트로이 전쟁 그리고 오디세우스가 트로이에서 고향으로 돌아오는 10년 동안의 여정에 대한 두 편의 위대한 서사시이다. 대부분의 사람들은 이 서사시들이 트로이를 신화 속의 장소로 묘사한다고 생각했다. 슐리만은 다르게 생각했다.

1868년, 그는 튀르키예의 히살릭이라는 도시가 호머의 트로이 유적 위에 자리잡고 있다고 확신하게 되었다. 1871년에 그는 그곳을 발굴하기 시작했고, 1873년, 엄청난 양의 보물을 발견했다. 그는 너무나 기뻐서 이것을 트로이의 전설 속 통치자, 프리아모스왕의 이름을 따 "프리아모스의 보물"이라고 불렀다. 이 일은 슐리만에게 전 세계적으로 엄청난 명성을 가져다 주었다.

슐리만은 후에 그리스에서 추가 발굴 작업을 진행하려고 했다. 그는 역사 속의 오디세우스를 찾는 데 관심을 가졌다. 그러나 그는 전혀 발견되지 않았다. 이후에 그는 튀르키예로 돌아가 계속해서 트로이를 발굴하였다. 그러나 그가 고대 트로이를 발견했다고 처음 공표했을 때 얻은 명성은 결코 되찾지 못했다.

Reading Skills
Ⓒ

• Exercise 7 • ——————————— p.154

정답 Q1 Ⓓ   Q2 Ⓓ   Q3 Ⓓ   Q4 Ⓐ

해석 **폼페이**

서기 79년 8월 24일, 폼페이 도시에 중대한 사건이 일어났다: 도시가 사라진 것이다. 폼페이는 로마 제국의 한 도시였다. 그곳은 지금의 이탈리아 나폴리 가까이에 위치해 있었다. 불행하게도 폼페이는 화산인 베수비오산 아래쪽에 위치해 있었다. 베수비오산이 갑자기 활동을 시작한 이틀 동안 도시는 완전히 파괴되었다. 거의 1,700년 동안 폼페이는 잊혀졌다.

그러다 1748년에 그곳이 우연히 다시 발견되었다. 이것은 고고학자들에게 엄청난 사건이었다. 그 이유는 베수비오산이 너무나 빠른 속도로 분출해서 폼페이의 시민들이 탈출할 시간이 없었기 때문이었다. 많은 사람들이 그들이 서 있던 바로 그 자리에서 죽었다. 그 화산은 또한 엄청난 양의 화산재로 도시를 뒤덮어 폼페이는 거의 완전하게 보존되어 있었다.

이렇게 보존된 덕택에, 고고학자들은 실제 한 로마 도시가 한때 어떤 모습이었는지를 연구할 수 있게 되었다. 실제로 많은 건물들이 완전히 그대로이다. 오늘날에도 고고학자들은 로마 제국에 대해 더 많은 것들을 알아내기 위해 여전히 건물들을 발굴하고 있다. 폼페이는 또한, 한때 평화로웠던 이 도시의 유적을 보기 위해 매년 약 250만 명의 방문객이 찾는 인기 있는 관광지이다.

Reading Skills
Ⓑ

• Exercise 8 • ——————————— p.156

정답 Q1 Ⓒ   Q2 Ⓒ   Q3 Ⓑ   Q4 Ⓒ

해석 **고고학의 도구들**

유물을 발굴할 때, 고고학자들은 최대한 정확해야 한다. 이러한 이유로 그들은 삽보다 큰 것은 무엇이든 거의 절대 사용하지 않는다. 무엇보다도 고고학자는 가능한 한 훼손을 최소화하면서 최대한 정밀하게 현장을 발굴하는 데 관심을 기울여야 한다. 그래서 발굴자는 발굴 현장에서 여러 다양한 도구들을 사용한다.

고고학자들은 훼손될 만한 유물이 없는 지역을 발굴할 때는 삽을 사용한다. 삽으로는 중요한 지점에 가능한 한 빠르게 도달할 수 있게 된다. 그러나 일단 토양의 일정한 층에 도달하면 그들은 좀 더 꼼꼼하게 작업하기 위해 파는 속도를 늦춘다. 이때 다른 도구가 필요하다.

가장 일반적인 것이 모종삽이다. 이 작은 도구로 발굴자들은 자신이 하고 있는 일을 살피면서 땅을 아주 조금씩 팔 수 있다. 모종삽을 사용하면 고고학자들은 땅을 너무 많이 뒤집어 엎지 못한다. 발견된 유물이 있다면 고고학자들은 그것을 훼손하지 않도록 훨씬 더 작은 도구로 교체한다. 이러한 도구들로는 숟가락, 솔, 심지어는 이쑤시개 등이 있다. 그에 따라 자연스럽게 발굴 속도는 눈에 띄게 느려진다. 그러나 이렇게 함으로써 고고학자들은 삽으로 모든 것을 파기 시작한다고 가정할 때보다 훨씬 더 정확하게 현장을 복원할 수 있게 된다.

Reading Skills

Ⓒ

Grammar Point p.158

Grammar Check-Up

A
1. are many sites
2. was Vesuvius
3. were golden treasures
4. Did the archaeologist
5. are some hobbyists

B 1 ⓓ   2 ⓑ   3 ⓒ

C
1. ☐ So many shipwrecks remain hidden deep under the water.
2. ☐ Looking for Troy was the lifelong goal of Heinrich Schliemann.
3. ☑ As brave as Indiana Jones was Allan Quartermain.
4. ☑ So amazing is Stonehenge that people are still not sure how it was built.
5. ☑ Had Machu Picchu been found earlier, many of its buildings might have been looted by treasure hunters.

Vocabulary Review p.160

A
1. recover
2. utterly
3. relics
4. sanitation
5. hunters

B 1 Ⓑ   2 Ⓒ   3 Ⓐ   4 Ⓒ   5 Ⓑ

C 1 Ⓑ   2 Ⓒ   3 Ⓐ   4 Ⓓ   5 Ⓐ

D
1. momentous
2. precise
3. graves
4. ancient
5. shipwrecks

Practice Test p.162

1 Ⓑ   2 Ⓓ   3 Ⓑ   4 Ⓒ   5 Ⓑ   6 Ⓐ
7 Ⓐ   8 Ⓑ   9 ❹   10 ②, ⑤, ⑥

해석 왕가의 계곡

고대 이집트의 도시인 테베는 이집트의 남부에 위치해 있었다. 오늘날 같은 자리에는 현대 도시인 룩소르가 자리잡고 있다. 도시 옆을 흐르는 나일강의 서쪽에는 왕가의 계곡이 있다. 이곳은 500년이 넘는 기간 동안 많은 파라오와 귀족들의 안식처였다.

기원전 1500년경 이집트인들은 피라미드 건설을 중단했다. 그 전에는 피라미드가 무덤으로 사용되었다. 하지만 쉽게 발견이 되었기 때문에 도적들이 종종 이곳을 약탈해서 보물을 훔쳐 갔다. 그 결과 이집트인들은 왕가의 계곡에 있는 산비탈에 무덤을 파기 시작했다.

지금까지 60개 이상의 무덤이 발견되었다. 어떤 것들은 크기가 작지만, 수백 피트에 이르면서 수많은 복도와 방을 갖춘 것들도 있다. 하트셉수트 여왕의 무덤은 입구에서 700피트 이상 떨어진 곳에서 발견되었다. (이곳은 지금껏 발견된 것 중 가장 길다.) 파라오인 람세스 1세, 람세스 2세, 아멘호테프 1세가 이곳에 매장되었다. 안타깝게도 이곳 대부분의 무덤들은 보물들을 도굴 당했다. 하지만 1992년에 하워드 카터가 킹 투트라고도 알려져 있는, 파라오 투탕카멘의 무덤을 발견했다. 그의 무덤은 대부분 그대로였으며 엄청난 양의 보물들이 그 안에 있었다.

보물은 없더라도 많은 무덤들에 벽화가 있었다. 이 벽화들은 고고학자들이 고대 이집트에서 일어난 일들을 이해하는 데 도움을 주고 있다. 킹 투트의 보물들 역시 고고학자들에게 많은 것들을 알려주고 있다. 또한 이러한 물건들로 인해 더 많은 사람들이 고대 이집트에 관심을 가지게 되었고 그 결과 더 많은 발굴이 이루어지도록 촉진하고 있다.

CHAPTER 7 Physics

Understanding TOEFL Question Types & Reading Skills p.166

① Question Types ▶ Sample Question

Ⓑ

해석 벤저민 프랭클린

대부분의 사람들이 미국 건국의 아버지 중 한 사람이었던 벤저민 프랭클린을 물리학과 연관시키지 않는다. 그러나 프랭클린은 미국에 많은 공헌을 하였을 뿐만 아니라 미국 최초의 물리학자이기도 했다.

1750년대에 프랭클린은 번개에 대해 생각하기 시작했다. 그가 천둥번개가 치는 폭풍우 속에서 연을 날렸다는 일화는 유명하다. 프랭클린은 연줄에 금속 열쇠를 매단 다음 금속 줄을 열쇠에서 항아리로 연결해 두었다. 번개가 연을 강타했을 때 그가 열쇠를 만지자 그는 충격을 느꼈다. 이 실험으로 프랭클린은 번개의 성질에 대해 자신이 의심했던 바가 옳았으며 번개가 실제로는 정전기라는 것을 증명했다. 그는 또한 전기가 양극과 음극을 모두를 띠고 있다는 것을 실험으로 증명했다.

2 Reading Skills ▶ Check-Up
When

• **Exercise 1** • ─────────── p.168

정답 Q1 Ⓓ Q2 Ⓑ Q3 ❷

해석 **단순 기계들**

물리학자들은 주로 우주의 각 물체가 다른 물체에 직간접적으로 미치는 두 영향에 대해 관심을 가지고 있다. 사람들은 또한 종종 기계를 사용하여 다른 물체에 직접적으로 영향을 미친다. 거의 모든 기계들은 지렛대, 경사면, 쐐기, 나사, 바퀴와 축, 도르래라는 6가지 종류의 단순 기계들이 복잡하게 변형된 것이다.

단순 기계들은 다양한 방식으로 작동하며 일을 좀 더 간단하고 어렵지 않게 만든다. 단순 기계들은 또한 움직이는 부분이 극히 적거나 아예 없고, 대신에 에너지의 도움을 받아 작동한다. 이 세상 구석구석에서 사용되고 있는 기계들을 보면 단순 기계들을 수없이 많이 볼 수 있다.

대부분의 건물 앞에 있는 휠체어 경사로는 경사면이다. 롤러 스케이트를 타는 사람들은 바퀴와 축을 사용하고 있다. (사람들이 매일 타는 엘리베이터 또한 바퀴와 축의 도움을 받아 사람들을 위아래로 수송한다.) 심지어 놀이터에서 시소를 타는 아이들조차도 지렛대를 사용하고 있는 것이다. 이러한 단순 기계들과 그것으로 만들어진 더 복잡한 발명품들 덕분에 사람들의 삶은 훨씬 덜 복잡해지고 있다.

Reading Skills
Ⓑ

• **Exercise 2** • ─────────── p.170

정답 Q1 ❷ Q2 ❶ Q3 Ⓒ

해석 **중력**

사람이 무언가를 공중으로 던지면 그것은 올라가긴 하지만 그러고 나서 땅으로 다시 떨어진다. (그 물체가 아무리 높이 올라가더라도, 여전히 결국에는 다시 내려올 것이다.) 마찬가지로 사람이 높은 구조물에서 무언가를 떨어뜨리면, 그것은 계속해서 떨어지고 결국 땅에 도달할 것이다. 이런 일이 발생하는 이유는 중력 때문이다.

중력은 만유인력의 법칙을 생각해 낸 아이작 뉴턴 경에 의해 처음으로 설명되었다. (일화에 따르면, 그는 사과 하나가 나무에서 떨어져 그 아래에 있던 그의 머리를 때렸을 때 중력의 법칙을 생각해 냈다.) 본질적으로 그는 우주의 모든 물체는 다른 모든 물체를 끌어당긴다고 생각했다. 그러나 그 인력의 세기는 물체가 얼마나 큰가 그리고 다른 물체와 얼마나 가까이에 있는가에 따라 달라진다고 생각했다. 이것은 곧 태양이 지구에 대해 강력한 인력을 가지고 있을 것이며, 그 인력작용은 더 멀리 떨어져 있는 토성에 대해서는 좀 더 약하다는 것을 의미했다.

애석하게도 과학자들은 아직까지 왜 각각의 원자가 다른 모든 원자를 끌어당기는지는 규명하지 못했다. 이것에 대해 몇 가지 이론들이 있으나 아무것도 과학계에 완전히 받아들여지지는 않고 있다. 따라서 물리학자들은 이 질문에 대한 답을 계속해서 찾고 있다.

Reading Skills

1 if 2 but

• **Exercise 3** • ─────────── p.172

정답 Q1 Ⓒ Q2 ❷ Q3 Ⓑ

해석 **탈출 속도**

어떤 사람이 공중으로 공을 던지면 그 공은 일정한 높이까지 올라가서 정지한 다음에 땅으로 떨어진다. 그러한 이유는 지구의 중력 때문인데, 중력이 공중에 있는 물체를 끌어당겨서 떨어지게 만든다. 국가들이 우주로 로켓을 보내기를 기대하기 시작했을 때 그들은 중력에 대해 신경 써야만 했다.

지구의 중력이 끌어당기는 힘을 벗어나기 위해서는 물체의 속도가 초속 11.2 킬로미터에 이르러야 한다. (그것은 음속의 30배 이상에 해당한다.) 이는 탈출 속도라고 알려져 있다. 이러한 속도에 도달하는 물체는 더 이상 지면으로 떨어지지 않고 우주로 날아갈 수 있다.

그러한 속도를 얻기 위해서는 막대한 양의 연료가 필요한데, 이것이 바로 로켓이 그처럼 커다란 주된 이유이다. 로켓이 탈출 속도에 도달하게 되려면 충분한 연료를 가지고 가야 한다. 우주비행사들을 달로 수송한 새턴 5호 로켓은 크기가 엄청났다. 그 거대한 크기 덕분에 이 로켓은 많은 적재물을 싣고도 탈출 속도에 도달했다.

Reading Skills
Ⓐ

• **Exercise 4** • ─────────── p.174

정답 Q1 Ⓒ Q2 ❸ Q3 ❷

해석 **물리학의 실용적인 적용**

물리학의 분야는 아주 광범위한 주제들을 다룬다. 빛, 전기, 자기, 심지어는 우주까지 포함하고 있다. 많은 물리학자들에 의해 이루어지는 연구는 너무나 복잡하고 대개는 대부분의 사람들이 이해하기 어렵다. 그러나 그들의 연구와 발견이 현대 세계를 오늘날만큼 진보할 수 있도록 도와주고 있다.

한 가지 예로, 물리학의 발전 없이는 텔레비전, 라디오, 컴퓨터, 또는 냉장고도 없을 것이다. 사람들이 소유하고 있는 그 밖의 모든 가전 제품들 또한 없을 것이다. (여기에는 토스터기, 다리미, 전자레인지 등이 포함된다.) 그 이유는 이러한 기계들이 모두 전기로 작동하며, 물리학자들이 전기에 대해 많은 발견을 이루고 있기 때문이다.

마찬가지로 인공위성과 사람을 모두 우주로 보내는 우주 프로그램도 물리학이 없이는 존재할 수 없을 것이다. 인공위성이 없다면 현대의 전기통신은 완전히 달라질 것이다. (우선 아무도 휴대전화와 같은 무선 도구를 사용하여 통신할 수 없을 것이다.) 이들은 물리학을 통해 가능해지고 있는 진보의 일부에 지나지 않는다. 미래에는 물리학자들 덕분에 확실히 사람들의 삶의 질이 훨씬 더 많이 향상될 것이다.

Reading Skills

1 However 2 Nor

• Exercise 5 • p.176

정답 Q1 １ Q2 Ⓑ Q3 ４ Q4 Ⓐ

해석 **아이작 뉴턴 경**

17세기와 18세기에 살았던 아이작 뉴턴 경은 초기 현대 시대의 가장 위대한 과학자였다. (그는 심지어 코페르니쿠스와 갈릴레오 같은 과학자들보다 훨씬 더 위대했다.) 사실 많은 사람들이 그를 현대 물리학의 아버지라고 부른다. 많은 것이 있었지만 그의 업적 중에서도 특히 두드러지는 것이 하나 있다. 바로 세 가지 운동법칙을 발표한 것이었다.

뉴턴의 운동 제1법칙은 관성의 법칙이라고 불리는데, 정지되어 있는 물체는 외부의 힘이 가해져 움직이기 전까지는 정지된 상태로 남아 있으려 한다는 것을 설명한다. 이것은 단지 물체가 스스로 움직이지 않으며 그것을 움직이게 하려면 무언가가 필요하다는 것을 의미한다. 제2법칙은 가장 중요한데, 이를 이용하여 다양한 물체의 역학을 계산할 수 있기 때문이다. 그 법칙은 물체의 힘이 가속도에 의해 증가된 물체의 질량과 같다는 것을 수학적인 용어로 설명한다. (심지어 한 물체가 얼마나 많은 힘을 가지고 있는지를 계산하게 해 주는 비교적 간단한 수학 방정식도 있다.) 마지막으로 제3법칙은 모든 작용에는 그와 동일한 반작용이 있다는 점을 설명하고 있다. 이 법칙 덕분에 물리학자들은 수많은 현상들을 설명할 수 있게 되었고 그중 하나가 비행기가 나는 원리에 관한 것이다.

이러한 세 가지 운동법칙은 세계에 대해 많은 것을 설명하도록 도와주었다. 뉴턴의 발견 때문에 세계는 그곳에 사는 사람들에게 훨씬 더 명확해졌다.

Reading Skills

Ⓓ

• Exercise 6 • p.178

정답 Q1 Ⓑ Q2 ４ Q3 Ⓓ Q4 ３

해석 **맨해튼 프로젝트**

1930년대, 세계는 전쟁으로 치닫고 있었다. 독일, 이탈리아, 일본의 억압 통치는 그 세력을 확장하려고 애쓰고 있었다. 게다가 1939년, 나치 독일이 원자폭탄 개발 방법을 발견하는 데 기대를 걸고 있다는 소문이 돌았다. 이 폭탄은 어마어마하게 강력한 폭발을 일으킬 수 있는 원자의 힘을 이용할 것이었다. 나치에 맞서기 위하여 미국은 1급 기밀로 맨해튼 프로젝트에 착수하기 시작했다. (이것은 결국 인류가 그때까지 시도했던 가장 비싼 프로젝트가 되었다.)

맨해튼 프로젝트란 자력으로 원자폭탄을 만들려는 미국의 시도였다. 미국 국방성 장관이었던 레슬리 그로브스의 지휘 아래, 세계에서 가장 뛰어난 지식인들 중 몇몇이 그 프로젝트에 참여하기 시작했다. 이 사람들에는 프로젝트를 이끈 J. 로버트 오펜하이머와 엔리코 페르미, 글렌 시보그, 리처드 파인만 등이 포함되어 있었다. 많은 연구 기지들이 있었는데, 그중 시카고 대학교, 오크리지, 테네시, 로스앨러모스, 뉴멕시코에 있는 것들이 가장 중요했다.

1942년, 시카고의 몇몇 물리학자들이 최초의 핵반응을 이끌어냈다. 그 이후로 그들은 폭탄의 실마리인 우라늄과 플루토늄에 대해 많은 것을 알아냈다. 그 후 7월 16일, 뉴멕시코의 앨라모고도에서 A-폭탄이 터졌다. (한 달 후, 미국이 일본에 두 개의 원자폭탄을 투하함으로써 제2차 세계 대전이 끝나게 되었다.) 핵의 시대가 열린 것이다.

Reading Skills

1 but 2 After

• Exercise 7 • p.180

정답 Q1 ３ Q2 ２ Q3 Ⓑ Q4 Ⓐ

해석 **시간 여행**

시간 여행은 많은 공상 과학 소설과 영화에 흔히 등장한다. 그러나 물리학자들은 그것이 가능한지 그렇지 않은지에 대해서는 동의하지 못한다. (어떤 물리학자들은 그런 일이 일어날 것이라고 말하는 반면, 또 다른 물리학자들은 그 일이 결코 가능하지 않을 것이라고 주장한다.) 많은 물리학자들이 단순히 현재에 있는 사람이 미래에서 온 사람과 만난 적이 없다는 이유로 시간 여행은 불가능하다고 주장한다. 그들은 만약 그것이 가능하다면 미래에서 온 여행자들로 현대 사회가 넘쳐야 한다고 주장한다.

반면, 어떤 물리학자들은 시간 여행이 이론상으로는 가능하다고 주장한다. 그들은 여러 가지 다양한 방법으로 그것이 이루어질 수 있음에 주목한다. (안타깝게도, 그 방안들이 시간 여행이 가능하다고 보여준다더라도, 현대의 기술은 그에 요구되는 기계를 만들 수 없다.) 한 가지 방법은 어떤 사람이 빛의 속도보다 더 빠르게 여행하는 것인데, 빛의 속도는 초당 약 30만미터로 이동한다. 이만큼 빠른 속도에 이르러야 사람은 시간을 거스를 수 있을 것이다. 그러나 현재 그 누구도 빛의 속도의 일부만큼이라도 가능한 기계를 발명하지 못했다.

어떤 물리학자들은 엄청나게 강한 중력이 작용하는 거대한 우주 공간인 블랙홀을 통해 여행하면 사람들이 시간 여행을 하게 될 거라고 믿는다. 마찬가지로 또 다른 물리학자들은 웜홀의 존재를 상정하는데, 웜홀은 근본적으로 사람들을 항성계에서 항성계로 이동시켜 줄 우주의 지름길이다. 지금으로서는 이러한 생각들은 모두 이론적인 것이며 꿈으로만 남아 있다.

Reading Skills

Ⓑ

• Exercise 8 • p.182

정답 Q1 Ⓒ Q2 ２ Q3 １ Q4 Ⓐ

해석 **알베르트 아인슈타인**

역사적으로 뛰어난 물리학자들이 많이 있어 왔지만 알베르트 아인슈타인만큼 똑똑한 사람은 거의 없었다. 그는 1879년에 독일에서 태어났는데, 그의 유년기는 그가 그렇게 위대해질 운명이라는 것을 보여주지 않았다. (사실, 아인슈타인은 물리학 수업에서 매우 나쁜 점수를 받은 일화로 유명하다.) 그는 1901년에 스위스의 특허 사무실에서 직장을 얻었고, 나머지 일생을 그곳에서 보내는 것처럼 보였다. 그러나 아인슈타인은 동시에 박사 과정을 밟았고, 1905년에 박사학위를 땄다. 그 이후 그는 전 세계를 깜짝 놀라게 한 많은 발견을 해냈다.

물리학의 여러 분야에 대해 연구하면서 아인슈타인은 물리학계를 뒤집을 만한 많은 결정적인 논문들을 발표했다. (바로 여러 다른 분야를 연구하는 이러한 능력이 그를 유명하게 만들어 주었다.) 그 첫 번째가 1905년, 공간과 시간을 다룬 특수 상대성 이론에 대한 그의 논문이었다. 이어서 1916년에는 일반 상대성 이론에 대한 연구를 연달아 발표했다. 아인슈타인은 또한 역학과 전자기학 분야도 연구했다. 그가 다룬 또 다른 물리학 분야는 빛이었다.

자타가 공인한 평화주의자였던 아인슈타인은 나치가 정권을 장악했을 때, 독일을 떠났다. 전쟁을 증오하였음에도 불구하고, 원자폭탄의 탄생을 이끌 연구를 시작하도록 미국 대통령 프랭클린 D. 루즈벨트를 설득한 것은 바로 그에게 보낸 아인슈타인의 편지였다.

Reading Skills
1 yet   2 and

Grammar Point   p.184

Grammar Check-Up

A   1 who
    2 which
    3 whose
    4 whom
    5 that

B   1 ⓒ   2 ⓐ   3 ⓑ   4 ⓑ

C   who, which, whose, that, whom

Vocabulary Review   p.186

A   1 shortcut
    2 theoretically
    3 axle
    4 doctorate
    5 dropped

B   1 ⓒ   2 ⓓ   3 ⓑ   4 ⓒ   5 ⓐ

C   1 ⓒ   2 ⓐ   3 ⓓ   4 ⓒ   5 ⓑ

D   1 key
    2 telecommunications
    3 calculate
    4 proved
    5 regime

Practice Test   p.188

1 ⓐ   2 ⓒ   3 ⓐ   4 ⓒ   5 ⓑ
6 ⓐ   7 ⓓ   8 ⓑ   9 4
10 Kinetic energy: 2, 7   Potential energy: 1, 3, 6

해석   운동 에너지와 위치 에너지

에너지는 일을 할 수 있는 능력을 가리킨다. 에너지는 두 가지 유형으로 존재한다: 바로 운동 에너지와 위치 에너지이다. 운동 에너지는 물체의 움직임에 의해 생성되는 에너지를 가리킨다. 위치 에너지는 물체의 위치와 관련된 에너지를 가리킨다.

두 유형의 에너지 모두에 대한 수많은 예가 존재한다. 예컨대 강물을 막는 댐 뒤에는 저수지가 만들어진다. 이처럼 저장된 물은 막대한 양의 위치 에너지를 가지고 있다. 댐의 수문이 열리면 물이 흐르기 시작한다. 이 경우, 물은 움직이기 때문에 물의 위치 에너지가 운동 에너지로 바뀌게 된다. 그러면 물은 전기 생산에 이용될 수 있으며, 이러한 전기는 위치 에너지로 저장되어 이후에 사용될 수 있다.

또 다른 예는 롤러코스터이다. 롤러코스터는 매우 높은 곳까지 굴러 올라간 다음 빠르게 하강하는 것으로 알려져 있다. 롤러코스터가 선로의 가장 높은 지점에 도달하면 그것은 굉장히 많은 위치 에너지를 갖게 된다. 이러한 에너지는 롤러코스터의 무게와 그 안에 타고 있는 사람들의 무게는 물론 롤러코스터의 높이가 더해져 생긴다. 롤러코스터가 선로 아래를 향해 내려가면 위치 에너지는 운동 에너지가 된다.

세 번째 예로는 사람들이 먹는 음식이 있다. 음식에는 신체가 소화하고 사용할 수 있는 영양분이 포함되어 있다. 이는 음식에 위치 에너지가 포함되어 있다는 것을 의미한다. 신체가 음식물을 소화시키면 이는 근본적으로 에너지로 바뀐다. (이런 형태에서는, 운동 에너지로 여겨진다.) 이로 인해 사람들이 움직이고, 말하고, 생각하고, 기타 다른 활동들을 할 수 있다.

CHAPTER 8 Political Science

Understanding TOEFL Question Types & Reading Skills   p.192

1 Question Types ▶ Sample Question
ⓑ, ⓒ, ⓔ

해석   사회주의와 자본주의

20세기에는 두 정치 체제가 세력을 두고 경쟁했다. 바로 사회주의와 자본주의가 그것이었다.

사회주의하에서는 모든 것이 인민의 소유이다. 사유재산은 없다. 이론에 따르면 인민은 그들 자신이 아니라 공동체의 이익을 위해 일한다. 반면 자본주의하에서는 생산물과 땅에 대해 개인적인 소유권이 존재한다. 사람들은 이익을 얻기 위해 일하고, 그 이익을 사적으로 보유할 수도 있다. 또한 사회주의 정부는 억압적인 경향이 있지만, 자본주의 국가는 많은 경우에 민주주의를 실행하고 개인의 자유를 존중한다.

20세기에, 미국은 자본주의를 실행한 반면 소련은 사회주의 정부를 갖췄다. 사회주의가 가진 많은 결함들 때문에 소련은 붕괴했다. 그러나 미국은 자본주의의 우월성을 보여주며 세계의 패권을 차지하게 되었다.

2 Reading Skills ▶ Check-Up
land

• Exercise 1 •   p.194

정답 Q1 ⓐ, ⓒ, ⓔ
Q2 Reasons for its signing: ⓐ, ⓓ
Effects of its signing: ⓑ, ⓔ, ⓖ

해석   대헌장

많은 사람들이 미국 헌법을 역사상 가장 중요한 정치 문서 중 하나로 여긴다. 그러나 대헌장이 없었다면 미국 건국의 아버지들이 결코 헌법을 쓰지 못했을 것이다.

"대헌장"이라는 뜻의 라틴어인 마그나 카르타는 1215년에 서명되었다. 그것은 영국의 관습법을 발전시키는 데 일조했다. 이것은 후에 미국의 법에도 영향을 미쳤다. 대헌장은 기본적으로 영국 왕이 가지는 권력과 그렇지 않은 권력을 정확히 명시함으로써 영국 왕의 권한을 엄격하게 제한했다.

13세기 영국의 존 왕은 종종 자신의 권력을 남용했다. 귀족들은 근본적으로 힘을 합쳐 대헌장을 썼고, 왕이 그것에 서명하도록 했다. 그것은 왕의 권력을 제한했을 뿐만 아니라 귀족과 영국의 국민들을 보호하고 그들에게 일정한 권력을 주었다. 대헌장이 항상 시행되지는 않았지만, 오늘날에도 사람들은 세상에서 가장 중요한 정치 문서 중 하나로서 대헌장을 존중하고 있다.

Reading Skills

American law

• Exercise 2 • ─────────── p.196

정답 Q1 Ⓐ, Ⓒ, Ⓔ
Q2 Political situation: Ⓔ, Ⓖ   Ideal ruler: Ⓐ, Ⓓ, Ⓕ

해석 니콜로 마키아벨리

니콜로 마키아벨리는 르네상스 시대에 살았다. 1469년에 이탈리아의 플로렌스에서 태어난 마키아벨리는 군주가 어떻게 통치해야 하는가에 대한 논문인 *군주론*을 썼다.

마키아벨리는 이탈리아 북부에서 정치적으로 격동의 시기에 살았다. 힘 있는 도시 국가였던 플로렌스, 밀란, 베니스가 세력을 두고 끊임없이 경쟁하고 있었다. 그들은 또한 스페인, 신성 로마 제국, 프랑스와 로마 가톨릭 교회의 간섭을 받고 있었다. 마키아벨리는 이를 염두에 두고 *군주론*에서 그가 생각하는 이상적인 통치자를 묘사했다.

그는 통치자가 폭력을 사용하는 것을 용납할 수 있다고 여겼다. 그러나 그것은 극단적인 상황에서 이루어져야 한다. 마찬가지로 좋은 통치는 사유 재산과 국민의 재산을 존중해야 하며, 그것이 결과적으로 국가의 부를 증대시킬 것이라고 여겼다. 마지막으로 마키아벨리는 통치자가 절대적인 규칙 체계를 따를 필요가 없다고 생각했다. 국가의 최우선 이익을 염두에 둔다면 통치자는 때로 비도덕적으로 행동해도 된다고 생각했다. 이러한 사상으로 인해 "마키아벨리식" 개인이라는 개념이 생겨나게 되었다.

Reading Skills

immorally

• Exercise 3 • ─────────── p.198

정답 Q1 Ⓑ, Ⓓ, Ⓔ
Q2 Reasons for its creation: Ⓒ, Ⓕ
Rights it gives: Ⓐ, Ⓓ, Ⓖ

해석 권리장전

1789년, 미국은 헌법의 비준을 고려하고 있었다. 그렇게 함으로써 미국의 탄생이 이루어질 예정이었다. 그러나 많은 미국인들은 헌법에 대해 염려했다. 그들은 국민의 권리가 충분히 잘 명시되어 있지 않다고 생각했다. 그들 생각에는 정부가 나중에 권력을 남용할 가능성이 있었다. 그들은 미국 정부가 영국이 그랬던 것처럼 억압적이 될까 걱정했다. 그래서 헌법에 10가지 조항이 추가되었다. 이는 현재 권리장전이라고 불린다.

이 조항들은 미국 시민들에게 가장 중요한 권리들 중 일부에 해당한다. 제1조항은 시민에게 종교, 연설, 출판의 자유를 준다. 제2조항은 개인이 무기를 소유할 수 있는 권리를 준다. 대부분의 미국인들이 이 두 조항을 중요시한다. 나머지 여덟 개의 조항에는 배심 재판과 과도한 보석금 부과 방지에 대한 권리가 포함되어 있다. 제10조항 또한 연방 정부의 권력을 제한하여 각 주와 시민들에게 더 많은 권력을 주고 있다.

Reading Skills

jury

• Exercise 4 • ─────────── p.200

정답 Q1 Ⓐ, Ⓒ, Ⓓ
Q2 Cause: Ⓒ, Ⓔ   Effect: Ⓐ, Ⓑ, Ⓖ

해석 왕권 신수설

수 세기 전 유럽의 많은 나라들은 군주에 의해 지배되었다. 대부분의 경우 이러한 왕들은 절대적인 권력을 가지고 있었다. 따라서 왕은 자신의 영토에서 자신이 원하는 것은 무엇이든 할 수 있었다. 이렇게 할 수 있었던 이유는 왕권 신수설이라고 불리는 개념 때문이었다.

이 개념에 따르면 왕은 신에 의해 통치하도록 선택받았다. 그 결과, 왕은 오직 신에게만 응답했다. 왕의 영토에서 그의 말은 법이었고, 왕은 자신이 원하는 것을 할 수 있었다. 왕의 백성들이 왕에게 복종하고 그의 말에 순종하는 것은 당연했다.

서구에서 왕권은 중세 시대는 물론 그 이후까지 존재했다. 1600년대에는 그 정점에 도달했다. 영국과 프랑스의 통치자들은 왕권 신수설을 믿었다. 하지만 시간이 지나면서 사람들은 왕의 전제적인 통치에 반대하기 시작했다. 두 나라 모두에서 혁명이 일어났고, 그 결과 왕은 권력을 빼앗기고 심지어 목숨을 잃기도 했으며, 국민들에게 더 많은 권력이 주어졌다.

Reading Skills

revolutions

• Exercise 5 • ─────────── p.202

정답 Q1 Ⓑ, Ⓔ, Ⓕ
Q2 Reasons for writing: Ⓔ, Ⓖ
Influences on its writing: Ⓐ, Ⓑ, Ⓓ

해석 토머스 제퍼슨과 독립선언문

18세기의 식민지 미국에는 정치적 수완이 뛰어난 사람들이 많았다. 그들은 미국 혁명의 시작을 도왔고 미국이 대영제국으로부터 독립을 선언하도록 이끌었다. 1776년 7월 4일, 몇몇 주의 대표자들이 독립선언문에 서명함으로써 미국은 독립을 이루어 냈다. 이 문서를 쓴 사람이 토머스 제퍼슨이었다.

독립선언문은 미국이 독립을 선언하는 이유에 대해 나열했다. 그것은 영국의 조지 3세 왕의 폭정에 대해 언급했다. 또한 모든 인간이 "생명, 자유, 그리고 행복을 추구할 권리"를 가지고 있다고 공표했다. 마지막으로, 그 누구도 왕의 통치하에 삶을 지배 받아서는 안 된다고 명시했다.

제퍼슨은 이 문서를 쓰면서 많은 사람들의 영향을 받았다. 그의 글의 많은 부분이 *통치론*을 비롯하여 많은 저서를 쓴 철학자 존 로크에게서 영감을 받았다. 상식의 저자 토머스 페인의 저술들도 역시 제퍼슨에게 여러 사상을 제공하는 데 도움을 주었다. 제퍼슨은 독립선언문을 완성하기 위해 1689년에 만들어진 영국의 권리장전의 일부를 사용하기도 했다. 이 모든 것이 합쳐져, 제퍼슨은 현대 시대에 가장 강력하고 영향력 있는 문서 중 하나를 썼다.

Reading Skills

July 4, 1776, independent, Thomas Paine's

• **Exercise 6** • p.204

정답 Q1 Ⓑ, Ⓒ, Ⓔ

Q2 Rise to power: Ⓐ, Ⓖ   Fall from power: Ⓑ, Ⓔ, Ⓕ

해석 독재 정권

때로는 한 사람이 나라 전반과 시민 전체에 대한 권력을 장악할 수도 있다. 이러한 사람을 독재자라고 하며, 그 사람이 통치하는 시기를 독재 정권이라고 부른다.

독재 정권의 가장 중요한 특성은 독재자가 무제한적이고 통제 불가능한 권력을 지니고 있다는 점이다. 독재자의 말이 곧 법이다. 일종의 의회나 국회가 존재할 수는 있다. 그러나 독재자에 대한 실질적인 힘은 없다.

유감스럽게도 독재 정권은 그 성격상 대개 억압적이다. 대다수 독재자들이 군인 출신이다. 최근에는 이라크의 사담 후세인, 북한의 김일성, 쿠바의 피델 카스트로가 그에 해당한다. 이 모든 경우에서, 그들은 그 나라 군대의 지지를 받았고, 그로 인해 자신들의 뜻을 국민들에게 강요할 수 있었다. 자비로운 독재자들이 있긴 하지만 극히 드물다.

다행스러운 것은 국제적인 압력과 그 나라 국민들에 의한 혁명의 가능성 때문에 대부분의 독재 정권이 오래 가지 않는다는 점이다. 최근 몇 년 동안 많은 동유럽 국가들의 국민들이 그들의 독재자에게 대항하여 봉기했다. 동독과 같은 어떤 경우에는 민주주의로의 이양이 평화롭게 이루어졌다. 그러나 1989년 루마니아에서는 그 나라의 독재자가 시민들에 의해 처형되었다.

Reading Skills

unlimited, Cuba, Romanian

• **Exercise 7** • p.206

정답 Q1 Ⓐ, Ⓑ, Ⓔ

Q2 Governments liked: Ⓑ, Ⓓ

Governments disliked: Ⓐ, Ⓒ, Ⓕ

해석 플라톤의 국가

2,300여년 전, 그리스의 철학자 플라톤은 국가에서 정부에 대한 자신의 사상을 기록해 두었다. 그 책은 논쟁의 여지가 많아 수 세기 동안 논쟁이 계속되고 있다. 플라톤은 국가에서 엄청난 양의 정보를 다루었는데, 그가 설명한 가장 중요한 두 가지 내용은 정부의 바람직하지 못한 형태와 이상적인 형태였다.

플라톤은 민주주의를 아주 경멸했다. 그는 민주주의가 다양한 사회 계급들 사이에 너무 많은 압박감을 일으킬 것이라고 생각했다. 또한 시민에게 너무 많은 권력을 주는 것에 반대했다. 부자들이 통치하는 과두 정치는 그가 피해야 한다고 주장했던 정부의 또 다른 형태였다. 그는 부자라고 해서 사람이 반드시 좋은 지도자가 되는 것은 아니라고 여겼다. 플라톤은 서로 다른 계층의 구성원들 사이에서 갈등을 이끌어 낼 수 있는 전제 정치 또한 경멸했다.

플라톤은 그가 경멸하는 정부의 형태를 기술하는 데 초점을 두었다. 그러면서도 이상적인 형태에 대해서도 기술했다. 이는 바로 철학자 왕이 이끄는 정부였다. 플라톤에 따르면 철학자들만이 사회에서 선을 인식할 수 있는 유일한 사람들이었다. 그러므로 그들이 사람들을 가르쳐 통치해야 하는 것이다. 또한 그런 통치자들은 탐욕스럽거나 난폭하지 않기 때문에 국가를 돕는 데 초점을 맞출 것이다. 오히려 그들은 개화된 존재로서 통치할 것이다.

Reading Skills

Plato, Democracy, philosopher-king

• **Exercise 8** • p.208

정답 Q1 Ⓑ, Ⓓ, Ⓔ

Q2 How it is needed to win: Ⓒ, Ⓕ

Makeup of the Electoral College: Ⓑ, Ⓔ, Ⓖ

해석 미국의 선거제도

많은 민주주의 국가들이 그들의 지도자를 직접 선출하며 따라서 일반 투표에서 승리한 사람이 대통령이 된다. 미국에서는 이러한 제도가 통용되지 않는데 미국은 공화국이기 때문이다. 대신에 미국은 선거인단에 의지하여 대통령을 선출한다.

선거인단에는 538명의 선거인이 있다. 각 주마다 선거인의 수가 다르다. 선거인단의 수는 각 주의 의회 대표자의 수와 같다. 각 주에는 두 명의 상원 의원과 각기 다른 수의 하원 의원이 있다. 와이오밍과 같은 몇몇 주에는 단 한 명의 하원 의원이 있다. 하원 의원이 굉장히 많은 주도 있다. 예를 들어 캘리포니아에는 52명이 있다.

미국의 대부분의 주에서, 그 주의 선거인단 표 전체가 각 주의 승자에게 주어진다. 그러므로 후보자는 270명의 선거인단 표를 얻어야 대통령이 된다. 대부분의 경우 일반 투표에서 승리한 사람이 선거인단 투표에서도 승리해 왔다. 그러나 아주 드물게, 일반 투표에서 승리한 사람이 선거인단 투표에서 승리하지 못해서 대통령이 되지 못한 경우도 있었다. 이러한 일이 아주 최근인 2016년에 있었는데 도널드 트럼프가 힐러리 클린턴에게 일반 투표에서는 졌지만 더 많은 선거인단 표를 얻어 대통령이 되었다.

Reading Skills

Wyoming, 270, president

Grammar Point p.210

Grammar Check-Up

A 1 active
2 passive
3 passive
4 active
5 passive

B 1 ⓓ   2 ⓑ   3 ⓐ   4 ⓒ   5 ⓒ

C given, written, added, pleased, ratified, founded

Vocabulary Review p.212

A
1 absolute
2 profits
3 enforce
4 dictator
5 restricted

B 1 Ⓐ 2 Ⓓ 3 Ⓑ 4 Ⓑ 5 Ⓒ

C 1 Ⓓ 2 Ⓒ 3 Ⓒ 4 Ⓑ 5 Ⓐ

D
1 treatise
2 deprived
3 transition
4 private
5 subjects

Practice Test p.214

1 Ⓐ 2 Ⓒ 3 Ⓓ 4 Ⓐ 5 Ⓒ
6 Ⓑ 7 Ⓐ 8 Ⓑ 9 ④
10 Executive: ②, ③ Legislative: ⑤, ⑥, ⑦ Judicial: ①, ⑨

해석 　　　　　　　　　삼권분립

많은 국가들이 정부를 세 개의 부로 나눈다. 이러한 권력 분립으로 인해 정부는 비교적 원활하고 효과적인 수준에서 기능할 수 있다. 세 가지 부는 행정부, 입법부, 사법부이다.

행정부는 국가의 법을 집행한다. 전형적으로는 대통령이나 수상이 행정부를 이끈다. 미국에서는 장관들로 구성된 대통령의 내각이 행정부에 소속되어 있다. 연방수사국(FBI)과 같은 기관도 마찬가지이다.

입법부는 국가의 법을 제정한다. 대부분의 국가에 다수의 대표자들로 구성되는 국회나 의회가 존재한다. 미국 및 영국과 같은 몇몇 국가들은 양원제를 채택하고 있기 때문에 입법부에 두 개의 원이 존재한다. 미국에서는 상원이 미 상원(Senate)이고, 하원이 미 하원(House of Representatives)이다. 미 상원에는 주 마다 두 명의 의원이 있는 반면, 미 하원에는 50개의 모든 주가 인구에 따라 서로 다른 수의 의원 수를 배정받는다. (이로써 각 주의 상원에는 균등대표제가 하원에는 비례대표제가 부여된다.)

사법부는 법을 해석하고 그 법이 합법인지 여부를 결정한다. 이곳은 국가의 전반적인 사법 체계를 구성한다. 미국에서는 최상위 법원이 대법원이며, 대법원에는 9명의 법관이 있다. 또한 연방 법원, 주 법원, 그리고 시 법원 및 지방 법원이 존재한다.

이 세 개의 부는 대개 함께 협력하여 잘 운영된다. 이들은 "견제와 균형"이라는 체계 위에서 작동한다. 각각의 부는 동등한 권한을 가지고 있기 때문에 다른 부와 균형을 이루어서 과도한 권력이 집중되는 것을 막는다. 이는 겉으로는 복잡한 체계로 보이지만, 그 단순성에 의해 작동한다.

Actual Test

Actual Test 1 p.218

1 Ⓑ 2 Ⓒ 3 Ⓒ 4 Ⓐ 5 Ⓓ
6 Ⓓ 7 Ⓐ 8 Ⓑ 9 ④
10 Roman Republic: ④, ⑤, ⑥ Roman Empire: ③, ⑦

해석 　　　　　　　　　고대 로마

전설에 따르면 로마는 기원전 753년에 건국되었다. 로마가 존재하는 동안, 로마의 정부는 여러 차례 바뀌었다. 약 500년 동안 로마는 공화정이었다. 이후 공화정 형태의 정부가 몰락한 후, 로마는 제국이 되었다. 로마는 서기 476년까지 제국으로 존재했다.

로마 공화정은 기원전 509년에 설립되었다. 이때는 복잡한 정부 형태를 가지고 있었는데, 기본적으로 로마의 시민들은 자신들을 통치할 공직자를 선출할 수 있었다. 또한 상당히 다양한 분야를 관할하는 매우 상세한 법들이 존재했다.

공화정에서 가장 높은 지위는 집정관의 직위였다. 임기가 같은 두 명의 집정관이 있었으며, 이들의 임기는 1년뿐이었다. 이로써 이들이 과도한 권력을 축적하지 못하게 방지했다. 집정관은 전쟁을 선포하고 세금을 징수할 수 있는 권한과 같은 권력을 가지고 있었다. 공화정에는 또한 원로원이 있었다. 의원직은 종신제였고, 집정관들에게 자문을 해주었다. 평의회에서는 평민이라고 불리던 일반 국민들이 지도자를 선출하고, 법을 통과시키고, 기타 정부의 역할들을 수행할 수 있었다.

공화정에는 그 외에도 다수의 정부 관리들이 존재했다. 각각은 고유한 책무를 가지고 있었고, 법을 준수해야 했다. 일반적으로 이러한 통치 방식은 단점이 있었음에도 불구하고, 로마에서 원활하게 이루어졌다. 예를 들어 다양한 정부 부서들이 존재했고, 부패한 공무원들은 처벌을 받을 수 있었다. 로마 공화정은 현대의 민주주의 정부의 기초로서 기능했다.

하지만 이러한 형태의 정부는 기원전 1세기에 끝이 났다. 이때는 내란과 독재의 시간이었다. 내부 갈등은 아우구스투스가 황제의 자리에 오른 기원전 27년에 끝이 났다. 황제인 아우구스투스는 – 그리고 그 이후의 통치자들은 – 권력을 독점하고 전제 군주로서 군림했다.

제국의 시기에도 원로원은 여전히 존재했다. 하지만 공화정 시기에 가졌던 것보다 권력이 크게 줄어들었다. 황제는 또한 다수의 공무원들에게 의지했다. 이들은 막대한 권력을 행사했는데, 그 이유는 로마 제국이 정말로 방대한 지역에 걸쳐 있었기 때문이었다. (사실, 부유한 지방을 관리했던 이들은 어떤 경우 거의 황제만큼의 권력을 가질 수 있었다.)

집정관과 달리 황제는 평생 동안, 혹은 장군과 같은 누군가에 의해 자리에서 물러날 때까지, 통치를 했다. 이들은 보통 친아들이나 양아들을 후계자로 선택했다. 제국의 힘이 막강했던 때에는 아들이 쉽게 왕좌를 물려받았다. 어수선한 시기에는 승계와 관련된 문제들이 자주 있었다.

Actual Test 2 p.222

1 Ⓐ 2 Ⓑ 3 Ⓒ 4 Ⓐ 5 Ⓒ 6 Ⓑ
7 Ⓒ 8 Ⓐ 9 ② 10 ①, ④, ⑥

24

해석
제인 오스틴

제인 오스틴은 *오만과 편견*이라는 소설의 저자로 잘 알려져 있다. 하지만 그녀는 단순한 소설가 그 이상이었다. 몇 가지 측면에서 그녀는 문학 분야의 선구자였다. 그녀는 여러 이유로 문학에 막대한 영향을 미쳤다.

오스틴은 1775년에서 1817년까지 살았다. 당시 여성 작가들은 극도로 드물었다. 글을 쓰는 일은 그저 여성들이 하기에 적합한 일로 여겨지지 않았다. 실제로 그녀가 쓰고 그녀 생전에 출판된 네 권의 책에서 오스틴의 이름은 저자로 표기되지 않았다. 대신 그 책들은 익명으로 출간되었다. 그녀가 죽은 뒤에야 그녀가 쓴 작품들이 그녀의 것으로 확인되었다. 오스틴의 소설들이 출간 즉시 베스트셀러가 된 것은 아니었다. 하지만 시간이 지나면서 인기를 얻었다. 실제로 그 책들은 200년이 넘는 기간 동안 거의 항상 인쇄되고 있다. 오스틴 덕분에 여성들이 작가가 되는 일이 점점 더 받아들여지게 되었다.

오스틴의 작풍 또한 영향력이 컸다. 그녀가 그 기법을 만든 것은 아니었지만, 그녀는 자유 간접 화법을 대중에게 알리는 데 도움을 주었다. 이러한 글쓰기 방식에서는 이야기의 서술자가 다양한 등장 인물들이 생각하고 있는 것을 독자들에게 알려줄 수 있다. 하지만 "그는 생각했다"와 "그녀는 생각했다"는 글에 등장하지 않는다. 이러한 기법으로 작가는 등장 인물들의 생각을 보여주면서 그에 대한 통찰을 덧붙여 제시할 수 있다. 오스틴은 이러한 방식을 상당히 많이 사용했다. 오늘날 이러한 방식은 작가들 사이에서 흔히 사용되고 있다.

오스틴의 소설들은 종종 보통 사람들에게 초점을 맞춘다. 이것은 *이성과 감성*, *오만과 편견*, *맨스필드 공원*, *엠마*에 드러나 있다. (이들은 그녀 생전에 출간된 소설들의 제목이다.) 그러한 점에서 그녀는, 종종 평범한 개인의 행위에 초점을 맞추는 현대 소설의 창시에 도움을 주었다. 왕이나 위대한 영웅의 행위를 다루는 대신, 오스틴의 소설들은 19세기 영국의 중산층에 관한 이야기를 들려주었다. 이러한 주제는 그녀의 작품이 인기를 얻는 데 도움이 되었다. 그것은 본질적으로 그 작품들을 문학계에서 읽힐 뿐만 아니라 재미있는 이야기를 원하는 독자들도 즐기는, 시대를 초월한 고전으로 만들어 주었다.

Actual Test 3   p.226

1 ⓓ   2 ⓒ   3 ⓑ   4 ⓑ   5 ⓒ   6 ⓑ
7 ⓒ   8 ⓓ   9 3   10 2, 3, 4

해석
허블 우주 망원경

망원경이 아무리 크고 강력해도 망원경이 포착하는 이미지는 여전히 왜곡될 수밖에 없다. 그 이유는 지구의 대기가 별빛이 나타나는 방식에 영향을 미치기 때문이다. 이러한 이유로 1990년에 우주 망원경이 발사되었다. 그것은 우주로 발사된 최초의 대형 망원경일 것이다. 허블 우주 망원경이라고 불리는 이 망원경은 천문학 분야에 막대한 영향을 끼치고 있다. 그것은 지구로부터 엄청나게 먼 거리에 있는 은하계의 사진을 찍고 있고, 우주에 대한 사람들의 지식을 확장시키는 데 도움을 주고 있다.

허블 망원경은 대략 스쿨버스 정도의 크기이다. 1990년에 그것을 우주 왕복선을 이용하여 궤도에 진입시켜야 했다. 그것은 지구 위로 약 600킬로미터 상공에 있는 지구 궤도에 안착했다. 하지만 허블 망원경이 작동을 시작하자 천문학자들은 실망을 했다. 이미지가 기대하고 있었던 것만큼 거의 뚜렷하지 않았다. 허블 망원경을 면밀히 조사하자 망원경 속 거울의 곡률이 잘못 구부러져 있다는 점이 밝혀졌다. 작은 실수였지만, 이것은 사진의 품질에 큰 영향을 끼쳤고 그 때문에 사진이 흐릿하게 보였다.

1993년, 또 다른 우주 왕복선에 탑승한 우주비행사들이 5일간에 걸쳐 허블 망원경을 가까스로 수리했다. 이 수리로 인해 허블 망원경은 마침내 기대했던 수준의 고화질 이미지를 생성할 수 있었다. 원래 허블 망원경의 수명은 약 15년으로 예정되어 있었다. 하지만 2023년 기준으로 그 망원경은 여전히 작동 중이었다. 주된 이유는 망원경을 수리하기 위해 5차례에 걸친 우주 비행이 수행되었기 때문이다. 이러한 우주 비행들로 인해 허블 망원경의 수명이 크게 연장되었다.

허블 망원경의 주요 업적 중 하나는 우주의 나이가 약 137억년이라는 점을 밝혀낸 것이었다. 허블 망원경은 스스로 찾아낸 먼 은하계의 사진들을 수없이 많이 찍고 있다. 또한 태양계 밖의 첫 번째 행성의 사진도 찍었다. 오늘날에는 CHEOPS 및 제임스 웹 우주 망원경과 같은 다른 우주 망원경들도 사진을 찍고 자체적인 발견을 한다. (허블 망원경이 작동을 하는 시기 동안에도 다른 망원경들이 발사되고 또 작동을 멈추고 있다.) 하지만 허블 망원경은 여전히 인류의 지식 발전에 기여하고 있다.